North of Danger

North of Danger
❅ Dale Fife ❅

Map and decorations by Haakon Sæther

A Unicorn Book

E. P. Dutton   New York

Library of Congress Cataloging in Publication Data

Fife, Dale.   North of danger.

SUMMARY: Twelve-year-old Arne undertakes a two-
hundred-mile trip on skis to warn his father of a
German invasion of their town on the Norwegian
archipelago of Svalbard.
1. Svalbard—History—Juvenile fiction. 2. World War,
1939-1945—Norway—Svalbard—Juvenile fiction.
[1. Svalbard—History—Fiction. 2. World War, 1939-
1945—Norway—Svalbard—Fiction] I. Title.
PZ7.F4793No 1978 [Fic] 77-26199 ISBN: 0-525-36035-2

Published in the United States by E. P. Dutton, a Division
of Sequoia-Elsevier Publishing Company, Inc., New York

Published simultaneously in Canada by Clarke,
Irwin & Company Limited, Toronto and Vancouver

Editor: Emilie McLeod   Designer: Rik; Levinson
Printed in the U.S.A.
10 9 8 7 6 5 4 3 2

To Lorene and Charles Beasley

Midsummer 1974

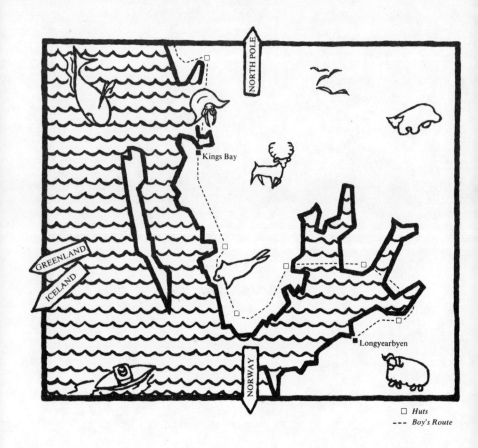

NORTH POLE

Kings Bay

GREENLAND

ICELAND

NORWAY

Longyearbyen

□ *Huts*
- - - *Boy's Route*

❋ Foreword ❋

The story of twelve-year-old Arne Kristiansen, in the Archipelago of Svalbard, is a fictionalized account of a true incident.

Svalbard, more often called Spitsbergen, lies within the Arctic Ocean approximately ten degrees, or four hundred nautical miles, from the North Pole. It is under the sovereignty of Norway.

In August of 1940, British warships stood in Advent Bay off Longyearbyen, the capital. Their mission was to evacuate the entire population, some three thousand people, most of them coal miners and their families.

The German Army, which had already taken over Norway, was expected to invade Spitsbergen to cut off the shipment of polar coal to Europe and to destroy or take over weather and radio stations critically necessary for the safety of Allied shipping.

Unknown to the authorities, one person, Arne Kristiansen, was left behind. This is the story of what happened after the ships moved out of the harbor and the long dark polar winter was about to close down.

Arne was the first to see the rescue ships creep into Longyearbyen Harbor under cover of early morning fog.

A battleship, two destroyers.

Apprehension jolted him down to his toes. Not the evacuation. Not yet. Not until his father returned.

He pushed away from the breakfast table so violently his chair banged against the cupboard, rattling the dishes. He sprang to the window.

The Paulsons—mother, father, Nils—with whom he had lived for the weeks his father was away, crowded behind him.

"The British!" Nils, who was Arne's friend and almost his age, shouted. "The British. They're here."

"Thank God," Fru Paulson said. "We're safe now. They'll evacuate us before the Nazis get here."

Arne's breakfast churned in his stomach.

His father, a glacialist, was at work two hundred miles north in the Arctic, unaware of what was happening. Arne turned anxiously to Schoolmaster Paulson. "They won't take us to England before Father gets back—they won't— they can't leave him behind alone."

Schoolmaster Paulson's eyes were solemn behind his thick glasses. He snatched his sweater from a peg on the wall. "I'll see what it's all about."

Arne made a rush for the door, pulling on his anorak as he ran.

"Wait, wait for me," Nils yelled.

When they reached the dock, the sysselmann, who governed Spitsbergen for Norway, was ahead of them. A broad-chested man, he stood stolidly at the end of the pier, his gaze riveted on the ships. Next to him waited the director of the mine.

Now the miners streamed down from the coal tunnels that bored into the black cliffs, already snow-crested at the end of August.

Women and children came hurrying along the town's lone street. They were all headed for the dock, to stand against the sharp wind blowing off the fjord, to watch the ships.

Nils pulled the hood of his anorak over his head. "I heard it's warm in England."

England! A faraway, strange land.

England. Without the assurance, the warmth of his

father's closeness, the very sound of it made Arne feel hollow. He caught at a straw. "Maybe the British have come to tell us the war is over. Then my father and I can go back to Norway."

Nils took his gaze from the ships for a moment. "They're here because the Nazis are going to invade Spitsbergen, just as they did in Norway." His face was without expression. Only his blue eyes showed what he felt for Arne.

Ugly memories welled up in Arne. The Nazis occupying the country, the resistance, quislings, traitors, pointing fingers and hostages sent to concentration camps.

Arne's father's bold defiance, fighting the occupation as a leader in the Underground. Clever, daring, the Gestapo on his tail—finally too close, too dangerous. The Underground schemed to save his father's life, contriving to get him to Spitsbergen as a member of an international scientific team.

The scheme was successful. The Nazis knew Arne's father only as a glacialist who had spent much time working in Spitsbergen. They became aware too late that a hunted prize had slipped from their grasp.

In Spitsbergen his father had joined the other member of the team, a Swiss scientist.

Out in the fjord, beyond the coal boats, a small vessel plowed a furrow from the battleship to the dock. A murmur ran through the crowd. A cheer as two officers jumped up to the pier.

The sysselmann, the mine director and Schoolmaster Paulson greeted them, shaking hands. Their faces were serious as they walked to the company office.

The crowd was quiet now, waiting.

The rumors: "They've come early. It's because the Nazis are bound to invade before the long darkness sets in. . . ."

3

"It's our radio and weather station they want. . . ." "It's our coal. . . . They're bound to stop our shipments to the Allies. . . ."

It seemed forever to Arne before the officers came out of the company building and returned to the ship.

Men came and went.

Official word passed mouth to mouth: "We leave tomorrow."

Arne felt as if he'd been hit in the stomach. He wormed his way through the crowd, close to the mine office. When the sysselmann came out the door, Arne rushed forward and planted himself in front of him. "My father isn't here. We can't leave without him."

Schoolmaster Paulson stood behind the sysselmann. "Bjørn Kristiansen is not expected to start back for three weeks," he said gently.

The sysselmann's face was grave. "Arne, the ships can't wait. The evacuation must be immediate and secret. Even the Gestapo will not harm a peaceful scientist."

They didn't know. His father would be a prize in the hands of the Nazis. He dared not tell them. He looked up into their faces, the worried sysselmann's, the kind schoolmaster's. Who might be a quisling? A traitor?

"Father has a radio," Arne said desperately. "He could be warned."

The sysselmann shook his head. "Our radio has been silenced. The Nazis would intercept any message we sent. If they should suspect what is happening, they would bomb the ships."

Schoolmaster Paulson put a hand on Arne's shoulder. "Your father is a clever man. He will manage. Get yourself ready to leave."

No one could help him.

4

His throat hurt from holding back tears. It was being squeezed tighter and tighter. He couldn't get his mind off the hurt to think. Things were happening too fast. If he could just stop everything, there must be something he could do to help his father.

※ **2** ※

Arne remembered the exact moment he knew what he must do. He was trudging along the coal-dust road toward Nils' house.

Everywhere families, little worlds—fathers, mothers, children—hurried home, talking, planning.

They were not his family.

His family was his father.

His father was far north. Unaware of the danger. He must not return, once the Nazis came.

It was up to Arne to stop him.

Somehow he must stay behind when the rescue ships sailed for England.

Fear, like an electric shock, coursed through his body at the boldness of his scheme.

He had no time to be afraid.

Could he manage it alone?

He must. He remembered the quislings in Norway. He dared not trust anyone, not even Nils.

Nils rushed out of the house at Arne's approach. "Maybe we'll be lucky enough to ride the battleship," he said, eyes shining. It was plain to see that Nils was excited about sailing off to England.

In the house, everything was turmoil.

"Arne," Nils' mother said, "take only the lighter clothing. It doesn't get very cold in England."

Fru Paulson had been good to Arne. She was not demonstrative, but now she put an arm around him. His mother had died when he was very young, and he was self-conscious about her embrace, even though it warmed him. "Remember, Arne, you will be with us in England, the same as here."

He wriggled away, guilty at not telling her his plan. He closed his mind to the guilt.

He began to pack his clothes, all the while mentally cataloging the supplies, the heavy clothing he must spirit away and hide. Where? In one of the mining tunnels high above the town.

His skis were the most important item. They were leaning against the back of the house. He must sneak them up to the mine immediately, before they were locked away in the cellar or shed.

He slipped out of the house, shouldered the skis and was well on his way when he heard a chuckle. Nils.

"You're not going to take them with you. There's no snow in England. What are you up to?"

Arne thought fast. "Hide them. I don't want any Nazi using them."

Nils kept step with him. "Where?"

"Oh, some mine."

"That's stupid," Nils said. "They say the Nazis are going to blow up the mines."

Arne kept walking up the hill. He hoped Nils would drop back.

"You're not making sense," Nils said. He grabbed Arne and spun him around.

"Leave me alone," Arne cried. "Get away from me." He thrust out his arm and punched Nils hard in the jaw.

Nils rocked back and rubbed his face. He looked at Arne, disbelief in his eyes.

Nils was Arne's best friend. Everything that had happened today was too much. Arne felt as if he were crumpling to pieces. He looked at his friend and shook his head. He couldn't speak. He sank to the ground.

Nils crouched beside him. "We all know how you feel, but you heard the sysselmann. He said even the Gestapo would not harm a neutral scientist."

"There's more to it than that, Nils. There's more. . . ." He clamped his lips together. He had said too much. He looked at his friend. He needed to tell his friend. He needed Nils.

Nils' face showed alarm as he listened to Arne's story of his father's work in the resistance.

"If it were your father, what would you do?" Arne asked when he had finished.

"What could I do?" Nils asked.

"What you'd have to do—stay behind when the ships leave."

Nils' eyes widened. "That wouldn't be easy. I'd need help. . . ."

"Yes," Arne said. "Someone to say, when they started looking for you, 'He must be on one of the other ships. He was on the dock.' "

"Ships radio to each other," Nils said.

"The radios will be silent until they're far away."

"What will you do when the ships leave? What's your plan?" Nils asked.

They talked in whispers now.

"I'll stay up at the mine. Keep watch. I'll wait for my father. If the Nazi ships come before he does, then I'll have to go to him."

"That's impossible," Nils exploded. "Two hundred miles with the sun less and less each day and the cold worse and worse. Arne, you haven't been through a winter here on Spitsbergen. You don't know what it's like. Cold, ice a thousand feet deep in places. Glaciers, three months of darkness. How will you find your father?"

"I have a map," Arne said and pulled it from his pocket. "Father marked it for me. He's along this fjord by the great glacial wall at around eighty degrees."

"What about food?"

"There should be some left behind. Then there are trappers' huts along the fjords."

"Some trappers are going with us, those who happened to be here and know about the evacuation."

"Their huts will still be there," Arne argued.

Nils put a finger on a circle on the map. It was marked: Trapper Hans Braun.

"Do you know him?" Arne asked.

"Nobody really knows him. I saw him once. He's a kind

9

of hermit. His hut is about halfway to where your father is. But he's weird, they say."

Nils looked worried.

The worry spilled over to Arne. "I shouldn't have gotten you into this," he said. "You'll get into trouble. Nils, I'm scared—my plan's no good."

"You can't stop now," Nils said. He grabbed the skis Arne had thrown to the ground and got to his feet. "No one can ski as well as you. That will be important. You might make it. Sure, I'll be in big trouble." He grinned. "It won't be the first time."

Nils' assurance caught fire in Arne. He jumped up. "When the war is over, we'll have yarns to swap."

"Right. You'll brag about the bears you fought. I'll tell about the bombs that missed me," Nils said. His words were joking, but his voice was rough. He turned away quickly, and, shouldering Arne's skis, headed for the mine.

Arne followed close behind his friend.

They were in big trouble, both of them.

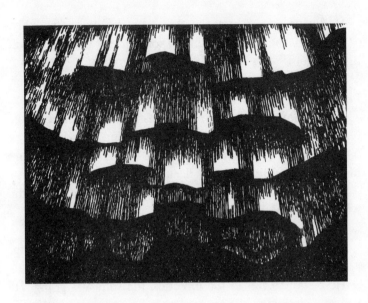

※ **3** ※

What was wrong?

Why didn't the battleship leave?

For what seemed forever, Arne crouched in the mouth of the coal mine and waited, tense, fearful.

The two destroyers had maneuvered out of sight.

The battleship's siren had long since shrieked its readiness to sail.

Still, it did not move.

Had they discovered he was not on any of the ships?

They'd gotten the truth out of Nils! Any second now, they would lower boats and come to get him, force him to go to England.

11

He began to perspire and then to shiver uncontrollably.

Abruptly the ship gave three short shrieks that sent a jolt through him.

The ship began to move—slowly at first, then faster, faster.

The backdrop of black mountains like heaps of coal, the blue water, the hundreds of gulls sweeping and diving low over the ship made the evacuation unreal. There was no hint that an entire town was fleeing the enemy.

The ship was moving rapidly now. His last tie with the world grew smaller, smaller.

He was alone.

ALONE! The awfulness of his solitude crashed over him. What had he done?

He began to run in the direction the ship was going. He waved frantically. "Wait for me," he screamed. "WAIT! Nils, NILS, tell your father—don't leave me here alone—it's Arne. . . ."

In his terror he stumbled and fell. He rolled. Faster and faster he rolled and tumbled down the hillside. Finally, he lay still, bruised and breathless.

He looked up. The sea was empty. Nothing stirred.

Never before had he been so alone.

His breath came in short, fearful gasps.

His legs and arms felt paralyzed. He'd never be able to move again.

He heard a clucking and turned his head. A covey of feather-legged grouse came pecking along the hillside. There was something alive besides himself, something familiar. "Hello," he said weakly.

The grouse paid no attention. They were unafraid. Arne's father had told him that the wildlife on Spitsbergen had not learned to be afraid of man. He felt better for the company of the grouse and for having talked—having heard the sound of his own voice.

On his feet, he turned from the sea. He could not bear to go down to the empty town. Not yet. He took his flashlight from the pocket of his anorak and plunged into the black silence of the mine. He walked over the bumpy iron rails to the place behind a coal car where he had hidden his supplies. They were just as he and Nils had left them—skis, rucksack, gloves, overgloves, tools, extra clothing. The two most vital items, his compass and map, were in the inside pocket of his anorak.

His wristwatch showed it was almost noon. He began to worry. What if the Nazis had arrived?

He went cautiously into the daylight.

There was nothing.

He would go down to the town. Busy himself with things that must be done, find the key to the Paulson house which Nils had hidden away for him.

By the time he climbed down the mountainside a wind had blown up, scattering the light covering of snow on the town's single street. Already the eerie feeling of a ghost town hung in the air. The crunch of the overhead coal gondolas was silenced, the school, church, houses—shuttered, boarded up. The sandy plot where he and Nils had played soccer with friends was sad in its desertion.

Nils' house looked strange, unfamiliar, desolate.

An alien sound vibrated from the sky.

Nazi planes?

He flattened himself against the side of the house and looked up.

A huge flock of geese was passing overhead, followed by a second flock, this one lower in the sky. The air was filled with gabbling.

13

The migration south had begun.

Arne imagined their flight over the Arctic Ocean and the Norwegian Sea. Maybe they'd fly right over Oslo. Would he ever see his old home again? Homesickness wrenched through him as he watched the smooth, orderly flight of the wild geese.

A young straggler lagged. "Honk! Honk!"

To Arne it sounded like a desperate cry. "Help! Help!"

"GO! GO!" Arne shouted to the gosling. "You'll make it."

He watched the straggler reach the flock. Good, he's with all the others.

And then Arne remembered something. His father's rule of the Arctic was never travel alone.

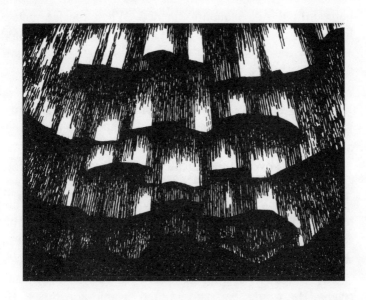

❊ 4 ❊

Each morning Arne scanned the sea.
Each day the temperature dropped.
Each day the sun stayed a shorter time.
But the Nazi ships did not come.
He became bolder in his thinking as the days passed. The Germans would not come with the long night approaching. They would wait until spring to invade.
Why sleep in the mine? He moved his skis and all his supplies into Nils' father's house.
His hopes rose. It was now just a little more than two weeks until his father would start back. They would stay

here until the dark months passed. When the ice melted in the fjords, they would find a small boat; they would escape. . . .

The German destroyer came on the seventh day.

Arne saw it from the same window he had seen the British ships. For a paralyzing instant all the feeling went out of his legs. They felt hollow, rubbery.

Then he moved automatically, with speed and precision, as he had rehearsed in his mind many times.

His rucksack was ready, with food and a thermos of hot tea. In moments it was on his back, his skis over his shoulder. He was on his way, trying to stay out of sight of the ship in the harbor.

The terrain was flat, crisscrossed by a network of small rivers. He would be exposed and visible for miles. He hugged the riverbanks and took refuge in the bends. The men on the ship would be sure to scan the area with binoculars. He could feel them burn into his back like eagles' eyes. He moved fast, but he felt as if he were living a nightmare. Running in one spot, not getting anywhere. Any moment now he would hear a round of shots from the ship's guns.

Not until he was several miles upvalley did he have any feeling of safety. He had been there before, the last time with his father. As he remembered the day, his aloneness was suddenly sharp and hurting. It had been midsummer, when the sun never sets in the Arctic. A three-month day without night, when grasses and wild flowers—bluebells, glacier crowfeet, reindeer roses—burst from the rocky land. His father knew all the growing things. He had picked a stem of oval leaves. "Scurvy-wort. The vitamin C of the Arctic. Men have died of scurvy with this plant growing practically under the soles of their boots."

16

Arne had run a finger over a leaf. "Why didn't they eat some?"

"They didn't know. It takes knowledge and patience to survive here."

Patience!

Arne had no time for patience now. His father would start back to Longyearbyen in fourteen days. To stop him, Arne must travel two hundred miles in thirteen days. The fourteenth day would be too late. Speed was the thing. For that he needed snow so he could ski. But there were only patches of it in the valley. The wind had swept the stony land almost bare.

This was a worry. But when he struggled to the crest of the mountain, he gazed into an endless white world of snowy plains, icy peaks, glittering glaciers. It was vast, boundless—a formidable enemy.

Fearful, he wanted to turn back. But the Nazi enemy was behind him. There was just one thing to do—go on.

He buckled on his skis. Suddenly he felt he was being watched. His neck muscles tensed. He pivoted slowly and searched the whiteness.

There, not twenty feet away, a fox stood against a snowbank, barely visible in its white coat. Arne let out his breath. "Well, hello there, Fox," he called, delighted to see something alive.

The fox stood motionless and ignored him.

"Well, I'm on my way," Arne said. He jabbed his ski poles into the snow and forged ahead.

Arne was sure of himself on skis. He felt that sureness—confidence—now. With the wind at his back, he raced effortlessly down the slopes. As he bent to the contour of the land, his skis were an extension of his feet, a part of the rhythm of muscle and bone.

Even though the wind was cold, he felt warm and, after a while, thirsty. He stopped in the lee of a boulder, took off his rucksack and stretched his arm and back muscles. He took from his pack the thermos of hot tea and drank sparingly, then filled the thermos to the top with snow.

He was ready to be off again when he sensed something moving.

He turned. The fox froze to a stop behind him.

"So you've been trailing me."

The fox took no notice.

"You're looking for company, same as I."

When Arne began to climb the hill ahead, the fox shot forward with long, graceful leaps, white against white, a ghostly fox.

"Good-bye," Arne yelled after him.

But when he reached the brow of the hill, the fox stood waiting, brown eyes glittering.

Arne propelled himself forward. "I'll beat you on the downhill," he shouted.

Partway down the slope he turned and stopped. The fox leaped and swam in the snow.

Arne leaned on his poles and waited for the fox to catch up. "Aren't you afraid of me?" he asked the fox. "Maybe I've got a gun. You might end up lining the hood of an anorak. You shouldn't trust people."

The fox lay down panting on the snow.

Their shadows on the snow were yards long and close.

"On your feet, Fox," Arne said.

There was no time to waste.

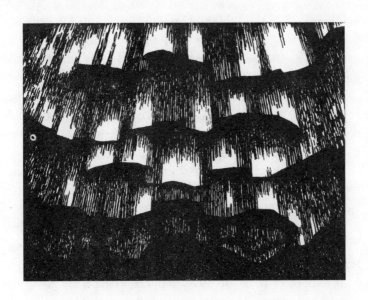

5

It was midafternoon, and nearly dark, when Arne reached the edge of Sassen Fjord. The fox had stayed with him.

Arne pulled the map from his anorak and unfolded it to study the black dots which pinpointed the huts and creep-ins of trappers. They were roughly ten to fifteen miles apart. The fox followed as he moved, searching.

He was lucky. It did not take long to find a tar-papered shack. It was really just a refuge hut, and it sat somewhat dizzily on a rise close to the shore. Arne shoved open the door to a single, smoke-blackened room. The ceiling was barely high enough for a man to stand. One wall was caved

19

in. Bear . . . Arne thought nervously. A big ice bear.

Still, it was shelter. The first thing to do was build a fire. As Arne headed for the shore to find wood, the fox was gone.

The sky over the water was noisy with seabirds. The beach was strewn with a jumble of things the sea had coughed up: planks, boxes, trunks of trees, driftwood bleached white. Sandpipers scattered as he approached.

The logs Arne gathered shone as if polished by their journey through polar seas. Where had they come from? he wondered. What continent? Which country?

He spied the fox running light-footed along the shore, his bushy tail streaming out behind him. The fox was looking for his supper. Arne must look for his.

It took three of his precious matches to get a fire going. It roared and spewed out inky smoke before steadying.

His father had told Arne the code of the trapper: wood and food of some kind must always be left in a hut. The last person to stay in this one must have been poor. All Arne found was a paper bag of pressed oatmeal. Still, it would make a hot meal. He'd leave something in exchange. Pemmican, he decided.

The only cooking utensil was a blackened frying pan. It would do to melt snow in which to cook the oats.

The warmth of the fire and the bubbling porridge gave the shack a homey feeling. He'd celebrate the good start of his trip. He opened one of the cans of condensed milk he had brought. It was frozen, and, after he thawed it, grainy, but it was still good. He allowed himself a heaping teaspoon of sugar to sprinkle over the gruel.

He thought of his friend Nils. He wished he were here. Was he in trouble on Arne's account?

Arne had just finished the meal when he heard an eerie

shrieking. He rushed outside to see terns diving at the fox, which had dragged a dead fish from the waves. With crafty aim, the birds shot down on him. The fox let out a thin, anguished yap as their sharp beaks ripped his fur. He flipped over on his back and struck out desperately with his paws.

Arne grabbed one of his ski poles from alongside the hut. "Thieves," he yelled and swung the pole around in a circle over his head. The marauding birds scattered. "Thieves, go find your own food."

The fox dragged his prize a distance from Arne, as if he too might steal it.

A strange blue light touched the icy mountains and snowy ground. The moon, a luminous disk, seemed close enough to grasp.

Finished with his food, the fox drew closer to the hut. He lay down, curled into a circle, tail over snout.

As Arne turned to go inside, a mist obscured the moon. He remembered his father saying, "Only one thing you can count on about Arctic weather. It's fickle."

Later, in his sleeping bag, he heard the wind whine mournfully through the cave-in the bear had made. He shivered. He did not want to meet up with a bear.

He heard the fox howl, a piercing, sad sound. Far away, a howl answered. Then all was quiet.

Arne wondered how many huts he would sleep in before he reached his father.

He started at every new sound. What if the bear came back?

He was afraid to go to sleep.

His eyes were heavy. He was snug and warm in his reindeer sleeping bag.

He was asleep.

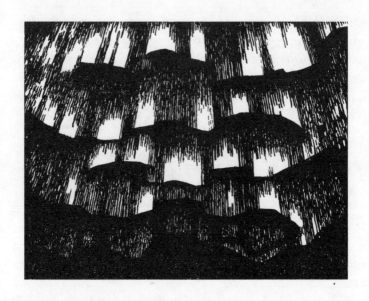

❊ 6 ❊

Arne awakened to a strange sight. The walls of the hut were white with hoarfrost. The temperature had dropped.

He yawned and stretched, and then he was on his feet. Even before he pulled on his boots and sweater, he opened the door. The fox was gone. He had expected as much, but he had a sense of loss. The fox had been company, someone to talk to.

It would take too much time to get the stove fired up again, so Arne drank a small amount of the hot tea he had poured into his thermos the night before, ate cold sausage and some biscuits.

He studied his map while he ate. The fjord waters that

lay north resembled, roughly, a left hand, palm down, fingers thrust into the terrain.

He traced the route he had traveled the day before. He was now past the base of the "first finger." From here he would be traveling over flatland along the fjord. He had made some twenty-five miles yesterday. If he averaged that much each day, it should take him eight days, in all, to reach his father's camp at the edge of a great glacial wall.

He drew a circle around the next hut marked on the map. It was a distance of about thirty miles. He would make it by nightfall.

Pocketing the map, he eased his shoulders into his rucksack and went outside. As he strapped on his skis and slid down to the fjord, he looked for the tracks of the fox. Fresh snow had obliterated them. He was moving in a silent, white world. The only sound was the long scraping of his skis.

At noon, pleased with his progress, Arne halted close by a lagoon, unfastened his rucksack and took from it dried fruit and crackers.

As he ate, he watched eiderducks fly close to the water, then glide down to join others snuggled like a feathery quilt across the pond. Migrating! "So you're leaving," he said out loud, for he needed to hear a voice, even his own. The ducks murmured drowsily but paid no heed to him.

The brief stop made Arne conscious of the numbing cold. He swung his arms and stamped with his skis. He wiggled his toes to get the circulation going in his feet. He dug in his poles and moved forward.

The sky darkened.

The terrain roughened.

No more easy skiing. He took off his skis to climb over masses of rocks deposited by glaciers.

The temperature kept plunging.

The sea spumed against the shore. A cruel wind blew snow, sharp as needles, against his face and under the hood of his anorak.

Would he ever reach the next hut? He had to find shelter.

He was almost upon it before he saw the sagging cluster of boards, the door banging open. The wreck was completely filled with snow.

It was unbelievable. Too much to comprehend. There was no shelter within thirty miles. Where would he sleep?

The wind, savage now, drove the snow before it in enormous drifts. He could see almost nothing.

BLIZZARD!

Dig in. Fast. No more time.

A snowdrift would have to do.

He struggled out of his rucksack and got his short-handled shovel. As he burrowed, ptarmigan flew out from under the cover of the snow and startled him.

No time to cut blocks of snow, dig a passageway, hollow out a shelter to sit up, lie down.

Falling snow—soon it would clog the opening—ram a ski pole into top of drift, ventilation.

Crawl inside, pull off boots and icy anorak, get into sleeping bag, pull flap over head—numb, exhausted.

Slowly, agonizingly, feeling came back in his fingers, toes. Then warmth, sleepiness. He must sit up, get matches and candle. Save the flashlight batteries. The candle flame was steady; hardly a puff of wind crept into the shelter. Snow was already blocking the opening.

Drink tea—still warm. Food frozen. Put raisins and

chocolate and boots in sleeping bag; they would thaw by morning.

Blow out candle. Listen. Snowhouse muted the rage of the blizzard. Battle of winds, might go on for hours, could rage for days. Fear! Panic! He might be so deeply buried in snow he could not dig himself out. No one knew where he was. Father. He would return to Longyearbyen, be shot. A terrible scream. Whose? His!

Control!

Pull the sleeping bag over head, shut out the storm.

Remember fun. Norway at midsummer, when the lilacs bloom, bonfires, singing, laughter.

Sleep!

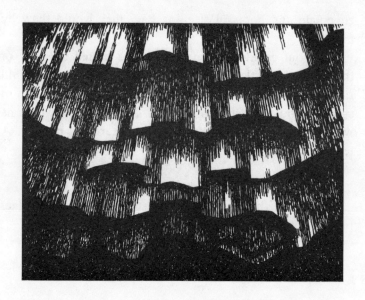

❋ 7 ❋

Arne awakened slowly to the darkness and silence.

He reached out. His hands struck a wall of snow.

He remembered. The horror of it brought him fully awake.

He fumbled for his flashlight and looked at his wristwatch. It had stopped at nine o'clock. Morning? Night? What day? How long had he been in this grave? How deeply was he buried?

He lay on his stomach and began to shovel his way through the snow that blocked the opening. Each shovelful had to be thrown behind him in the shelter.

He would never reach the outside.

26

At the first glimpse of gray light, he felt reborn. He lay gasping, observing the miracle. He burrowed to the outside. The blizzard was over. The nightmare, he decided, had happened just yesterday.

After the warmth of the snowhouse, he felt the rasping cold keenly. He hurried into motion, dug out his belongings. He ate the thawed raisins and chocolate. Then he buckled on his skis and slid down to the fjord. It had iced over during the night.

His map showed he was still about twenty miles from the tip of the fjord's "middle finger" and the next shelter, which, from the size of the circle on the map, was probably just a creep-in.

If he could, however, cross the fjord at this point, he would be close by the hut of the trapper Hans Braun, the hermit that Nils had told him about. If he went all the way around the fjord, it was some sixty miles. If he crossed the fjord, he would save at least two days' journey. This was important. He had made only ten miles yesterday.

He crossed to the edge of the ice and prodded it with a ski pole. Water bubbled up.

Too thin.

He'd have to go the long way.

At first there were stretches along the shore where he rhythmically thrust his poles into the snow and his skis swished smoothly over the surface. But those stretches became rarer as the morning wore on. Often he had to make wide circles around cliffs that rose starkly from the sea.

Again and again, detours slowed him.

At noon he ate only crackers with a mouthful of snow to quench his thirst. He knew this was foolhardy. Cold in the stomach took away energy. But he was impatient to be on his way.

The frozen fjord was tempting. The other side seemed so close. He'd test the ice once more. He put his weight on it. It held.

He stabbed it with his ski pole.

Thick.

Should he risk it?

At the rate he was traveling, he'd never reach his father on time. He needed the two days he would save by crossing the ice.

He was already tired, miserable. Across the fjord there was a trapper, a warm hut.

On skis, if one moved fast and did not stop, even thin ice held.

The sky began to cloud over.

Another blizzard?

He'd try the ice.

He jabbed his poles into it and thrust forward.

The wind was at his back. The ice was smooth as silk. He raced, thrilling.

He was in control.

Confident.

There was nothing to fear.

Until halfway across the fjord, he felt the ice begin to sway. Slowly, up and down it heaved.

He heard an ominous cracking.

With horror he saw a narrow lead fill with black water. Speed carried him over it.

He was safe.

Then he heard a loud grinding, gnashing explosion. All around him the ice broke into giant slabs.

Frantically he jabbed his ski poles into the slab he stood on, while ice blocks smashed each other with a crashing roar.

His only chance to survive would be if the current pressed the ice floes against the land to make a bridge.

A tremendous block crashed into his floe and almost jolted him into the water. He could not keep his balance. His rucksack weighted him down. He cast it off into the sea of ice and lunged forward with all his strength, around cracks, across the weaving floes.

A lead opened and widened in the last stretch of ice before the shore. A cracking bent the ice beneath his flying skis.

Desperately he tore open his anorak and held it wide to the wind, making a sail. He shot across the open water and catapulted onto the icy bank, limp, gasping.

Only his ski tracks proved he had crossed the impossible ice pack.

His rucksack was gone.

His hands in his mittens were lumps of ice.

He must find the hut of Trapper Braun soon.

With numb fingers he managed to get his compass from his pocket. This far north it might not be accurate. He'd follow its direction nonetheless.

His legs were as stiff as ski poles.

His eyelashes were frozen together.

He dragged on, frozen, barely conscious.

A light!

Or was it a star?

Stars were not square.

He brushed the ice from his face.

A hut.

He was almost there. Another few steps.

From out of nowhere something white and furry lunged at him.

A bear?

He fell to the ground.

"Kara," he heard a gruff voice shout.

A giant stood silhouetted in the doorway of the hut, a gun in his hand.

The white world turned black.

❋ 8 ❋

Arne jerked upright.

Where was he?

A hut, rough, smoke-blackened.

He craned his neck to look into the bunk above him. Empty.

The room was warm, filled with the smell of coffee. There was a table, two stools and little else.

Now he remembered. The beast, the giant with a gun. The trapper Hans Braun. He fell back on the bunk. He was safe.

His bones ached. He could go on sleeping forever.

The door burst open, and freezing air whooshed in.

Through half-closed eyelids he saw the giant. His shaggy head just missed the ceiling. His face was covered with so much hair, he looked more troll than man.

The giant did not glance at Arne.

Arne watched him toss his gun on a shelf, then go to the stove and dump a fish into a frying pan. When he took off his anorak, Arne saw the width of the man's back—big muscles moving under a thick shirt.

When the fish was cooked, he flipped it right onto the table. He set the coffeepot alongside it, then slammed a loaf of bread down and stabbed it with an oversize knife.

He turned abruptly. For the first time he acknowledged Arne. "Alive, are you?" he growled. "Then sit up and eat."

Arne slid from the bunk. His stomach felt queer. He looked at the food. He was going to be sick. He looked away.

"From what fine place have you come that you turn your nose up?" the trapper asked.

"My home is in Oslo."

"Ho! From Oslo. So we have fine manners. Well, here we do not eat for pleasure. We eat to survive."

He cut a hunk of bread from the loaf and shoved it across to Arne. Then he grasped the coffeepot in a hand big as a bear paw and drank from the spout, mockery in his deep-set eyes.

It was unreal. The trapper seemed an actor playing a part. Nils had said the man was strange.

Arne tasted the fish. It was better than it looked. Now he was ravenous. He reached for more bread.

"Takk for maten," he said when the meal was finished.

The trapper did not answer his thank-you with the usual *Velbekomme*. He stabbed a toothpick between his teeth and fixed a hypnotic eye on Arne. "How is it you came here half-dead?"

Arne felt his face redden with embarrassment.

"I took a shortcut across the fjord. I thought the ice would hold."

The trapper chewed on his toothpick. "Why are you here alone?"

Arne squirmed under his gaze. "I'm on my way to see" —something in the trapper's eyes stopped him—"to see a friend," he finished lamely.

"A friend? And where is this friend?"

Arne was on guard. "North. . . ."

"How far?"

Arne shrank from the questioning, but the trapper's eyes bored into him, demanded answers.

"From here—maybe a hundred miles."

The trapper laughed—a derisive sound. "IGNOMIN-IOUS," he shouted. "You intend to travel that far north? A stupid boy who tries to cross thin ice and has already lost his provisions? The winter is almost at hand, and yet you are headed toward the Pole—to see a friend. Where did you start this crazy journey?"

Arne's face grew hot, but he stifled his anger. He needed the man's help. "From Longyearbyen. I have a map. I have money. I can pay if you will give me supplies."

"MONEY!" Hans sputtered. He roared that word again: "IGNOMINIOUS! What is money here? When did you begin this journey?"

"Three days ago."

The trapper crossed his arms over his wide chest and glared. "Let's have the truth. Longyearbyen was evacuated."

Arne was caught.

"Out with it. Why were you left?"

"I didn't want to go. I hid when the ships left."

"Why did you do such a stupid thing?"

Arne squirmed in his chair. "Because, because of my— friend. He wouldn't know what had happened."

"This friend—what is he doing up north?"

"He's a glacialist."

"A scientific man. He should be able to take care of himself and not need the help of a boy."

Arne swallowed his anger and pride. "Will you help me?" he asked again.

The trapper's eyes seemed to bore straight through Arne. "Not until you tell me the whole truth. Then I'll think about it."

Arne felt as if his insides were crumbling. How could he tell this stranger about his father? He wished he had more experience at judging people. How could one tell who was a quisling, a traitor?

The trapper shrugged. Turned away.

Arne had to tell if he were to have help. He blurted, "I'm going to my father. The Gestapo hunted him in Norway. He escaped. If he returns to Longyearbyen and they get hold of him, they'll put him in prison camp or worse. . . ."

The trapper's eyes glinted. "His name?"

"Bjørn Kristiansen," Arne gasped, with what seemed to him his last breath. He rubbed his eyes.

The trapper's face was expressionless. He pushed away from the table, hauled a rucksack from a shelf and tossed it to Arne. "It needs repairs. You can have a sleeping bag and what supplies you need."

Arne was too overcome with thankfulness to express it in

34

words. Now he had a friend. He set to work immediately on the rucksack. "I must be ready tomorrow."

"In the Arctic the weather decides such things," the trapper said. "You have a map showing where your father is." He held out his hand. "Give it to me."

Arne stiffened.

At that moment there was a scratching at the door.

"Kara," the trapper said and opened it.

A huge white dog bounded into the room.

"So that's the beast that attacked me last night!" Arne said. "I thought it was a bear."

"Attacked! Huskies love man."

Kara made a leap at Arne, almost knocking him to the floor. She licked his face. Nuzzled him.

Arne wrestled with the dog. Thanks to Kara, the trapper seemed to have forgotten about the map.

Later, when the trapper left the hut, Arne took the map from the pocket of his anorak and hid it inside his shirt.

Kara kept Arne company while he repaired the rucksack and stored in it the supplies Hans gave him. He sharpened tools and tarred skis.

The dog nuzzled Arne as he worked, teasing for attention.

Arne took Kara's head into his hands. "You're curious about me, same as the trapper," he said. "You'd like to pester me with questions, too."

Hans had pulled too much information out of Arne. Still, he reasoned, if someone fell into my hut half-dead, asking for help, I'd ask questions, too.

He got to his feet. "Let's see how these skis feel. Come on, Kara."

With the dog bounding at his side, Arne skied toward the fjord.

The regular order of day and night was changing. The stony land was passing into the long night. The sun was later each day in bobbing up over the horizon, and its course was shorter. There was only dawn and twilight. It was almost noon, and the sun was just rising. Again he counted the days he had left to reach his father. HURRY seemed burned into his brain.

In the distance, he saw the trapper, hand on the stock of his gun.

Silently, with just a gentle swish of his skis, Arne came closer.

A seal lay on the ice in the pale sunlight.

The trapper had a perfect shot at it.

He was taking too long.

Kara bounded to the shore. Barked.

Instantly the seal disappeared into a hole in the ice.

Arne laughed as he skied down to Hans.

Hans turned, raised a fist. "Ignominious," he shouted. "We could have had fresh meat."

Arne knew it had not been his or the dog's fault that the seal had escaped.

Hans' beard was covered with hoarfrost. He looked like a wild man. "The seal's blood would have given us energy for our journey tomorrow."

Arne stiffened. "OUR journey?"

It was the trapper's turn to laugh. "I'm going to make sure you don't fall through ice again."

"I don't need a bodyguard," Arne spat out.

The trapper turned toward the hut. "I have traplines to repair north along the fjord. For that distance I'll see you don't get into trouble."

Arne knew Hans' plan was sensible. The trapper knew the area. He could save Arne much time. But he felt uneasy. Why had Hans missed the seal? Trappers never missed.

And the word *ignominious*. A strange word for a trapper. The trappers Arne had known at Longyearbyen sometimes used colorful language. They swore. They would never say "ignominious."

Arne shrugged off the worry. He should be thankful for the trapper's help. What would he have done without Hans?

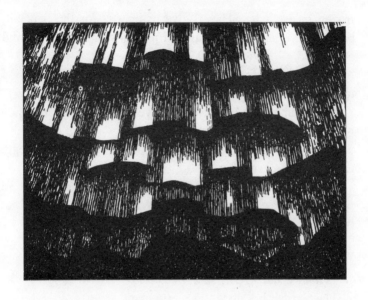

❄ 10 ❄

NIGHTMARE!

Arne was running, fast and away from the trapper.

But his feet stayed in one place.

Terror!

The trapper reached out, grabbed him.

Arne jerked awake.

Hans was shaking him.

"Weather's good," he said. "Time to be on our way. Eggs are ready."

"Eggs?" Arne said, trying to shake off the dream, sliding out of his bunk.

"Gulls' eggs. Saved since the laying season. I keep them

frozen in a glacier. They'll give us energy for the trip. Sit, boy, they've been boiling away for almost half an hour and are done."

The egg Hans set before him was enormous. Arne tried to crack it. The shell was like cement.

"Don't spare your muscles. Give it a bang on the side with your knife," Hans instructed.

Arne gagged a little at the transparent white of the egg. He managed to swallow it.

"I've some chores," Hans said. "You saw up some frozen meat for Kara. Then chain her. We'll leave soon as I get back."

"Chain her?"

"She'll slow us."

"That's cruel," Arne said.

The trapper nodded. "It's a cruel land."

He took his gun from the shelf. There was a strange gleam in his eyes as he ran his fingers down the barrel. "Would you rather I shot her?"

The trapper stamped out, and Arne patted Kara. Then he took seal meat and a saw outside and began to cut it into pieces. He threw a few to Kara. And then he stared. The trapper's ski tracks were etched plainly in the snow.

Something about them worried Arne.

Where had he seen such tracks before? They had not been made by Norwegian skis.

A picture flashed into his mind. He was skiing with his father outside Oslo. His father pointed to ski tracks. "German," he pronounced.

All of the things that had bothered him about Hans now raced through Arne's mind. The trapper's way of speaking. His Norwegian was different from that spoken in Norway, not the same as in Spitsbergen. He had wormed out of Arne information about his father, information Arne had been determined to tell no one. He had known about the evacuation, yet radios were silent. Did Hans really have traplines? Was he going to them? If so, why would he not take Kara?

Pure terror washed over Arne. He had been about to lead this stranger to his father. He had been a fool.

Feverishly now he prepared to leave.

He grabbed his rucksack and all his supplies from the hut. He buckled on his skis.

Kara sensed his panic. She raced about, excited. She jumped up, putting her paws on Arne's shoulders.

Had Hans been joking about shooting the dog?

Kara trembled in her eagerness.

"You want to go with me, don't you? Well, why not?"

He thrust the seal meat he had sawed for her into his rucksack.

"We'll have to move fast. Let's go."

He dug his poles into the snow.

He was off.

The dog raced on ahead.

❋ 11 ❋

Arne had an eerie feeling that he was being followed. Again and again he broke his fast pace to search the frozen landscape.

Nothing!

He was making such good time on the flatlands along the fjord that he began to relax. His spirits soared. The going was easy. He sang to Kara. She seemed to understand. "We'll see Father sooner than I thought," he told her as they halted at the base of a steep cliff which blocked the shore-line. "Now we'll eat."

Kara snuggled up against him, tilting her head sideways, watching.

"Imagine how surprised he'll be to see us."

Kara nudged him.

He reached down and tugged at her heavy coat. "You're hungry. Is that what you're saying?"

Kara wagged her tail enthusiastically.

Arne gave her some of the seal meat. "I should have taken time to saw more. But when we get to Kings Bay, we'll get some."

Kara was finished with the food in seconds. Arne threw her a piece of the pemmican he was chewing. He scanned the trail behind him. Safe. "Let's go," he said.

Kara beat Arne easily on the climb up the cliff. With a smug look on her face, she waited for him on the crest of the ridge.

A glacier gleamed ahead. Wedged between twin peaks, the congealed river was a frozen highway. Northward rose an eternity of ice mountains. The sun was a flaming circle low over the horizon. How soon would it disappear alto-gether?

HURRY!

Arne dug in his poles and flew on the wind. As he fol-lowed the smooth curve of the glacier, he was constantly on the alert for concealed crevasses, for the grayish look of indented snow, a warning that wind and pressure had bridged over the top of a split.

There were ravines to skirt and boulders of ice at the glacier's sides to stay clear of. The way was strange, un-canny, exhilarating, but he felt in control. Nothing could stop him now.

He had not reckoned with Kara.

She could not keep up with him on the downhills. He waited for her time and again.

That night they slept in a creep-in, huddled together.

Arne had given the dog the last of the seal meat. "We'll be in Kings Bay tomorrow. By noon," he promised her.

But by noon that day they had traveled only half the distance to Kings Bay.

The cold was intense, the wind violent. It tore into the hood of his anorak and bit into his ears. It surrounded him, grabbing from all sides. At times it seemed to cut the skis from under him.

By late afternoon it wound down. Still, they had not reached Kings Bay.

Arne felt despair. He was tired and so was the dog. They moved slowly, clumsily.

It was night when they stood on a knoll and looked down at the village, a crescent along the shore. On the snow, gleaming under a polished moon, everything stood out plainly—houses, mine buildings.

Arne reached down and patted Kara where she lay panting in the snow. "Down there we'll get food, and I'll have a warm place to sleep."

But something was wrong.

There were no lights.

No smoke came from chimneys.

With a sinking feeling that gave way to nausea, he realized the town was deserted.

Then he saw a figure moving on skis.

Joyfully he started down the slope.

A big hulk emerged from the shadows. Familiar.

Kara ran toward the skier.

Arne shifted his weight, turned his skis abruptly to stop.
THE TRAPPER!

"Kara," Arne cried as he dug his poles into the snow and lunged in the opposite direction.

"Stop," Hans shouted.

44

Arne hurtled down the incline and across the frozen fjord.

A quick glance behind. The trapper was trailing.

Faster! FASTER!

A cliff loomed ahead.

Skis sideways, Arne climbed to a crest, then slid onto a glacier, a narrow ice road hemmed in by gigantic ice boulders.

Kara sprang ahead.

Arne glanced behind. The trapper was not in sight.

But Arne had failed to see the slight depression ahead, the grayness. Danger signal, CREVASSE!

Too late he felt the air roar up. At the same moment Kara made a gigantic leap over the abyss, Arne's skis struck at the edge. He plunged down.

He crunched to a sickening stop, one ski wedged against the wall of ice.

He clawed the sides of the crevasse, trying to grip and pull himself up. His mittened hands slid off the slippery wall.

Above his head he heard Kara's whimper. He could not see her.

How far down in the ice slit was he?

He tried to free his ski. Slowly, agonizingly, he did, only to slide down another foot. The ski caught again.

He was going to fall to the bottom of the crevasse.

He beat at the ice, flailed his arms and thrashed. Still he slid.

The cold crept into his bones. He must rest. Then try again.

He thought of his family, of his father, his long-ago father. He had called him "Papa."

His mother. Strange how he remembered her clearly

now. She was helping him build a snow troll. He heard her laughter . . . soft, chuckly. She sang him to sleep sometimes. He would sleep now.

From far off he heard a whimper.

Kara. Why was Kara whimpering?

Suddenly a light blinded him.

"ARNE! ARNE!"

The trapper's face loomed above him, casting a shadow.

❈ 12 ❈

Arne expected jeers, mockery.

"Hang on," Hans shouted. "I'll drop a rope."

Arne lunged for it. The pain in his arms brought life back to his body.

"Can you knot it around you?" Hans shouted down.

Slowly, with numb fingers, Arne managed the knot.

Then, agonizingly, he felt himself hauled to the surface.

Hans untied the knot. He did not rage at Arne. "Are you in one piece?" he asked.

"I think so," Arne said, untangling himself from skis and rope.

He staggered to his feet, and pain shot through his right ankle. It buckled under him.

Across, on the other side of the crevasse, Kara ran wildly.

"Lie down," Hans yelled.

Obediently the dog groveled in the snow.

"We've got to get over to that side," Hans said. "There's no way to get around the crevasse. There are ice bulges along both sides."

Arne limped to the edge of the dark slit. "It's not so wide. We could make a running jump."

"The way you're limping? We need a bridge. We'll have to make one."

"With what?"

"With what we've got. Our skis and rope. I'll bind the two pairs together. You toss our backpacks to the other side."

Arne watched as Hans lashed the skis double, knotted his rope and placed the "bridge" over the narrowest part of the crevasse. It looked flimsy over the dark abyss. He held his breath as Hans crawled out and flattened himself on the skis.

"Climb over me," Hans ordered. "It's the only way to be sure you won't slip."

Arne was too scared to think. He did as he was told.

Slowly, slowly, he crept on his hands and knees over the prostrate Hans.

Freezing air surged up from the black depths of the crevasse with a ghostly whine. The blood pounded in his ears, and, after an eternity, he was on the other side.

In terror he watched the big man crawl forward and off the ski bridge to regain his feet.

Kara greeted them as if they'd come back from the grave.

Hans untied the skis. "If you can ski down to the fjord, we'll make a sled for you."

It was a slow, painful journey. At the bottom there was an abandoned hut. When they reached it, Hans ripped planks from the sagging door. "We'll use your skis for the runners."

Kara, meanwhile, raced in circles. "Huskies like to pull. She knows something's up," Hans said.

"She's hungry," Arne said. "I ran out of food for her."

"It's not a long run. She'll make it all right. I'll fix her a make-do rope harness."

Arne marveled at the trapper's ingenuity with the few tools he had. Finally, he watched him tie a rope for steering at the end of the crude sled. He remembered his father's words about knowledge and patience being necessary to survive in the Arctic.

Kara was wild with excitement, ready to be off.

Hans packed the sledge with their rucksacks.

"All right, Arne, get on," he said.

Arne hobbled onto the sled.

"Go, Kara," Hans shouted.

Off they soared, the trapper alongside shouting commands: "Left, steady, right."

Arne's ankle did not hurt as much now that he was off it. As he lay snug and warm on the sled, he felt overwhelming gratitude toward Hans.

How could he have doubted the motives of the trapper? He had saved his life twice, even risked his own.

"HALT!" The trapper's voice rang out as they approached a hut built on a rise along the fjord. Even in the darkness, Arne could tell that this was a strong hut. The moon hung over it like a lantern, close and big, silvering the snow on the roof.

After he had limped inside and the trapper had lighted a lamp, he saw that the hut was clean and well cared for. There was kindling, logs, coal.

Soon a fire was blazing in the stove and water was boiling in the kettle.

"How is it that we can use any hut?" Arne asked.

"It goes back a thousand years. King Øystein of Norway decreed the death sentence for the ones who did not leave a hut in the same condition they found it. It's a matter of survival. And now, let's have a look at your ankle."

Arne had a hard time getting off the right boot. "Swollen," Hans said as he probed gently. "No bones broken. I'll get a bucket of snow, and we'll put on some cold compresses."

By the time that was done and Kara had been fed, tea was ready, and Hans brought Arne a mugful.

"*Takk,*" Arne said. He felt guilty, ashamed, for all the trouble he had caused Hans. "Why aren't you angry?" he asked.

Hans shrugged. "I was young once. I understand impatience. You were in a hurry to reach your father."

"Why didn't you abandon me? Why did you follow me?"

"You had my dog."

Arne reached down and petted Kara, who was lying at his feet. What had made him even think Hans would harm the dog? Remorseful, he was about to say so, but the trapper was on his feet. "We must have a feast to celebrate your safety."

The feast turned out to be a can of fish balls and flat-bread. It did indeed taste like a feast.

The hut was cozy in the lamplight. A bearskin was nailed to the wall. The bunks were covered with deerskin pelts. Black-and-white drawings of peaked mountains and frozen

50

seas were on the walls. There was a shelf of books. Another shelf held a row of bears carved from driftwood.

The hut, Arne thought, was that of an educated man.

It had been a long day. Arne's eyes were heavy. He climbed into bed. He thought about tomorrow. Would his ankle be strong enough to travel? He had maybe seventy more miles to go. At twenty miles or so each day, he would see his father in three days.

Tomorrow he would show Hans the map. Hans would help him plot the way.

Tomorrow . . .

❋ 13 ❋

Arne had a nightmare.

An ice bear, towering over the cabin, banged against the roof with huge paws.

He awakened with a start. Jerked upright.

BANG! There it was again.

"Bear . . ." he yelled down to the trapper, who was stoking the stove.

"Just the wind slamming scraps of corrugated iron around the chimney," Hans said.

Arne came fully awake. He swung out of bed. Slid to the floor. Pain, like fire, shot through his ankle.

"A bad morning," Hans growled. "The wind is from the east. We're in for some unweather."

"Unweather?"

"You'll see."

Arne limped to the window. All he could see was snow flashing against it. Everything in the hut rattled.

"Sit," Hans said. "This morning it's oatmeal. There's yeast in the cupboard but no bread."

Arne bolted his breakfast.

"Let me have a look at your ankle," Hans said.

"It's better," Arne said. "It won't slow me today."

"Today?" Hans exploded. "You're not going anywhere today on that ankle and in this weather."

"Look," Arne said, pulling up his pants leg. "The swelling is down. I'm used to storms. We have them in Norway."

Hans pounded a fist on the table. "You just think you know storms. You'll not travel today. Maybe not for a week. But then again, maybe in a day or two."

Arne pushed away from the table. "I must go."

"Going now would be a waste of energy," Hans said. "Here we learn to conserve energy."

"I can't just sit when every day counts," Arne shouted.

"All right," Hans said calmly. "Go. But first, bring in wood. You'll find it, all cut, on the west side of the hut. Take a sack to drag it."

Arne's ankle began to thump when he pulled on his boots. It would stop.

He put on sweater, anorak, gloves, and made for the outdoors.

The wind grabbed him the second he was out of the hut. It came from all directions. It cut his legs from under him. He stumbled. His ankle throbbed.

53

By the time he reached the wood, ice crystals clung to his face, and his hands in his mittens were stiff.

The wind had swept the wood clean of snow, but it took an eternity to fill the sack and drag it into the hut. He stumbled inside, exhausted, his lungs aching. He fell into a chair, gasping.

Hans handed him a mug of steaming cocoa. "How soon you leaving?"

Arne gritted his teeth. "You win."

"It's early for this kind of storm," Hans said. "It could die down by tomorrow. Don't worry too much. I know safe shortcuts." He grinned. "Without crevasses to fall into."

Arne pulled off his boots and rubbed his ankle. The trapper did know best, and he was a friend.

"Let's go over your map," Hans said.

For a moment Arne hesitated. I must trust him, he thought.

He took the map from its hiding place and handed it to Hans.

They began to plot the route.

❊ 14 ❊

The blizzard did not let up. It worsened as the day crept on.

Disheartened, Arne fidgeted while Hans calmly went about making bread: punching it down, shaping it into loaves, shoving them into the oven.

"The wind is like a thousand voices, all untrained," Hans said.

But to Arne, the wind was like the long-drawn-out screech of some fearful monster.

It started far away, got louder and louder, closer and closer, hurled itself against the hut, clutching at loose boards—anything in its way. It wound around and around the hut, shaking it until the curtains stood out like sails and the next moment were sucked back onto the windowpane. Tongues of snow, fine as smoke, sharp as needles, came through cracks in the walls.

Then, suddenly, the wind faded, only to begin all over again—again—and again—until Arne pounded on the wall and yelled, "STOP."

"It will," Hans said. "In its own time."

"It will blow the hut away before it stops," Arne cried.

Hans shook his head. "This hut has stood for many winters. Here, ignorance is the killer."

"Ignorance?"

"Of how to survive," Hans said. "It killed a hutful of soldiers just a few months ago, not many miles from this very spot."

"Soldiers?"

"Frozen. All of them. They took refuge in a hut. When the door was opened, they fell out like so many matchsticks."

"Where did they come from?"

"That's not known. Maybe a landing party, maybe from a torpedoed German warship. . . ."

"Germans. GOOD!" Arne spat out.

"NO," Hans shouted, raising a fist.

Arne drew back.

The wind roared down the iron stovepipe, blew the door of the oven open, and clouds of cinders scattered into the room.

"IGNOMINIOUS!" Hans raved. He rushed to the oven, brushed cinders from his browning loaves. "Done," he said, smiling broadly now. "And what do you think we have to go with it? Cloudberry jam."

Cloudberry jam! Arne had not had any since Norway. He devoured half a loaf of the bread and a good part of the jam before he really thought about it. To borrow a hut and find such treats as flour and jam was certainly a surprise.

Other things here were strange.

He hobbled about the hut, examining the books. They were in several languages. In one corner was a row of Bibles, again in different languages.

He ran his hands over the carved bears. He thought they were very good.

An old trunk stood against one wall. Arne tried to lift the lid. Locked.

When he glanced up, the trapper's gaze was on him. For that instant, Hans seemed threatening. A prickle of apprehension ran through Arne. Was Hans really a trapper? He'd test him. "When I was outside, I saw ptarmigan. They would be good with the fresh bread for supper."

"There are lentils here," Hans said. "Lentil soup is also good with fresh bread. Who wants to go out in this un-weather to bag ptarmigan?"

Arne could not fault the answer.

That night Arne lay awake in the upper bunk. Questions twirled about in his mind. Why had Hans been so angry at Arne's reaction to the death of the German soldiers? All Norwegians, unless they were quislings, were against the invader.

There was something mysterious about the hut. Hans was very much at home in it, almost as if it were his. Could this be? There were animals skins—bear, deer, walrus—on the walls and on the bunks, but had Hans really bagged them? Hans, who could not shoot a sleeping seal?

Questions, many questions. All unanswered. While Arne

brooded, the savagery of the storm diminished. Did that mean they could leave tomorrow? He'd ask Hans. The lamp was still lit.

He sat up and looked over the edge of his bunk. Hans was close to the stove, doing something with his hands. He was carving a bear.

Arne lay back. His mind did flip-flops. The hut must belong to Hans.

No, not possible. It belonged to an educated man.

Below, he heard the chair scrape against the floor. The light went out. Hans moved in the lower bunk.

Why, Arne wondered, had he not come out and asked Hans directly about the hut?

Deep down, Arne knew the answer. He was afraid.

Of what?

He did not know.

Arne came awake with a start. Had he dreamed that
frightening moan?

He sat up.

The storm?

No, outside it was deadly quiet. The storm was over.
Jubilantly, he slid down from his bunk and tested his ankle.
Good.

Kara got up from where she lay next to Hans' bed,
stretched and came to him.

The moan again. It came from Hans' bunk. A nightmare
probably.

Arne turned toward him, shook his shoulder. "The storm is over. We can go," he said.

Hans turned feverish eyes toward him. "I'm freezing. Keep the fire going," he gasped.

Arne heaped wood on the dying embers, put on the kettle.

Hans was shivering. "Arne, malaria back again, medicine in the chest, key on a hook behind the clock."

Arne sprang to the chest and unlocked it.

The lid creaked as he raised it. A murky smell came from the chest's interior. He dug through photographs, books, clothing, to find a box with medicines, which he took to Hans.

"Quinine," Hans said, pointing to a bottle of tablets.

Arne brought a mugful of water to Hans, who was shaking so violently he spilled it.

Arne hurried to find more bedclothes. He made tea, gruel. All the while his mind groped with his problems. His need to reach his father, Hans' sudden sickness.

Hans was quieter now.

Arne gulped breakfast, his map propped up against the medicine box.

He figured seventy more miles to his father. Six days left to reach him. Time was running out. As he folded the map, his glance fell on the box of medicines. It was old, made of some kind of metal. He had not noticed the lid before—an etching of a city, some of it worn off. At the bottom, the name of the city—Hamburg. Hamburg, GERMANY. GERMANY!

Fear shot through him with needle pricks. The box meant nothing, a souvenir box. Now unexplained things jumped into Arne's mind to nag him. The trapper's insistence on helping find Arne's father, the many kindnesses, all of them leading to his father—*after* Hans knew his father was wanted by the Nazis.

Hans was asleep now. Arne stood next to his bed and studied his face. If Hans shaved, what would he look like? Far different. Only the hair on his face made him appear rough, uncouth.

The man was helpless, yet Arne felt unsafe, as if he were teetering on the edge of a crevasse.

Foolish. Hans had been good to him. And yet . . .

Across the room, the lid of the chest still stood open and drew Arne. Quietly he went over to the corner, knelt before the chest, began to go through its contents. A fine suit, black. The label inside the coat—a Hamburg tailor. There were many photographs, family pictures, all with the imprint of a German photographer.

All but one—of a young man in the uniform of a German officer and taken in a desert country. On the back of the photograph in heavy script, he read, "AFRICA, 1917."

Something about the face was familiar. The eyes—deepset, intense. The young man clean-shaven, but if he had hair on his face . . . HANS!

Softly, Arne closed the chest.

Now he knew.

His legs were weak as he got to his feet.

"Arne, the fever, a little water," Hans begged. "Thank you, thank you, Arne."

Arne put on sweater and anorak and went outside for more wood.

He sawed meat for the dog.

He gave the trapper his medicine. He put food close by. Water.

"Tonight and tomorrow will be the worst," Hans mumbled. "The crisis. We'll reach your father in time. I know shortcuts."

Arne pulled his rucksack over his shoulders.

The trapper watched, eyes wild. He tried to sit up and fell back. "Wait, Arne, wait."

Arne went to the door, looked back.

Hans seemed more dead than alive.

The dog followed Arne outside.

Arne buckled on his skis and pushed off.

He looked back. The dog was following. Well, why not?

The smooth snow was marked with an occasional track.

He saw the mark of a fox. Once he saw the print of a bear. He did not want to meet up with a bear.

Suddenly Arne realized Kara was no longer with him.

He turned.

She was way behind, standing still, her tail lowered.

"Kara!"

She ran to him.

"Let's go."

The dog seemed puzzled.

Arne thrust his poles into the snow and went forward. He looked back. Kara was running the other way.

Arne did not call her again. But as he skimmed over the snow and glided around curving hills, her puzzled look haunted him.

After a time he stopped to check his compass and look at his map.

He was ready to go again when, racing toward him came a herd of reindeer. They halted abruptly some thirty feet from him, their white coats blending with the snow. They turned away.

Before Arne could recover from his surprise, they were

back again. Closer now, watching him. If he were a trapper with a gun, he could pick off whichever one he wanted. Didn't they know that?

Their curiosity satisfied, they walked away lazily.

They trusted him. Didn't they know that was dangerous?

He didn't trust, and because he didn't, he had left a man who might die. If he could not reach his medicine, if he could not keep the fire going, Hans would die. A man who twice had saved his life. Should he have tried to trust Hans in spite of what he had discovered in the chest? He didn't know.

He stood there and he realized how young he was. Twelve years old, and he must make a decision about life and death.

He remembered the disbelief in Hans' eyes when he had left.

Hans had begged for time. "We'll reach your father. I know shortcuts."

In order to give Hans what he asked for, Arne had to trust him.

"I have to go back," Arne said. "I have to go back."

❆ 16 ❆

From far off he saw Kara waiting at the door of the hut. She ran to meet him, wagging her tail furiously. When Arne took off his skis and pushed in the door, the dog squeezed in ahead and ran to Hans' bed.

He was just as Arne had left him.

The fire was almost out.

The gruel was untasted.

Even before taking off his anorak, Arne piled wood onto the embers and took medicine to Hans. He was burning up, throwing off the covers, delirious.

Arne nursed him for two more days, frightened for Hans, frightened for his own father. During the second night the fever broke. Hans was drenched in sweat. Arne brought him warm, dry clothes. They had to be changed again and again.

Toward morning, Arne dozed in a chair beside him. When he awakened, the trapper was trying to sit up. He was rational. His eyes were steady on Arne. "You came back. Why?"

"I don't know. You're a German, a German officer. I saw what was in the chest. The Gestapo is after my father. We can't go home to Norway. I don't know why I came back. Maybe I'm like the reindeer I saw. They came back for a second look at me, to see what I really was, I guess. Maybe I had to do the same."

Hans managed a wan smile. "Whatever the reason, I'm grateful." He sighed. "There was a time I too ran away. Unlike the reindeer, I never went back."

He closed his eyes. Arne wanted him to go on. "Why did you run?"

Hans seemed to come back from some far-off place. "I was a chaplain. For four years I saw the stupidity, the waste of war."

He paused, as if the memories were too painful.

After a moment he went on. "After it was over, I had a church in Hamburg. When the second war was coming, I knew I could not go through it again."

Hans looked spent, but Arne wanted to hear the rest. "How did you get away?"

"As a student I had spent much time in Norway. I knew Spitsbergen. Norwegian ships often came into the port of Hamburg. One day I boarded a freighter. I came here to lead my life alone, without disorder, ugliness. I brought my books, and I made a nest for myself. I would kill only when I had no other food. War would never touch me again."

He smiled. "Then you came. War did touch me." He held out his hand. "Give me a lift. I'm shaky, but I can get up. Tomorrow we will go to your father."

As Arne went about getting ready for their departure, one thing still bothered him. How had Hans known about the evacuation? The radio at Longyearbyen had been silenced. Also those on the British ships. And yet, when Arne had arrived half-dead at Hans' hut, he had known about it.

No, Arne decided, he would not ask.

He believed Hans' story.

He would trust.

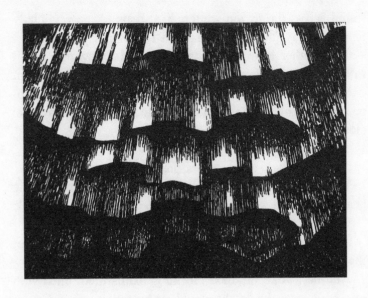

❇ 17 ❇

Images—frightening, thrilling, awesome—imprinted themselves on Arne's mind as they sped north. Icebergs, blue-tinged in the wan sunshine. Snow, fine as flour, squeaking beneath skis. A yellow moon present day and night. Air so clear the ends of the earth were visible. A glimpse of musk-oxen, the fresh tracks of hugh bear paws.

Worries. Could Hans keep up the terrific pace? Would he become ill again? How about Kara? Would they reach the great ice wall in time? Or would they find his father had already left and was returning to Longyearbyen and the Nazis?

There was a moment of terror. An ice bear and two cubs

stared across the frozen whiteness at them. Arne was ready to bolt. "Stay," Hans commanded both Arne and Kara.

The mother bear turned tail, the cubs following. "She'd rather eat seal," Hans said, taking his hands from the gun.

Shreds of pale sunshine hung in the clouds and disappeared into blue night. Hans announced, "I know a hotel close by."

"Hotel?"

"An old bear's cave. Abandoned," Hans said. "Safe."

The two-room bear hotel—dry and warm. Hans heating beans on a Primus.

Cozy.

Arne watched the shadows, unable to completely forget the former owner.

And he awoke the next morning, exhilarated, filled with joy. Today was the day he would see his father.

Apprehension.

The hunt for the camp amid sheer walls of ice, domes of crystal, bizarre, unreal shapes.

They were too late.

Had it all been for nothing?

Hans faltering, Kara tired, Arne felt defeat. Cold chilled him to the bone.

Suddenly he saw thin smoke rising. A mirage?

Closer now. A tent, two men, Father's voice. Arne falling into strong arms. Tears freezing on his face. A heavy weight lifted, and Arne was a child again, home with his father.

Hans forgotten, then remembered and pulled into the circle.

Father moved them toward shelter, warmth, food.

The Swiss scientist served up boiling soup.

Thawing, emerging from an ice cocoon. Arne was alive again.

Now Father asked questions. "What has happened? Why are you here?"

Arne told him.

His father was shocked.

"There was no way to let you know that you must not come back to Longyearbyen, that the Nazis were expected to invade," Arne said. "The radio was silenced. The evacuation had to be secret."

Arne's father struggled to control his feelings. "You stayed behind, you came all this distance. . . ."

"Father, I had no choice, not after I saw the first Nazi ship in the harbor. I could not have made it if I had not found Hans' hut. He saved my life."

"And you saved mine," Hans said.

Arne's father covered his face with his hands. Then he grasped Arne's shoulders tightly. "My son," he said, "how you have grown up."

The Swiss passed a steaming platter. "We thought our radio had failed. Tomorrow we would have been on our way to Longyearbyen."

Kara, well fed, lay under the table, content.

The meal finished, the talk turned to escape.

"Arne and I shall take our chances on a passing boat," Arne's father said.

"That is what an old trapper hoped to do," Hans interrupted. "He stopped by my hut just before Arne came. He had come from Longyearbyen, and he told me of the evacuation. He did not want to leave the Arctic. He said he would sit out the war in Iceland. I hope he made it."

Arne, listening, was thankful he had not asked Hans how

he had known about the evacuation. He was glad he had trusted.

The Swiss decided to return via Longyearbyen. "The Germans will allow a Swiss to pass, and I shall have Hans' company part of the way."

"I had hoped Hans would come with us," Arne's father said.

Hans shook his head. "Kara and I will stay. But after the war is over, we shall meet again."

They gripped hands with the promise.

Later Arne went outside the tent. Kara snuggled up against him.

Arne dug his fingers into the dog's thick fur. How could he say good-bye? His father came to stand beside him, his arm across Arne's shoulder.

They watched the Northern Lights move against the sky. Often Arne had seen them, but never as they were now, shining extravagantly, greenish to white, the stars and the moon glowing through the transparent veils.

The lights flashed across the sky continuously, as if they were sending a message of hope. The war would end one day. Arne and his father would return to Norway. The world would be right again.

✳ Epilogue ✳

Arne and his father made their escape via a fishing boat to the Shetland Islands and, eventually, to England.

On September 3, 1943, the German superbattleship *Tirpitz,* a cruiser and ten destroyers left the Norwegian fjord where they were hiding and headed for Spitsbergen. Longyearbyen was burned to the ground. The mines were set on fire.

On November 15–16, 1944, a British bomber spied the *Tirpitz* as she hid along an island in the neighborhood of Tromso, Norway, and dropped a bomb. It fell so close in the shallow sea that the battleship tipped over and lay bottom side up.

When the war was over and Norway was finally liberated, Arne and his father returned.

Arne was now seventeen.

They kept their pact to meet with Hans. They came together in Tromso, gateway to Spitsbergen. It was the time of the Midnight Sun, of music and laughter.

It took half the midsummer golden night to catch up on what had happened. . . . Longyearbyen was being rebuilt. There were greetings from Nils, from the Paulsons, warm invitations to Arne and his father to visit.

Later, Father, Arne and Hans got a lift on a small motorboat to the place where the capsized *Tirpitz* stuck out of the water. Together they walked over its flat hull.

"It was all so useless," Father said.

"Ignominious," Hans said.

"Ignominious," Arne echoed.

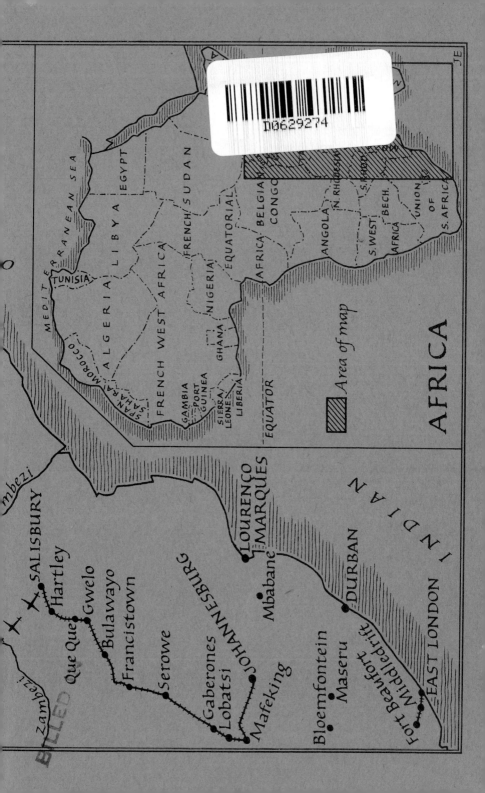

DRAWN IN COLOR

DRAWN

NONI JABAVU

IN COLOR

African Contrasts

T MARTIN'S PRESS • NEW YORK

For my Husband
Michael Cadbury Crosfield
with dearest love

Contents

vii

Author's Note

I BELONG to two worlds with two loyalties; South Africa where I was born and England where I was educated. When I received a cable sent by my father from my home in South Africa I flew back there to be amongst my Bantu people, leaving my English husband behind in London.

Later that year, he and I went to live in East Africa to be near my only sister who had married out there.

I have told here something of my own background and circumstances since this is a personal account of an individual African's experiences and impressions of the differences between East and South Africa in their contact with Westernisation.

Acknowledgements

THE following friends, not all of whom agree or identify themselves with everything I think or say, have solicitously cheered me at my work and I thank them from the bottom of my heart: Mr Robert Graves, who invited me to stay with him and his family in Mallorca, thus giving me inestimable peace and quiet during the last arduous weeks of typing; The Baroness Ravensdale, for generosity most imaginative, elegant and kind; Mr Norman Prouting, for giving me the freedom of his charming house in Chelsea when I grew weary of the furnished flat I had taken in Westminster to do my revisions of this book. And I can never give enough thanks for continual moral support during the whole time I worked in London, to Mr & Mrs Richard Chilver, Mr James Cameron, The Hon. Anthony Grigg, Mr Charles Lewis, Mr Philip Mason; or to The Countess of Clarendon, for being the first to urge me years ago not to be content with merely reminiscing to her and other close friends about my Bantu background but to 'write it all down in a book so that other people might share it'. And I can never thank my family in South Africa enough for the part they have played.

I am most deeply and affectionately grateful to Mrs Osyth Leeston for her very great understanding, her unfailing encouragement, as well as for the incomparable assistance she has given me throughout the writing of this book.

And I thank Sir John Murray very warmly indeed for his interest and for his most helpful advice.

I would also like to thank Mr Cyrus Brooks for his immense sympathy and for showing his faith in my efforts over many months.

Finally, I am much indebted to Mr Roland Brown for most

xi

kindly checking the manuscript and making valuable corrections on technicalities and facts.

N.J.

Acknowledgement is also made for permission to quote from copyright works as follows: J. McLaren's *A Xhosa Grammar* published by Messrs Longmans, Green & Co. Ltd (used on p. 57); 'Restoration Comedy' from *Punch*, 9 November 1955 (pp. 167–8); Professor Kenneth Ingham's 'Some Aspects of the History of Buganda' from the *Uganda Journal*, Vol. 20, No. 1, March 1956 (pp. 173–4).

A Cable from the Cape

THE CABLE arrived for me in London from South Africa. It was from my father, about my only brother, Tengo, twenty-six years old, reading medicine at the University of the Witwatersrand in Johannesburg. The week before, I had had a letter from him outlining plans he was making for when he would qualify in a few months' time. My sister and I hoped he would take a holiday abroad after the long years of training, stay with her in Uganda, East Africa, where she had married and gone to live, then come on to stay with me in London where I had married and lived. He would thus see both countries of his sisters' adoption. He was the youngest of the three of us, the only son, and it was some time since we had all seen one another.

But on March 8th, a young messenger boy whistled up to my house, stamped jauntily on the steps and rubbing his fingers to keep warm while waiting for a possible answer to the message he delivered:

'TENGO SHOT DEAD BY GANGSTERS FUNERAL SUNDAY
13TH JABAVU'

Before this I had always travelled between the Cape and England by sea, so to fly thousands of miles down the length of Africa was for me to see the size of my country for the first time; and as I looked down, the sight stirred the imagination far more than I had somehow expected it would.

But as the plane flew on and Africa unfolded below, that bizarre message jostled in my mind not letting my impressions develop as they would under more normal circumstances.

Now we were leaving the Rhodesias, were on the final lap to Johannesburg.

The air-hostess came round with sheets of paper for each passenger to fill in. We had got used to one another by this, almost our second night together. It was dark and we knew we were over the Transvaal. I studied my form and started to work on it trying to push my father's incredible message to one side for a while. Scanning the form I came to the paragraph in which they ask what brings you to South Africa. After some time I saw that I had to fill this in. I wrote: 'Coming home to my family for the funeral of my brother shot dead last Sunday by Johannesburg gangsters.' I still could not believe it and therefore wrote, I think, like an automaton; if I had fully believed, I doubt if I could have stated the reason like that, or at all.

Presently our forms were collected and the air-hostess glanced at each one to check before putting it away in her folder. I saw her glance at mine, saw her read it again and found myself thinking with a sudden pang of hope, 'So she too can't believe!' And watching her re-read my form several times the insidious notion haunting me reared up even more: my brother might have been shot, yes, this could happen to almost anyone in Johannesburg as the whole world knows. But let him not be dead. He would not, could not, must not be when I finally reach home. Tengo might perhaps be silent when I got there, unconscious, what, oh what could my father mean by 'funeral'?

I think that such attempts at self-deception torture everyone at some time in their life. Who hasn't felt it? Yet knowing this does not curb the terrible, wishful thoughts. They stampede in this uncontrollable fashion. At that moment the bizarreness that had been with me for the whole flight, through Paris, Athens, Cairo, Khartoum, Nairobi, Lusaka, reared like a dragon so that I did not know what to do with myself. But the thing that helped just then was totally unexpected; as the lights of the Rand now twinkled below and we all started to shuffle about collecting ourselves to the usual warning about seat-belts and landing regulations, the air-hostess walked up and stopped by me, bent down and whispered in my ear in a strong South African accent, 'When we get out, come with me. I'll see you get done first so you won't be kept waiting. All right?'

Our eyes met and she smiled, warm, human, womanly. I was almost overcome and, momentarily putting wishful thinking aside, asked myself, why does this girl move me so deeply? Had not other people shown this same human quality back in England when they heard what had happened?

Months afterwards I thought I had the answer—that it was perhaps because it is wonderful if you are a South African, when a South African of another 'colour' peeps through the prison bars of 'race' and you see another human being, warm, kind and nice. That girl was striking when I had first seen her at London Airport, extremely handsome with beautiful smooth skin, bright brown eyes; a little later she had impressed me even more when I realised that she greeted me and spoke as courteously as she did to the other ('white') passengers. After that, when the flight schedule had been handed round I particularly studied it to see what her name was and saw that it was a Boer one, that she was none the less 'a proper Boer' as we say at home.

We landed, taxied and stopped. As soon as I stepped out of the plane with its relaxed international atmosphere, I could feel the racial atmosphere congeal and freeze round me. The old South African hostility, cruelty, harshness; it was all there, somehow harsher than ever because Afrikaans was now the language. You heard nothing but those glottal stops, staccato tones; saw only hard, alert, pale blue eyes set in craggy sun-tanned faces.

As soon as I appeared in the doorway of the aircraft, black and white men flashed press photographers' bulbs at me making me blink and draw back. I had not expected this and was surprised. Voices shouted peremptorily at me from these men who milled round in their grey flannels, tweed jackets, mackintoshes, trilby hats, 'Make a statement about the death of Tengo!' 'Hey, will you arrive at Middledrift in time for the funeral?' 'When did you get the news?' 'Make a statement!' 'Statement!' 'Statement!'

In the clamour it was difficult to absorb the fact that on this night I was one of the victims of the Press, whose 'statements'

3

one so often saw splashed across picture papers under headlines laying personal agonies bare. I realised how until that moment I had not known what such people must feel when journalists swoop upon them in this way.

But what took my breath away was that black men were being every whit as impersonal, unfeeling as white. Africans who are inclined to the idea of 'Pan-Africanism' as many are in recent years, claim that black people have the quality of *ubuntu*, human feeling, and that white people lack it. Well, here was sophisticated westernisation in both colours, white and black.

I did not answer. The air-hostess turned and beckoned me to come in spite of them and I again stepped forward.

She kept the promise she had made, and thanks to her the Boers did indeed attend to me first, before the white passengers. As they scrutinised my papers throwing me glances of curiosity, I noticed their faces, hard as granite as we blacks always say, mouths set, lips blenched and tight, jaw muscles clenched. It was as if they were doing some kind of violence to themselves in acting on the prompting of the Boer girl's human feeling and being led to violate their racial code.

Months afterwards however, on returning to Europe partly overland and crossing into Southern Rhodesia by train, I was to discover that in their confusion in breaking their custom they had forgotten to stamp my 'entry' into South Africa, and I was to have an interesting word about this with yet another Boer.

On reaching Johannesburg the first lap of my journey was over. The following morning, Saturday, I had two more laps to do, first to the airport outside East London which is the one nearest my home; after that, seventy miles by road to Middledrift, our village in the Ciskei Native Reserve which lies across the Kei River from the better-known Transkei Native Reserve.

I caught the internal airline plane *Teevink*. We halted at Durban in Natal Province. More English was audible there than in the Transvaal, it being of course the former stronghold of British rather than Boers. I telephoned a friend, Rabia Ebrahim. At that time the public telephone booth was not

4

labelled 'Europeans Only' or 'Non-Europeans Only', but while I dialled and spoke there were kicks on the door and I looked up to see one of those harsh, tight-lipped, sun-tanned, pale blue-eyed faces glowering at me through the glass.

Rabia said how it was only two days before that she too had first heard the news, had opened her paper and was confronted with the account of the murder of my brother. 'Yusuf and I have been wondering if you could come,' and then her voice breaking a little, 'Oh Noni! . . .'

When the plane landed at East London, I saw through the porthole a reassuring little bank of relations and friends standing there waiting. Cordelia drove me to her house. From there my cousin Jeannie Jolobe was to drive me home. She had come that morning from Lovedale, nearly ninety miles. Her husband, who was a minister, was to help officiate at our funeral. She was able to tell me a little about what was happening at home, about my father.

'What about my sister? Is she here?'

Jeannie replied, stricken, 'My dear, we don't know if she even knows. We have heard nothing from Uganda.'

When Cordelia and her husband Sonny, a kinsman of mine, had given us something to eat, Jeannie and I at once set off.

I looked out at the countryside and thought how unchanging it was while people lived and died. The tarred road that I knew so well between East London and King William's Town across 'the land of the Ama-Ndlambe and the Ama-Ntinde' as we call it in our language, disintegrates into its old dusty corrugations after · passing King William's Town and goes on through stunted bush, country that was once the 'park' kind of African landscape but is now dotted only with scanty thorn trees; a land of droughts, overpopulated, overstocked. But across the wide, open land and on the distant horizon sharply drawn in the crisp sunlight, I saw the typical, wonderful Cape Province frieze of grandiose mountains.

When we had passed Blaney Junction we saw a small blue van ahead of us striking a following plume of dust and because of this we had to drop speed a little. We crossed the Xesi River

5

and drove through Middledrift proper, then out towards the railway station on the other side. The small blue van went before us. Presently we saw it leave the parched white corrugated road, take to the veld and bump along through the location of huts and African houses of Annshaw; it was going our way, drew up at our house. And what did I see there but hundreds of people milling about in the afternoon sunshine, so many that the stark euphorbia trees that fringe our garden were almost hidden; neither could I see our Bird of Paradise shrubs nor the fresh thickets of blue plumbago that I knew.

That little van stopped at the gate. The driver got out, and as we too drew up in my cousin's car we saw that it was Mr Mpulu, the teacher at the local school whose white-washed rondavel class-rooms are a few hundred yards from our house. It was then that I remembered that Mr Mpulu did run a small delivery van. And now I began to realise that some men among the people gathered outside our house detached themselves from the crowd and, taking off their hats, approached the back of the van, opened the doors, flexed themselves and bent their grey heads to lift and carry.

For in his van Mr Mpulu had travelled to Blaney Junction to meet the Jo'burg train that had brought my brother's body home. So it had happened, as the people exclaimed and pointed out to console my father, that his eldest child had left London six thousand miles away at the same time as his youngest had been put on the train nearly a thousand miles away on the Rand and they had reached home together. And since this was a gathering of people in mourning who were tempted to seize comfort from any aspect of what was happening, they murmured to him, 'This is God's work, bringing the children home together. He is still with you. Be comforted.'

So too it was only now that I fully understood that my brother was dead; for I had last seen him in the flesh here by these euphorbias and plumbagos and Birds of Paradise shrubs leading to this very verandah. I suddenly saw in my mind's eye how, just arrived for the university holidays, he had bounded into the house on those long muscular legs. I tried to look away

6

but could not help watching the six elderly men struggle to carry him. And I understood at last that we would never see his youthful leaps and bounds again.

They carried him through the plants in the garden, across the verandah, slowly, slowly through my father's book-lined study and into the big bedroom beyond it where they had carried my mother too, under our eyes four years before. And he too was being taken in to lie and wait so that hundreds should file past to look on his face and 'greet him for the last time'. The custom was being observed in everything; in the bare room, all furniture and pictures removed, my maternal uncles had already taken their places at each end of the improvised platform where the coffin would rest that night. Custom and rite demanded that they should guard their sister's son.

While they did so the house began to resound with the traditional exhortations and speeches 'to strengthen the bereaved', and I thought how more striking and stark these seemed when directed at oneself and one's own. There came a point during these impromptu speeches when it was felt that it would add to the 'strengthening' if Mr Mpulu would relate how he had fared when he had gone on his 'errand' to Blaney Junction.

So he started to tell in a deep voice and deliberate manner, in detail about the Blaney station-master, Mr van der Merwe; how 'that Boer had co-operated' to get the box unloaded and away; the wonderful way 'that Boer' had manipulated goods trains and waggons off the lines, had personally seen to it that the death-party should be spared the struggle of carrying the box all the way along the new, circuitous 'Non-Europeans Only' entrance and exit which, naturally, is the longest way round at all stations in South Africa nowadays, and instead had conducted them the most direct way, through the 'European Only'.

The mourners heard and exclaimed, 'My, the humanity of that Boer.' And someone elderly cried, *'Ama-Bulu asingabantu kakade?* Are Boers not people after all?'

That night the 'big people', the elders, were served dinner in

7

the dining-room. The house was so full that meals had to be held in relays; big people (heads of families, elders) in the dining-room; girls and young women who had come to help ate in the kitchen; and bucolic relations and such as felt too shy about their imperfect Western table manners were served out of doors in the yard, *braaivleis*, (barbecue style), next to our small cattle kraal where we keep two or three cows for milk. The full herd lives twelve miles away at our farm at Zanyokwe, where the family takes trips from time to time to see them. But as no home is a home without cattle, custom enjoins the presence of a kraal even if only a token one and even if milking-cows are only an ostensible reason. We were thus in a position to observe custom in this too, that there was a kraal next to which some of the men could eat food, the women at a distance from it.

Indoors in the dining-room my father sat at the head of the table, next to him my maternal uncles Cecil and Tennyson Makiwane, grey now, I saw, and stout, their faces much lined. Beyond them sat senior members of the paternal side including the oldest of all, my father's own maternal uncle whom I was seeing for the first time in my life, Henry Sakuba, last remaining brother of our paternal grandmother who had died in 1898 and to us children was that beautiful almost imaginary lady in huge Edwardian dresses with mutton-chop sleeves whose pictures had hung on the walls of our house ever since we could remember, fading daguerreotypes. There was one of these in the dining-room now, gazing down at the big people as they ate and talked.

Suddenly their buzz of voices was interrupted. At the door-way a deputation had appeared, of the family's young men and women in their twenties and nearly all Makiwanes; theirs was a flourishing clan unlike our Jabavus whose existence had been finally extinguished this week by my brother's death.

The young Makiwanes stood waiting, as was the custom, until one of the elders should speak to them first. As it is un-heard of for the young to interrupt the old at a meal, one of my aunts at once addressed them. She was not an 'aunt' in the

8

western sense, more of a 'second cousin once removed'; but because we acknowledge distant relationships in our extended family system which classified her within my parents' generation, she was my father's classificatory sister as anthropologists would say. She asked the young people what was the matter, and the moment she heard the opening sentences of their story she cried out loud to the consternation of everyone at table 'Oh my God, our child, our child!'

Everyone stopped eating; a hush extended through the door, through the house along the passages, to the kitchen where the helping women were busy. And finally the story came out, told by Cobham Makiwane who, though younger than some of us, was our senior maternal cousin, therefore it was for him to tell it.

This deputation of cousins and contemporaries or 'agemates' by generation, together with intimate friends of the dead son of the house, had been detailed to go to the station to meet the evening train bringing more batches of relatives from Johannesburg and bringing, too, some belongings of 'the late one' (as he was now called all the time) railed home by the Witwatersrand University authorities.

The young people's story was that one of them, Xola Makiwane, had become involved in one of those inevitable arguments with a white police officer. It had ended with the policeman arresting, handcuffing and marching him off to the cells over at the village, Middledrift. He was there at this moment, to be taken by the Black Maria in the morning with other 'pick-ups' over to Fort Beaufort prison twenty miles away to await trial.

From then on when the news penetrated, what eating could there be in the house? Food congealed on plates. The next morning, Sunday, was to be the day of the funeral; this arrest of Xola (his name meant 'Be-at-peace') was like a burying alive. (He was to be again buried alive when he and other relations were arrested for the famous Treason Trial some years later, but we were not to know this then.) The faces of the family glowed brown and stricken under the light of the Aladdin lamp on the dining-room table.

9

Long afterwards we all agreed about one thing: we would never forget the superhuman effort my father made that night on the telephone for three-quarters of an hour, pleading with the Boer police officer, appealing to the humanity we all know (how often we remark on it in South Africa!) lurks behind those granite-hard, sun-tanned faces, behind those glittering blue eyes.

'Please, *asseblief baas*, please! I ask you, *my baas*, what did this youngster do to you? "Cheeky" was he? What's that? "Fort Hare University cheek"? But *baas*, only this morning you met me at the station when I went to sign that chit for my boy's coffin. You shook my hand, squeezed it, didn't you? Said you felt sorry for me, didn't you, *baas*? Reminded me how you had known my son. Now how can you *do* this to me tonight? How can you arrest this boy? You know that he has come to help me bury my son. You know that he too is my child, he is my late wife's brother child, my boy's own cousin. What you *do* it for, *baas*?'

The house was filled with silence, women relatives pulling their rugs and thick shawls closer round their shoulders against the bitter cold South African night, everyone waiting, some praying, the men's gaze fixed on the floor.

A pressure lamp hung from the white match-board ceiling of the adjoining sitting-room. It hissed relentlessly over the shared humiliation.

At last all of us sitting there heard my father's voice in the next room alter in tone. From pleading it brightened and began to stutter and stammer, as usual with him when he became excited and in this a typical man of a clan which even the traditional 'praise-names' and 'clan salutations' describe as excitable. His changed tones electrified us.

'*Ja man, ja!* Aw right! I'll *come* to the cells! Wha' time? Four-thirty tomorrow morning? Yes, yes, yes! Thank you, *dankie baas, dankie!*'

And with that mixture of Afrikaans and English my father hung up and wound off the apparatus of our cumbersome rural instrument. He turned a tired face towards the roomful of people. Before him were mourners everywhere, on sofas, arm-chairs, stools, on the carpet. You could not move without care-fully picking your step. He now told how the Boer police officer had relented; how he had at first insisted that Xola had been cheeky, 'A cheeky bloody Fort Hare student kaffir boy', my father quoted. We all know the Boer attitude towards 'educated kaffirs'.

'But any'ow he softened: "Aw right, aw right, I'll talk things with you, Professor. But look yere, you gotta atten' at the cells yere at yarf-pars four tomorrow morning." ' My father involun-tarily mimicked, an aspect of his personality that asserts itself under any circumstances.

A gasp from everyone. 'Is that Boer mad? He *knows* it is the funeral tomorrow, *knows* that we are burying, that we're "con-cealing". How does he expect you, the father, to be up and over there across the valley at four-thirty in the morning? Does *he* rise at that hour?'

My father shrugged his shoulders. What was the use? Then to make us gently laugh, someone suggested, wry-voiced, that the police did rise as early as that in order to go raiding black people in their homes to fill the pick-up vans to the prison; he said grimly, 'You can always catch Natives sleeping in their houses.'

We resigned ourselves to the inevitable and shrugged our shoulders with my father.

But now spoke my father's 'mother', the very old white-haired maternal uncle whom we younger generation had been instructed when he arrived and was 'explained' or introduced, that 'by custom, *isiko*' we must call him 'Grand*mother*'. His white goatee twitched on the nut-brown toothless chin. '*Kulun-gile, mtshana. Akukhonto mntan'am*,' he said opening his remarks to my father with traditional phrases: 'All is well, nephew. It is nothing, my child. The Boer will release. He will free our child's child. You see, you knew how to speak to him. You spoke as befitted the occasion. You gave him the "*baas*" a Boer wants!'

At that our aunt, my father's classificatory sister, reared up like a stung mare. She was elderly, stout, had turned professional evangelist in her old age. Her eyes flashed as she turned, her greying eyebrows beetling at the part of the room where all we young were heaped on chairs, on the floor, even on the lid of the upright piano.

'You see, you young!' she harangued. 'You and your disdain when it comes to using wiles in dealing with the Boer, you with your insistence on looking the European straight in the eyes! Where does that get you? In the cells! Yet give him his *"baas baas baas"*, what does it cost when you would *see* how such a creature can be persuaded to be human? *Lino buntu i-Bulu*, it has humanity has the Boer. But one has to use tricks to drag its humanity out of it. Why disdain those tricks?'

2

The Family

I THOUGHT of all these things in church next day. It was packed
with Africans, liberally sprinkled with Boers, and 'Europeans'
(as we say for English), Coloureds, Indians. It was hot because
of the numbers; outside through the doors and windows, one
could see the spreading hillside where we lived covered with
motor-cars, buses, lorries. People had come on horseback too
and on foot, by train, by air, in their thousands.

Many of them explained to me why they had covered these
vast southern distances, and of course they had spoken, the
occasion being one so emotional, in our language *isi-Xhosa*,
expressive, forceful, not Biblical as some writers lead you to
think, more like Elizabethan English; words are pliable, can be
manipulated and therefore impregnated with subtle, often
startling shades of meaning; and 'from the shoulder', yet poetic
in allusion and illustration.

'Child!' they said. 'This news burst on us like the report of a
cannon! We heard but could not believe, COULD NOT BELIEVE!
Our Tengo dead so young, in his last few months of becoming
a trained doctor? Oh God-in-heaven! He who would have been
a precious doctor for our people, our only Tengo, of-Tengo-the-
Professor who is in turn Tengo-of-the-grand-old-one *u-Mhleli*,
Editor of our first newspaper-of-our-people-1884! We had to
come in order to see this "miracle" with our own eyes, only thus
could we *believe* that the Jabavus are now gone, finished, finally
departed. God gave them to us black South Africans. Now he
takes them away. Only by acting our part in this burial, this
concealment, could we be *resigned* to what has happened. We
had to come, child-of-our-child, else had we condemned ourselves
to go to our own deaths not satisfied, because not believing.'

And indeed, from my seat with the family (for this occasion

13

in the choir), I saw them listening with the utmost concentration when the officiating ministers announced that an account of the death was to be given, in an especially arranged interval during the service.

For this was indeed an especial day that the people had lived to see, this end of their leaders' line. My great-grandfather (who took his father's given name Jabavu, 'warrior-like', as a surname for himself and his children when the white man's law made surnames obligatory) had set his progeny's course in becoming a Christian convert; had been the first in the region to fit his hut with glazed windows; had educated my grandfather who became teacher then journalist then editor and owner of the first African newspaper in the land (as the people kept reminding me, 'way back in 1884'), and was 'the finest English speaker in this Border province', and politician associated with the great parliamentarians of the Cape Colony, Schreiner, Merriman, Rose Innes, C. J. Rhodes. In turn he had educated his sons, my uncles, sending my father, his eldest, 'to London, England, whence', as people said proudly, 'he had returned with a degree'. My father had later 'reared the young men and women of our people' in his capacity as a foundation member of the lecturing staff at Fort Hare, the college for higher education for which my grandfather had lobbied and campaigned while my father studied overseas that he might serve at such a seat of learning; and the campaign had succeeded, the college materialised in 1916 soon after my father returned.

The congregation looked at him now as he sat before them with, this day, his youngest, '*his* Tengo, the son who had been being educated too; that the people might benefit, this calf of noble animals', lying in the gleaming coffin in front of their eyes. How had the unthinkable thing come to pass? The people were now about to be told by one of my father's 'brothers', a classificatory uncle of mine who lived in Johannesburg and acted *in loco parentis* up there to my brother while he studied. One of the ministers now announced that my uncle would Tell How it Had Happened so that this huge congregation should know and be satisfied.

14

This uncle, 'Little Father' to my generation, was a succinct speaker who knew how to proceed from point to point in a way that the simplest country people present could follow. He started with a graphic description of the vicious slum conditions of '*e-Goli*, Johannesburg, where', he said, 'no man's life is safe, where people live insecure like fowls with their chicks ever liable at any moment whatsoever to be snatched by hawks diving from the skies!'

As he spoke in these terms that were common knowledge to all, moans and groans and spontaneous exclamations rippled uneasily through the church; he made the people's flesh creep and spontaneously they gave expression to their feelings, crying out loud, '*Taru Tixo!* Have mercy oh God!'

He explained about gangsters and protection rackets and how 'people who have backgrounds and futures and possessions are forced to yield to "protectioners" '; how the police up there, black as well as white, are themselves corrupt and vicious persecutors fattening on the people; how as a result many Africans in Johannesburg come to make arrangements with known gangsters to bodyguard them. 'For', he put it, 'the only way to shelter from gangsters is under the armpit of another gangster whom they fear and respect!' The people exclaimed.

He now told how my brother had been shot by his protectioner, as anyone might be, 'Because, my friends gathered here in God's name today, how are we mortals to fathom the gangster's soul? All we can do here in this quiet peaceful country scene is to make an effort of the imagination and guess that "once a gangster, always a gangster". We can imagine, can we not? how even if a gangster were to control himself for a time, for a purpose, he might be unable to control that gangster instinct were it suddenly to rear up within him. My own, my neighbour's, anybody's "protectioner"!'

Here tension had risen to such a pitch that an unknown woman burst out praying, her Xhosa voice ringing to the rafters. As I listened to her I marvelled, as so often, at the power with which quite ordinary unassuming people express themselves.

'Let us PRAY for that gangster, let us commend that twisted soul to Almighty God! Let us *do* this, *do* this, lest we find ourselves committing the sin of judging him. Let us remember, oh-community-of-ours, that that bullet would not have found its target if God had not pointed the way for it with His finger!'

Her voice pierced the huge overflowing church in the shrillest tones. My uncle had halted the moment she had called out, 'Let us pray'.

It was clearly a moment for pause, because everyone was staggered by the thoughts that had been aroused in them. There was a fearsome hush while the woman's exhortation was brought home to us all, for were not our hearts filling with thoughts of revenge, were not many of us at that moment swearing: 'An eye for an eye, a tooth for a tooth'?

We were and knew it, therefore the unknown woman's reminder of Christian ethics fought in our hearts with the instinctive, the unethical.

I could not possibly agree with the concept that God knew what He was doing in letting my brother be brutally murdered and it made me writhe. At the same time I was curiously aware of the mixture of sentiments being expressed here, pagan and Christian, not to say of the latter how Western, outmoded Victorian middle-class.

The atmosphere was tense. Mercifully, a man sensing the conflict raging in us all offered a safety-valve by 'spearing' (leading) the tune of 'Amen'. This was an apt intercession on his part, for in our African Wesleyan Methodist church service 'Amen' is set to a variety of tunes and is sung like a hymn in several verses repeating the word over and over again, usually spontaneously to cover up a halt in the service such as during a collection or other, unforeseen, emergencies. In a voice a concert baritone might envy, the man now took it on himself to cover the emergency aroused by this collective tension. He sang out alone as in a long pleading recitative, 'A-men, Am-e-hen! Ah-men, ah-men, ah-men!' The effect was to make people collect their senses. They recovered their breath, whereupon they spontaneously joined in, trebles, altos, tenors, basses, finding the correct pitch and sliding into the different parts. And it was in this joint act that all of us now turned the woman's difficult injunction over in our hearts and minds.

As the 'Amen' finished another man shouted a speech in Xhosa, 'The way is hard, *hard* for us Christians, it is hard to forgive but forgive we must!' As he went on speaking the people again spontaneously struck up another verse of 'Amen', the man's voice ringing on above the singing, combining with it in a strangely cathartic, shared performance. He gradually spent himself, his shouts getting softer, 'Show us, Lord, *show* your people how to forgive!' We sang on now as if to comfort and help him as well as ourselves, 'A-men, am-e-hen! Ah-men, ah-men, ah-men!'

It was when his speech finally died away and with it spontaneous interjections from all over the church and we wound up the final swooping 'Amens' that we realised how this outbreak of singing had so to speak allayed the wounds we had been on the point of inflicting on ourselves, had calmed the savagery that had reared within, the primitive in us all.

After that the service resumed its prescribed course of arranged speeches and tributes. Speaker after speaker called on the two families in extraordinarily fulsome vein, praising us that we might be consoled. This was according to custom. On another occasion the fulsomeness would have been unbearable but the underlying belief in the ritual was the healing property of it. And judging from the effect it was having on me for one, I could not help feeling how profoundly custom—*isiko*—is based on psychological need. '*Mzi wakwa Jili, nawe mzi wakwa Gambu!* House of *Jili* (Jabavus), you too, house of *Gambu* (Makiwanes)', and we were implored to accept God's Will. God had lent us a son and brother, He had given, now He had taken away. And they referred to us or addressed us direct, by our clan names *Jili* and *Gambu*, never by our modern surnames. I noticed how even when the speaker was European, Coloured or Indian and had therefore to be translated, whenever he spoke of Jabavu or Makiwane families, the Xhosa interpreter instinctively

17

substituted the clans. Again I thought how persistent and basic was *isiko*.

I remembered how like this it had been four years before when we were all in this same church because of my mother and I had heard them recount her achievements in helping 'rear the new women of our people', how she had 'built up and supported' my father in all he did, how they had described her, for me so revealingly, as his 'wife and Friend'; we had listened to these flowery accounts about families like hers of which she was a member of the fourth generation of *ubugqoboka*, with all that that implied to South African blacks in acceptance of the standards of an incoming culture and repudiating 'such things of Africa as were incompatible'.

I and my contemporaries had taken our present condition utterly for granted, never given past history or progress a thought. Hearing about it for what seemed the first time we began in our surprise to compare notes about Makiwanes and Jabavus and had suddenly become aware that our clan, despite its spectacular achievements, was not as steady, civilised, refined as *Gambu* people; we *Jili* were an aggressive crowd we now realised, warm-hearted, hot-headed, capable of rising high and falling mightily. I and my generation were flabbergasted. All these things had been under our noses all our lives, known by everyone evidently, yet it was only so late in the day that we were waking up to understand.

And now my brother, another *Jili*, had gone, nipped in the bud—people were saying one after the other—the last of a spectacular line. 'In the fifth generation of Westernisation,' speaker after speaker proudly declaimed, 'this family has finished.' They said it not so much in sadness as in the ritual spirit of '*Akukhonto*, it is nothing', which means 'such is life'; and they said, 'Therefore be consoled. Your deprivation and injury is not yours alone. The *Jili* clan was our spearhead, it is God's Wish that we should be without them now.'

Days afterwards we in the house would catch ourselves privately going over again in our minds the things that had been said to us, the exhortations and injunctions, and the ceremonies that had been performed.

In old-fashioned Xhosa parlance still current, the family were still 'in the forest', meaning ritual seclusion. We were not supposed to go about among other people until a final ceremony had been performed to purify, release, bring us out of the forest. The older people explained the reason, and I thought how there was nothing like family crises to enable custom and tradition to be handed down.

'The bereaved have to be secluded,' they said, 'because if the public are suddenly confronted with them at such times, they, too, suffer pangs of the heart since they are at a loss how to comfort them.' This seclusion therefore was *isiko*, to protect people from these pangs and embarrassments which tend to make adjustment difficult and thus disrupt the even flow of life. They explained that according to custom, only after a bereaved family had been ritually 'cleansed, doctored' by incantations and the 'spilling of blood'—meaning the slaying of an ox and feasting on it—could everyone then face the bereaved without embarrassment, without pangs; for a new leaf would then be turned over, the tragedy now consigned to forefathers and ancestors, the injury healed. References to the dead person after that should not be loaded with sad or bitter connotations. That would be the height of bad manners because 'Feeling must by then be adjusted, for Life must Go On'.

Until then we had to be secluded, in mourning, be in the forest, and this for some weeks. The final ceremony to 'release' would, because we were modern, consist first of a private service that our minister of religion would hold in our house followed by the *isiko* of olden days: the 'felling of an ox, the spilling of blood', the ritual provision of meat to be ceremonially tasted by family, friends and all passers-by without favour.

During the seclusion we were all supposed to try to deal with our incommunicable thoughts and memories. The observance of the custom seemed to be another of those instinctive ways of expressing a basic need.

3

The Pagan Woman

WE WENT to the station one morning to see off a party of relatives who were leaving us to return to their homes.

We congregated with other people at the far end of the platform on ground level, a good way beyond the top end of the platform which is where the 'Non-European' carriages tend to halt at stations in the Union since they were at present attached immediately behind the engine. The authorities are always changing the position of railway carriages of the races. Sometimes ours are at the tail end of the train, sometimes in the middle, sometimes at the engine end, the policy being to ensure (after the occasional derailments) that the safest part of the train should be for Europeans—or so we Africans firmly believed.

When the train comes in, however, you forget about this for its arrival is quite an occasion. You enjoy going to see people off or to catch a train yourself, or merely to go and watch and talk to travellers even when it is the morning train, which at our village arrives at that awkward time before breakfast.

The morning sun, newly risen, shone with its broad African smile on the sweeping expanse of shallow hills dotted with thorn trees, the hill-tops looking fresh and green in the clean new sunlight. In summer when pink and mauve and yellow flowers peep from between the boulders making tufts of colour along the ridges, 'the land looks beautiful like a young girl' as we say in Xhosa.

We watched the train approach, snaking its way along the sweeping contours, short green grass and trees and flowers until it slid to a standstill, in our case high above us so that we had to jerk our necks right back to speak to the travellers hanging out of the windows. Black and brown shining faces leant out greeting everybody known and unknown on the ground below.

And arms of raggedly dressed labourers going to work in the towns along the line handed out the luggage of passengers alighting from the third-class, luggage consisting of thin suitcases or pillowcases filled with belongings and tied with string or rope.

From the second-class windows more neatly dressed people, teachers mostly, looked out. And Europeans hung out of their windows, necks craned towards our part of the train as always at country stations; at the bustling ones like Port Elizabeth or Jo'burg they do not bother, but at rural stations it is as though Europeans are fascinated and mesmerised by the spectacle of Africans with their great bursts of exclamations and laughter and greetings; they gaze with set, unsmiling faces as if this African jollity is hard to tolerate. They hang on our every word and gesture, red-faced, tight-lipped. You sometimes hear a guard or linesman mutter in Afrikaans, '*Allemagtig*, what a lot of bloody Kaffirs travelling today!' Once I heard an African woman shout in Xhosa and laugh, 'My, who would be a European? Folks, these people rise up angry at everything even from their sleep! First thing in the morning angry, always angry, they were conceived on a twisted mat, those!'

While we were handing our relatives their things, a pagan woman walked up and down along the 'Non-Europeans Only' carriages balancing a basket of cactus pears on her turbanned head. She was a 'dressed' pagan, wearing an ankle-length cotton skirt that flared out in an immense fullness behind her not unlike the flared style of the red ochre-smeared pagan costume she would wear as a rule. There were many petticoats underneath this skirt, also full; and she wore an Edwardian style cotton blouse. I could tell she was pagan by the tiny bead circlets round each of her ankles.

The passengers began to clamour to buy prickly pears from her. 'Give them here, *mama*, what money are they?'

'Tickey a dozen!' she shouted back, and an exchange hurriedly ensued amid cries and loud laments from her for she was fearful of missing the tiny threepenny piece, the silver 'tickey' thrown down to her or passed from hand to hand. It was clearly a big thing for her to part with the fruit that she picked so laboriously and prepared; not only must she pick, dodging the long sharp-spiked cactus leaves but wipe each fruit clean of its own tiny, soft but devilish thorns arranged in harmless-looking furry tufts all over the peel. All that for a tickey a dozen. If she charged more, nobody would buy.

My Jo'burg uncle pounced on her and started to bargain, struck that moment by the idea of buying up the entire bucketful to give these departing relatives as *umpako*, provision, for their long journey north.

The train was about to pull out now, so 'Little Father' accelerated his efforts to beat her price down. I wished he wouldn't and so did all my cousins, but we knew that being a Johannesburg man he felt it necessary to demonstrate city smartness to these pagans and 'country pumpkins', that being the punning English term town relatives call us in the Reserves since country bumpkins grow and eat many pumpkins!

She cried shrilly, 'Make haste, brother, make haste. My money, I want my money!' handing her bucket up to the window. Many hands grabbed it to help her, helped my cousins empty it, then passed it back to her anxious clutch. The station master waved his green flag, the train whistled, its departure imminent, both making her cry out in ringing tones, 'Oh my God, who will pay me?'—a noble voice, stentorian and musical like an actress in an Elizabethan play.

My uncle answered, 'Hush, hush, sister-of-ours. Come with us. We are of course going to pay you your *ndaliso*, one shilling and sixpence.'

'But who are you with your "come with us"? I don't know you.' She appealed to strangers standing near by, at which those of them who had finished waving farewells to their friends now turned to my uncle and me and took it on themselves to reassure her. The matter became everyone's business.

'It's all right, *mama*, they belong here these people. Go with this man and this girl.'

' "Go"? Go where?' eyes flashing. How could she trust anyone with this *ndaliso*, might she not find she had braved those spikes and thorns for nothing? She said so and explained in bell-like tones how *indaliso* was the wherewithal to live for the best part of a week. 'Not, doubtless, to enjoy life,' she added, telling how she was a widow with children, 'but to live, to exist!' and people echoed the sentiment on all sides, urging her all the more to go with us.

'*Pi?* Where?' in despair, and was assured by a chorus.

'*Kwa Pro . . . fe . . . sa!* To Professor's, down there through the village!'

My Little Father started to walk. The train had pulled right out, the tail end of it about to round the first wide sweeping shallow contour of our Eastern Cape landscape. He strode out fingering his watch-chain as if to show that even if he had no ready cash on him at that time in the morning, nevertheless a well-dressed city man like himself possessed a watch and chain and that meant resources somewhere.

The pagan woman fell in behind my uncle and me, a few respectful paces to one side, skirts rustling and swinging and tossing from heel to heel as she strode holding herself so very erect, with the empty bucket on her head.

She said, 'What people are you, brother?'

'Of here.' I thought my uncle answered rather curtly, but said nothing. We walked on, his eyes roving round the green countryside drinking in its girl-like beauty. We passed through the village of rondavels and square-houses, the hunger a city man feels for the country, of which he was often telling us during this family gathering, clearly intensifying his pace as we walked.

We went past little patches of early mauve vetch and by tufts of yellow onion-plants. Some of the households of the village were hedged with the red-blossomed *ichakatha*, others with the exquisite pale blue plumbago shrub which we call *umthi ka-Maqoma*, the tree of Chief Maqoma. Some homes looked bare because the owners did not care, but the more sensitive occupants of others had planted azaleas, clumps of the flamboyantly feathered red and yellow Bird of Paradise bush, bouganvillaea, geraniums. As far as the eye could see the landscape was a typically South African one, wide expanse of rolling

23

shallow bare hills and in the distance a jagged blue frieze of mountainous edge; and there were the dark forested apron-like folds, *kloofs* we called them colloquially in Afrikaans, of the local Amatola mountain range. You could see how the gritty veld was dotted with bright yellow gazania, looking like big buttercups.

I remembered how as children on our way to school at Lovedale we used to pick gazania petals and put them to our lips one at a time and make kazoos of them, then eat the stalks full of sweet creamy milk. And pagans like this woman following us, had the custom of beating this plant, *u-bendle* we call it, to a pulp in order to isolate the fibres and make the soft stringy mass into a little pubic apron for baby girls. We walked on past cactus, mauve wild scabious, yellow mimosa, morning-glory. And my uncle repeated, 'We're people of here,' his thoughts evidently on other matters. 'Here' was very different from the Rand where he had lived for many years and where, if you come from the Eastern Cape as he does, the country seems dismal, featureless, a land worn with exploitation; its bowels, those white and ghostly mine dumps, lie heaped on the skyline, the barren soil marred by huge hoarding signs bearing chilly commercial legends: 'Such-and-such a Company, Pty'. I could understand why today he fairly 'feasted his eyes' on the scene as he walked. The woman took up his reply.

'O—h,' she said drawing it out in the undulating interrogative tone of speech. 'Of here then? Do you mean precisely, really, truly, in fact?'

'Ah, well *mandithi*, let me say rather, we are of-the-Professor. He is my elder brother.'

'Ah!' At last the penny dropped. She had not really heard before when she had been told at the station how we belonged here and now exclaimed greatly and made sure of it by asking for repetition. My uncle gave it and added, 'We are staying here. We came on the errand of this Concealment of my son.'

'Aha, now I see! Oh my God, that was a terrible thing. What badness to happen to father Jabavu, his only son. My God, oh my God!' She paused, momentarily at a loss, but presently was able to continue. '*Kanti*, and yet, we too had wanted to come,

24

brother-of-mine, to that Concealment for those are people we know. But we are "red" you see, pagans. This put us in a difficulty. All the same we prayed to God to bind you all, house-of-Jili. I pray for it the more now that I see you with my own eyes, "Let Him bind you, let Him make this heavy cloud pass from you." *It is nothing, akukhonto, it is nothing.*'

'Thank you, thank you, sister,' my classificatory uncle said, not slackening his step. The three of us were walking quite fast now. But I saw that he too was as moved by her outburst as I was, for he withdrew his sharp eyes from the landscape and fixed them in the middle distance, left his watch-chain alone and said with the formality which in our language covers up grief:

'That was nicely spoken, nicely spoken indeed, sister. The house-of-Jili thanks you for those words. Truly, such words bind us at such times. This so painful manner of passing of this son of mine, after all, then, demonstrates a wonderful thing to us all here at home: that the house-of-my-brother is loved even by pagans, even by such as you,' which she at once confirmed with a tremendous reiteration, 'But that is so indeed, young man, it is *so*, brother-of-mine!'

My uncle prepared himself to reply, in Xhosa fullness, thrusting his hands out in front of him now as he walked, as though to measure a rectangle. He looked down on the path in front of him, watching out for the potholes which were filled with brackish water from the heavy rain of the night and days since the funeral.

'Now then, do you understand this thing?' he was saying, stretching his outheld arms out more to loosen his sleeves. 'Is this something that you will understand when I explain it, friend-of-mine-who-is-much-prized? It is this: you pagan people should *come* to us Christian ones. You should come. You should have come to our son's Concealment, understand? You should not have felt yourselves in a difficulty. We are one people now here in South Africa. That other thing of old is no more, now, that idea that pagans who have not received the Word are different people from us converts who have received it. Oh, we are all one! That other was a thing brought by the missionaries,

25

these missionaries who now *live* off us, themselves forgetting The Word. We were separated into pagans and converts, yet it is nothing, it is wrong. We are one! You see that, you understand that thing?' His baritone voice rang, fairly filling the countryside as we went.

'Yes, brother,' she said, her skirts swishing. 'Yes, yes. You say so.'

'*Eh-weh*, yes indeed I say it! Now then, you and yours should also come to us at church, often, just as you are; never mind coming only to pray for rain when the drought has got us by the short horns, when even then when you come, you spoil your presence by wearing borrowed dress—tut! Leave the dresses to the converts, I say! Dresses mean nothing. Come in your pagan habit, and *dress* in it, then! Embellish yourselves, my dear good person. Adorn yourselves, oh adorn, *dress*, embellish, make yourselves beautiful, *thrust* your ochre on! Pile your beads on, make everything about you speak of pride, sister, confidence, yes pride in yourselves. For you are beautiful! Nothing is ugly in God, not even pagan dress. Therefore wear it proudly and hold out your chests! And *then* come and pray too, along with us!'

I could see why this uncle was considered a speaker. He was a politician, had a magnetic personality. He was a celebrated organiser of men, gifted with a masterful voice. But I also knew, the way those in families know these things, how he was something else too, not exactly celebrated, in business matters. A man of ability, of parts, but mercurial, with the clan temperament; also, he could have been kinder to my aunt and to other ladies. Among his virtues were fastidious and unrelenting neatness, breath-taking poetry in expressing himself in our language. Currently, too, he was not drinking. I thought of the old days when he was a horseman, how he used to gallop up to our house smiling, and we children would run to hold his horse and water it, and he would stuff sweets into our pockets.

He had one of those active brains, his brows almost always drawn, countenance preoccupied as now, always hard at work as all of us close to him knew, figuring out plans. He had the Jili initiative and aggressiveness; we all felt a constant regret

26

that his undeniable gifts should so often be put to 'these schemes of his', as we in the family called them, since few men are prophets in the eyes of their own relatives, and we would cry, 'What would become of him?' But oh, how we loved him for he was indeed a poet, as we put it: *skilled and delicate in language, i-ciko!*

There was a silence, broken only by the sound of our footsteps on the grass verge of the path.

At last the woman spoke. She was calm and at peace, no longer alarmed, flashing, crying out as she had done at the station when afraid about her tickey and her *ndaliso*; all that was put to one side and her mind was now occupied with higher things. She said, 'After all, our pagan dress *was* our first dress, when we were a NATION!'

'Aha!' triumphed my uncle. 'You understand it, you see it.'

'Indeed I see it, Jili,' she said simply as we approached the house.

We went in by the back gate that you come to when you walk from the station. My uncle went indoors, through the passage by the kitchen, but calling out to her, 'Stay here!' So she stood by the kniphofia and cacti in the backyard where there were already standing groups of women, also wearing the kind of dress, the Edwardian style full skirts and mutton-sleeved blouses that she had borrowed.

Some of them were our house-servants, others callers who had come to 'exclaim' (at our bereavement) but were too respectful to go to the verandah at the front of the house, preferring to wait here demurely for my father to come. They had been promised that sooner or later he would appear at this side. The sun shone on their faces, and all were sad, serious, as if the loss of a son had happened to them.

Presently my uncle came back with *indaliso* in his hand. And the pagan woman received it in the customary way, cupping both her hands and genuflecting a little. 'You have helped me, brother,' she said; a gracious way, I thought, of thanking for what was after all her due. 'Let the Lord bind you all.' And she

27

made to move away, but my uncle said, '*Kanene*, by the way: you said your clan name was *Makowane?*'

'Yes,' she said. 'One hails me thus: "*Makowane, Mathumbu, Masulelo, Sokhela* . . ." '

Before she could finish, exclamations broke out on all sides from the people standing and seated round about. 'Goodness! What people are those, what clan is that, where are you from? Never heard that one before.'

My uncle held up the palm of his hand to her. 'Don't go yet, stay, sister, stay. Let me call my elder brother. I mentioned your clan to him in asking him for the *indaliso*, and at once he said he would speak with you. Say no more about your clan now, keep it for him!' He dashed indoors again, and after a while came out, this time walking slowly, accompanying my father who held a pencil and a small sheaf of plain white postcards covered with his handwritten notes.

My father never missed an opportunity to take down rare or unknown clan names, or of checking those he had already collected; he had been at this antiquarian hobby for more than thirty years.

Everyone fell back a little; a teenage boy, on his way past the group and going to the kraal at the far end of the back enclosure, leapt aside to pick up a battered orange box and brought it up to my father who slowly lowered himself on to it and arranged his file of postcards in one hand and said:

'*Kha-utsho, dade*, be good enough to say, then, sister'; it was too urgent a matter to be held up with preliminary greetings. They would follow afterwards, as everyone knew.

The pagan woman again started the recital of her clan names, and there were three more from where she had left off before, '*Magidigidi, Mafan'avele* . . .' That one made us smile and start to interrupt with comments, for it meant 'They-who-appear-for-no-apparent-reason'; and when she had repetitiously explained the reason for it until she was satisfied that we understood, there was a further little hold up because my father repeated all of them after her and mistakenly chanted, '. . . *Sokhela, Mafan'avele, Magidigidi* . . .' but the woman stopped

28

him, protesting that he had fouled the order, he should say, *'Sokhela, Magidigidi, Mafan'avele'*, and lastly, *'Ntlongontlongo'*.

My father took great pains. At the end he carefully folded up his files and squared them like a card-player, slipped them into his waistcoat pocket, then addressed the entire group:

'You see then, all of you good ladies here today, these clan names and praise names—*zifumaneka nzima! kuba abanye abazazi* —are procured with extreme difficulty! for some do not *know* them.' He talked solemnly of the passing into oblivion of our nationhood, our traditions, our background as a people, who had travelled from the far north, East Africa; about our Hamitic forefathers with their cattle, always searching for grasslands, and mingling their blood with Bantu and Hottentot and Bushman and who knows what other peoples as they went during those unknown centuries? For decades now he had been trying to gather up what he could of known genealogies and praise verses, which often threw light on the journey and adventures of their owners' group of forebears. In his travels up and down South Africa on educational and political missions, at public gatherings from agricultural shows, athletic sports displays, from concerts to religious gatherings like revival meetings, in chance encounters with strangers on trains and buses, he had carried on enquiries until at last he had published his findings in his book, *Imbumba yama Nyama*. And he told the attentive group:

'That book has galvanised many Xhosa readers into writing and sending me more names, more praise verses. And now, among the many things I am doing in my retirement from Fort Hare, I am working on a further edition and will incorporate the masses of fresh news I have received from people like *these!*' here lifting his hand and pointing to the pagan. Everyone looked at her as if for the first time, and older ladies showered congratulations on her. She gave a most engaging grin on finding herself the centre of an uplifting little scene.

And now, the time having come, my father greeted her formally, which gave her the opportunity to tell him, also formally, how she and hers prayed that the Lord would bind him.

My father nodded gravely at each sentence. She spoke at length, expressing deep-seated philosophies about Life and Death, Parenthood and the human condition, with a grace and flow and unselfconsciousness that dumbfounded me. My father acknowledged in simple yet moving words, sitting on his up-turned orange box, and wound up the perorations:

'Well, I am glad it is you, sister, who have come to say those things to us here-at-home, even though it was truly speaking through the prickly pears that you came. Nevertheless we now take it as if you had been with us on that day, since you show us that it was only the difficulty of the dress that prevented you. Would it had not. But this brother-of-mine-here,' pointing at him, 'did well to bring you to me. You have spoken to me of your progenitors, names I did not know. But there are hints in these praise names and verses you have given which link with some that I do know . . .' And he recounted some of the traditions which he thought were linked.

The pagan woman was all smiles now. She had quite lost herself and forgotten daily cares as the splendour of her lineage, her *i-mvelapi*, her *where-from*, as we say, shone in glory before her and before my father, 'A man who,' as she put it to the company but indirectly addressing him, 'was dazzling to her and hers because of his deeds, his fame, illustriousness, and blinding to behold now that he was in so dark a forest (of grief).'

She told him smiling, 'We are few left of that lineage, that house, oh few indeed, father!' He discussed this decline and decimation with her at some length. Then changing his tone, my father teased her by punning on the praise name '*Mafan'avele*', about how, decimated though they might be and almost vanished, yet there was that recorded knack of her stock that it might reappear-for-no-apparent-reason, which naturally wound up the interview on a note that everyone appreciated! And then he said, 'Go then, *Ntlongontlongo*, and the Lord go with you.'

She turned her radiant face away, in a smooth movement, that empty bucket poised on her head, and walked away, her skirts sweeping her heels.

4

'A Friend and Mother'

IN SPITE of the fact that the rhythm of life in our home in the Reserve pulses gently, and weeks of quiet country existence engulfed us in which we consciously as well as instinctively 'observed the customs' intended to allay our feelings, nevertheless the pace of modern life was also pressing and could not be ignored.

Like so many so-called Westernised southern Bantu families, we were bound to behave in a proper manner, according to the dictates of the life old and new, the essence of our African life which outsiders tend to interpret as 'spoilt by Europeanisation'. In fact it is neither spoilt nor improved, it is simply different from what it used to be because of the elements from English and Boer life which have impinged on us.

One of the things we had to adjust as a family was my father's condition, that of widower. My mother had died four years before, leaving at home only my father and my brother. My brother was only by token at home, being most of the time far away up at Witwatersrand University. My sister and I had married abroad, our own homes and families thousands of miles away.

Now that my brother had gone, my father was alone in the house. One of his children was home for the present, but only for the present. The gathered relations also were bound to depart, indeed were already departing in ones and twos; the pace of events had to be accelerated in accordance with the times we lived in, we had to hasten the speed with which we must 'emerge from the forest'.

Even before my brother was killed, the matter of a new mother for the family had been gradually raising itself. Different elders had selected candidates on whom they looked with

31

approval, an act hanging over from the traditional way of marrying off members of families; had not my own mother been similarly selected for my father, *waganwa*, as we say, and her people picked him for her, sent her to England too on betrothal to share his background, and had it not worked?

My father too, a long time after her death, had little by little 'seen someone', as our phrase goes, for himself. The obstacle necessitating caution had been the children, his and hers, for the lady of his choice was a widow. This choice of his own had overcome the selections made by the various elders and coevals, suitable though they had been. Modernity again.

My late brother had met her, though nothing whatever, naturally, had been 'spoken' at the time. So had my sister when she had come home, as of ritual, to give birth to her first-born. As for me, a letter had been sent to England to sound me out. To my surprise, I had felt startled and jealous at the thought of my mother's place being usurped, even though at the same time I fully recognised the need and approved of my father's marrying again; in the end, forcing myself to exercise common sense in this struggle between old and new, traditional and modern, instinctive and cerebral, I saw that I must accept. Both my mother's children had already done so.

Now at this gathering therefore, the minds of both big and young people were occupied with the unwelcome prospect of leaving my father in his loneliness. It was tacitly agreed that this must be ended. As the weeks quietly passed, it became understood that 'the family must marry', we must 'acquire A Person, a mother for the home, A Friend for the head of the family'. In our inflected language, these literal translations seem more elemental and can have the effect when declaimed in formal speech by a member of the older generation of wrenching the heart of the listener, or as we say in Xhosa, of 'rending the bowels'.

This acquisition must be achieved almost at once, an awkward necessity in the midst of the elemental rituals we had to undergo. But it had to be, for when we all had to leave presently we could not leave our old father solitary in the house. In traditional days we would have stayed with him for many months.

32

One Sunday therefore, after lunch, my father announced to nobody in particular, that before taking his usual afternoon nap he would walk down to our African minister's house: had something of importance to discuss with him. We all exchanged looks, knowing what that something was.

We were aware how our elders had selected possible 'mothers' for us, gone into the questions of the backgrounds of each, health, age, personality. Unobtrusive conferences had taken place at different levels. Certain representatives of the older generation, women, had sounded us young people out. After that my classificatory paternal aunt representing the male clan discreetly spoke with me and my maternal cousins, who always addressed her colloquially by a term indicating their connection with her, different from my own which was 'Sister of my Father', in quick ordinary speech 'Si' Father'; and then, most important, my father's brothers-in-law had their feeling in the matter conveyed to me. I stood throughout not for myself but for my absent sister and late brother, even the other sister of whom we had been deprived many years before, when I was small. I was spoken to collectively, in this instance, *'nina'* rather than *'wena'*; and my uncles were important because they were the instinctive (in our language 'umbilical') custodians of us children, a matter of human relationships, not legal in either European law or Xhosa customary law since ours is a patrilineal not a matrilineal tribe. But in all things, human relationships with us rank supreme. All these groups conferred directly with my father, etiquette requiring a softening of the approach of so delicate a subject by much use of his clan salutations. But to me they expressed themselves indirectly, through the proper 'mouths' or intermediaries.

We children, whom I represented, were expected to indicate feeling with the utmost delicacy, almost not speaking, for traditionally we would not even have been consulted. But in these days things are changing, so we had to pretend that we were as of tradition in the dark, although naturally, being modern, we had been consulted. It was wonderful to see how proprieties are observed in all things.

33

So on that Sunday the household watched my father unfurl his black umbrella against the noonday sun, and my mother's eldest brother fasten his large Edwardian boots, rise from his cane chair and walk with him 'slowly slowly' down towards the minister's house where, we knew, ways and means would be discussed how to achieve the 'acquisition of a friend and mother' in a 'seemly' manner bearing in mind the symbiosis of custom and modernity.

In due course then, the day we waited for arrived. Mr Ntloko, a friend who lectured on Native Administration at Fort Hare, came out in his spare time to drive us the eleven miles from our village to our old town, Alice.

The marriage could have been transacted locally at Middledrift, but because we were so very lately and hastily out of the forest, our minister and the big people felt it would be more private and therefore more seemly farther away at Alice.

So we arrived at the family lawyer's office, my father, my 'aunt', our courtesy title for my prospective mother during her present status; we used the English word. I went, representing 'the children'.

5

The Out of Community Contract

THE LAWYER's office in Alice was in an elderly colonial house, the floorboards bare and well-scrubbed, the walls white-washed and the ceiling made of narrow matchboard slats painted white. The doors and window frames had not been painted for many years and were faded and peeling, as if many days of brilliant unrelieved sunshine had baked them. It had a typical look, wholesome, pioneer, colonial, bare essentials only. A current yearly calendar hung on the wall displaying the names of the foremost shops, businesses and farms in and around our small town. The calendar too had an air of dusty, friendly, colonial sleepiness.

At a table in a corner was a grey-haired African man, thin faced and hollow cheeked as if lacking some teeth, wearing a heavy khaki-coloured army jacket that seemed large for his slight frame. He held torn scraps of paper, earnestly reading and scrutinising each before doubtfully consigning it to the waste-paper basket. He glanced up as we came in, whispered 'good morning' and dropped his eyes again on his scraps of paper as the lawyer rose from the opposite corner, came forward holding out his hand to my father.

They met, both stiffer in the limbs these days, grasped each other's hands for a long time, the black man and the white man. Each searched the other's eyes, evidently with feeling, for each smiled a little, sadly. I knew that they had known each other for over fifty years, working and maturing together in this small town. Later on that day my father reminded us how he had dealt always only with E. E. P. Burl; there were newer lawyers nowadays in the town, younger, smart and fashionable no doubt, but he would never leave his old friend.

Still holding hands, my father said in a sibilant whisper,

35

'Mr Burl, I want you to draw me up an ante-nuptial contract now, now, now. I am due at the registrar's at ten o'clock; Mr Crossman, Mr Crossman. And he said the contract only takes five minutes and is the best thing for a man in my position.'

The lawyer gave a great start, dropped the other's hand and threw both his up above his head. ' "Five minutes"? "Five minutes"? What is the matter with Mr Crossman, "five minutes"? And my clerk still away! . . .'

My father interrupted, echoing him, startled too now. 'Still away?' and he turned to me and my aunt and shrugged, 'Mr Burl's typist,' as though we had not heard. Both old men stood shrugging their shoulders. At that moment a white man came in wearing a stetson hat, rough tweed jacket. His wide flannel trousers stopped short well above his ankles and his face was very sun-tanned. A farmer. As soon as this man came in I noticed an incongruous look flash across my father's face, an expression of cunning and hurried thinking and, surprised, I saw him instantly dart towards a door leading to an inner office. As he went, he said in Xhosa to me and our aunt, 'Come on, come on!' We obeyed without hesitation. Once in there, the lawyer's private sanctuary, my father explained:

'I did not want that white man to get in first, we would be delayed here all morning. Mr Burl won't turn us out once we're in here. Sit down, sit down.' Again we obeyed, though gingerly.

This inner office looked much like the outer one, bleached, rather bare, and as if much sunshine and heat had poured into it over the years. The partition boards were painted white and under the electric light switch by the door jamb was a miscellaneous collection of lawyers' papers and official notices in the two official languages; also a dressmaker's pink paper sheet symmetrically stuck through with rows of steel pins. A small room and we at once seemed to fill it, sitting on straight-backed dining-chairs round the lawyer's desk. We were silent, my father at intervals wiping his face with his hands, a gesture which we used to complain, when we were children, pressed his aquiline nose flat.

Presently Mr Burl followed us into the room. He was stout in his ancient, good-quality brown tweed jacket which sat on him comfortably. He came in reiterating the complaint he had started when the farmer had arrived and interrupted.

'Oh Doctor, oh Doctor!' The compliment that Rhodes University had recently paid my father in according him the 'Ll.D., *honoris causa*' had captivated our small town so that everyone was delightedly changing his day-to-day title and style from 'Professor' to 'Doctor'. 'Oh Doctor, you don't *know* what you are asking me. This thing takes *days*, has to go to *Capetown*!'—pointing in a westerly direction out beyond the office. 'I just don't know how I can do it, Professor, Doctor!' he said, growing more agitated.

My father stood up. 'Mr Crossman said . . .'

' "Five minutes"! I don't know what is the matter with him, *he* knows it takes more than——'

'He said it's a printed form, and a shilling stamp,' and my father felt in his pocket for a shilling, in the little yellow cotton tobacco bags in which he always kept small change, but at this the lawyer started to dance up and down, rushing to this shelf and that, snatching up documents and soon had a sheaf in his hand, foolscap size and in four parts each. He cried:

'A *shilling*? Oh Doctor, I don't want your shilling, don't take it out! "Five minutes"! Why, this thing is a *pound* stamp, man, a pound, let alone a shilling, shillings are nothing! I've got to type it all out four times, must be dead accurate, oh man, you don't know what it is!' He then flung himself at the desk, in front of him an ancient, trusty-looking upright office typewriter; just above his snowy head I noticed an equally ancient kind of telephone made by Ericcson of Stockholm, the name picked out in gold letters; it seemed to lend the occasion an even remoter air than before.

Mr Burl thrust into my hand one of the foolscap forms he had been collecting. I saw that it was printed in the principal official language of these days, Afrikaans. Glancing at it but keeping my ears open because of the agitation of the old men, I read:

Ras—man . . . vrou . . . (Race, man, woman)
Volle name van eggenote . . . (Full names of Persons married)

37

Persoonlik staat . . . (Personal status)

Beroep . . . (Occupation)

Magistraat en naturellekommissaris . . . (Magistrate and Native Commissioner).

I looked up. My father was still on his feet, and both men were now terribly excited, one waving a document about, getting ready to set it in the typewriter, the other searching and rustling in his brief-case and pockets for pencils and pens.

At last he produced a lead pencil and walked gingerly up to the desk, rummaged among the papers in front of his old friend for a clean piece, speaking hoarsely because of the agitation he was trying to suppress:

'Let me wri' down my names for you, then.'

'Oh my goodness, I ought to know your names by now!' cried the other impatiently and promptly recited all four of them as he set papers into the typewriter.

My father called out vigorously, '*Ja!* You ought to know them, oughtn't you?' Then they both began to laugh, a little recklessly, and shake their heads as if suddenly seeing themselves as being somewhat ridiculous. My father started telling one of his histrionic anecdotes about these names of his, something to do with his recent stay in Bechuanaland. Our lawyer's hand fell idle on his machine and he peered anxiously up at my father through his spectacles.

'What's that? What about Bechuanaland?'

I could no longer restrain myself. 'Father, don't talk! Hadn't you better keep quiet and let Mr Burl get on with it? Stop talking about Bechuanaland!'—at which my aunt also burst out gently to her elderly fiancé, 'Yes, father, do as Noni says. You, too, sit! Look, Mr Burl is sitting. Just leave him alone, my-dear-you, just leave him alone and let him work.' She spoke so kindly and softly.

My father looked at us as though he had forgotten us, his eyes very bright. He always became excited in this way if a time schedule of his were upset. Had he not carefully arranged everything beforehand, noting on white postcards filed away in his waistcoat pocket? The time Mr Ntloko's motor car was to fetch us from Middledrift, 9 a.m.; five minutes to be spent at Mr Burl's; then at 10 a.m. in front of the magistrate, married; at 11 a.m. to be picked up again in the town after a little shopping. He had therefore particularly arranged to be at the magistrate's office well before 10 o'clock, about twenty minutes. He had been congratulating himself and us, reminding me, by way of another of the fatherly anecdotes I had known since childhood, how he had learnt the value of punctuality from the terrifying example of my grandfather, John Tengo Jabavu as a grown man, actually *running* to catch trains. 'Your grandfather was a big man, over six feet and *heavy*! "Father, Father," we used to beg, "Father, let us *start* for the station, time is short." But he would say in his slow bass, "*Hayi*, no. Not yet. I have this and that to see to." Invariably it ended in the terrible spectacle of a dignified, adult man running, out of breath. *Mna?* Me? I vowed then and there!' And today here was my father's careful schedule ruined; it was nearly 10 o'clock, yet we were still at the lawyer's, on top of which Mr Burl was talking about 'four copies, accurate typing, everything having to be *dead right*, names to be given in full every time they occurred, pound sterling stamps, Capetown', why, the marriage might never take place this day! He looked at my aunt and me, gave a low whistle of despair, stood up, sat down, stood up; finally gathered up the tail of his overcoat and stood first on one foot then the other, making ready to sit once again. He looked round behind him as he lowered himself, eyeing the distance between himself and his chair and at last sat down, saying wearily in Xhosa:

'Perhaps you are right, children-of-mine.'

'Ah! *Now* then, Doctor,' said Mr Burl, and both wiped their foreheads with large white handkerchiefs, relieved. 'Don't worry yourself, my good man. I'll do this thing for you. I'll *do* it! I warned you yesterday about it, didn't I? And you wouldn't listen! But never mind. You know that I would do anything for you, my dear man. Now, these names. As long as you appreciate that this is more than a five-minute job, I'll do my best.' We were starting at last.

When it came to my aunt's name, our lawyer looked up and asked, 'Is this the bride, then?' He looked from her to me; he had really not noticed us before in the excitement and alarm. He now rose from his desk, took a couple of steps and shook her by the hand. She was overcome with shyness and only smiled, not speaking. He said, 'You are getting a good man, I can tell you. Known him all my life.' Then he looked wonderingly at me and turned to shake my hand. And when my father told him that this was his daughter, he exclaimed, 'My goodness, so *you* are here?' but he suppressed whatever he had been about to say and sat down again.

He typed for nearly an hour. Towards the end he said, sighing wearily, 'Repetition, repetition. That's the worst of the law.' Each time he had to insert the names of the contracting parties, he spelled them out loud: 'D-a-v-i-d-s-o-n D-o-n T-e-n-g-o J-a-b-a-v-u, B-e-t-t-y M-a-r-a-m-b-a-n-a.' At one point he started to spell out loud his own name but hastily checked himself, saying, 'I *should* know how to spell mine! Edward Ernest Ponsonby Burl. You know that I registered the initials, don't you, Professor? That was the best way out. Too long, my name. Especially this Ponsonby. That's an old English name,' he said to my aunt and me, 'it came from England, do you know that?' And we smiled.

Then he asked me to check each copy of the work he had done. 'Will you do that, Mrs——? What is your daughter's name, Doctor?' My father told him. 'Oh, so is this the one who flew from London? Not the one married to a barrister, then?' My father explained that my sister had not been able to come from Uganda.

'Oh, I see. Then what does *your* husband do?'

'A film director,' I told him.

'What! A film di——? He is in the big money, then!' And both old men laughed heartily. It was useless for me to explain so I did not try. Then Mr Burl said to me, 'Well, you won't mind checking this. I'll read out the typing only, not the printed text, only the typing you understand?'

We set to work checking through. There were no mistakes. It

seemed correct in every detail despite the hurry, the alarm, the excitement. However, I noticed that in one instance, Ernest, of the Edward Ernest Ponsonby Burl had been spelt 'Ernezt'. At that, he exclaimed delightedly, 'Professor, you've got a good child here!' And my father at once replied, 'Mr Burl, I can't tell you how I love that child of mine. My support always, I rely on her in everything that requires common sense. That's why I said to you just now you needn't read me the contract. If she reads it, that's enough for me; it means that I have read it!'

The lawyer started, all earnestness again, put out by the remark. 'Ah, but it was my *duty* to read it to you, my man. I had to do it. My duty. That's why I still had to read it to you, in spite of your daughter, in spite of anything! And look here, you do understand the contract, don't you? And the lady understands it?'—here turning to her.

Aunt Betty and my father nodded vigorously, heads bobbing up and down, anxious to have done with the thing and to establish that they were fully responsible.

The lawyer persisted however. 'You are marrying "Out of Community", you see? It means you will be man and wife in every sense of the word, just as I am married to *my* wife and everybody is married to theirs. But your property, that's yours separately under this contract. It's because of the grown-up children in the case.' My father and Aunt Betty were impatient, did not in the least want this all over again; had it not all been thoroughly ventilated, everything, including the question of property and the almost inevitable disputes between children in such unions? Hence these documents about 'Out of Community'. My 'new mother' had four or five whom we had not even met as yet, and to my surprise I for one already felt in that family atmosphere twinges of traditional hostility towards them. And some uneasiness in our relationship did indeed arise from time to time later on.

At last the lawyer held the completed papers in his hands and now rose, saying it would be more comfortable for us to sign in the other room on the wider table. As we went he turned to ask

41

how long I was going to stay and said, 'Oh, my girl, I am glad to hear that. And I am so glad you are to be a witness. That will be nice, won't it, Doctor?' My father chimed in happily, 'That's why she is here, my friend.' And they looked in each other's eyes. One said, 'It is good when your children are with you in this.'

I couldn't help thinking of this afterwards and of the relationship of the two men when, back home, I was to hear my father telling my maternal uncles and classificatory aunt about this morning's events. 'You see, Burl feels for me as for an own brother. We have known each other all our lives. The day before when I went to see him, I had to stop him from shedding tears, shedding tears I tell you, on the death of my son. And he is a man who has himself lost sons. In the War. Oh, terrible. A fine man. Felt for me, was on the point of tears! I said to him, "Don't do it, man, Burl man. You are going to make *me* break down now if you do this thing. You have experienced it; it was you first, now it's my turn to lose my son. That's all. So don't cry, my dear friend; you were strong when it was your time. Now it's my time, you must be strong again now." ' But for the moment in the office we had to busy ourselves signing the documents and their copies.

Another witness was needed, so Mr Burl called the employee, the African man who had been scrutinising scraps of paper destined for the waste-paper basket when we arrived. He signed, his surname being the resounding one of 'Balfour' since he was on the fringes of the celebrated family of one of the early converts, *umKwayi* by clan, who had adopted as 'official surname' that of the British statesman. A further excitement almost flared up again during the signing, our seniors dancing round each other at the table, the lawyer trying to indicate the spot we all had to initial—where 'Ernezt' had had to be corrected to 'Ernest'. We heard him say almost gruffly to my father, '*Here*, man, here, here!' and my father meekly, 'Ah, I get you, *here*?'

'*Ja!*'

'*Ja, ja. Alles reg*, here.'

42

When all was safely over, the lawyer looked at his wrist-watch and exclaimed, 'That's the fastest! I've never prepared a pre-nuptial contract in such a short time in my life! I did my best for you, Doctor, didn't I?'

'Oh man, record time, record time!'

'*Yo!*' cried the other, firing into the air an African expression in perfect pronunciation, with no relaxed vowel, not seeming to be aware that he did so, and mopped his lined forehead just as an African might when ejaculating in a similar context. '*Yo!* For someone to come in and say he is getting married in less than an hour and will I draw him up a pre-nuptial contract—you see *now* how Mr Crossman was talking nonsense, man, with his "five minutes"!' They laughed and agreed in their intimate small-town way, how Mr Crossman was a kind young man, liked to be helpful and not to disappoint people; he must have *wished* the contract might be drawn up in five minutes. My father said, 'But then, *he* isn't a notary, is he?' and dug his finger into the breast-bone of his friend, who seemed mollified by this comment, for he now said, 'He must have been thinking about *his* part of it, that's all. The ceremony, now that is only five minutes, oh yes! But the Out of Community contract? *Yo!*'

Now he asked my father to be sure to call in and see him on coming out from the magistrate's office which was directly opposite the office across the dusty white road. It was a red, Victorian colonial building whose roof was of corrugated iron painted the same red. My father began to protest. What else was he to come back here for, hadn't he finished all business with Mr Burl for today?

But his friend said reprovingly, with an engaging shy smile, '*Ag, man,* I shall want to *congratulate* you and wish you happiness, don't you know that?'

43

6

'The Business of Getting Old'

So now came the ceremony. The preliminaries were marked by numerous entries and signings in wide, long documents, but not before a pause for greetings to take place between my father and the European woman clerk who had to note down the particulars; it turned out that her namo was that of an old English family in the Transkei Native Reserve. She and my father promptly halted things in order to exchange genealogies, dates, reminiscences; only after that to business.

Alas, now it appeared that the young Boer clerk in the office had mislaid some papers vital to the ceremony. The magistrate was a South African of English descent. He looked young, perhaps early forties, hair thinning on top; he was tanned and I thought very good-looking. He coughed, smiled anxiously and said to my father:

'Professor Jabavu, if we can't find these papers we won't be able to marry you.'

My father firmly stood his ground and said, 'I'll pray, Mr Crossman. I will pray hard.' Aunt Betty and I stood agonised. My father relapsed into silence, eyes closed; he was praying. The English lady turned away to join the young Boer and both began to hunt industriously, with tremendous concentration. There was a heavy silence, then in some desultory remarks it transpired that the young Boer had mislaid other papers in this way, being new to this office. His name was a 'proper Boer' one, but he was so nice and clearly anxious that it did not occur to us to have hard feelings against him.

At last the papers were found. The young man brought them to my father with a gentle and sensitive smile. 'I'm very sorry to have kept you waiting, Professor,' he said, then explained at length what had unexpectedly happened to the file, including

44

the details of where it had finally turned up. 'Things always do turn up,' he finished cheerfully. We listened politely for he was courteous; my father had opened his eyes and I noticed how he regarded the clerk, with that look of African approval on beholding 'a well-brought-up young person', and he said, simply, 'My prayers have been answered, you see.' He so patently meant it that although the remark caused us younger ones, the Boer and me, to exchange a glance, the others beamed, obviously not dreaming of dissociating themselves from his happy sentiment.

As we were about to go into the magistrate's room for the last time my father suddenly noticed that I was wearing gloves and stopped short, 'Hey, this is supposed to be a quiet wedding, everybody will notice us now!' As if there had been any secrecy in this small town! 'How like a man!' I thought, but said nothing. He gazed, transfixed, at my gloves as if they mesmerised him until I could no longer refrain and protested that people usually wore them, they were not a mark of celebration—but before I finished, Aunt Betty intervened and, I noticed helplessly, changing the ground of my argument. ('How like a woman!' I thought, but could not say so.) '*Kaloku Tata*, you see, Father, this person of ours is in overseas dress. Everybody knows she is an overseas person. They would only suspect something if I, a person of-here, wore them since it is so seldom.' My father somehow pulled his eyes away from my hands and with bowed head resigned himself.

The marriage did indeed 'only take five minutes', and afterwards we walked back as asked to our lawyer's office. 'E.E.P.B.' at once came forward with his congratulations. 'You know, Doctor, I am *glad* my clerk was away today after all, otherwise I would not have had the chance to *do* this thing for you. As it was there were no interruptions. And you know now that I would do anything for you, don't you?'

'Oh yes, I know now. Record time, record time.' While his friend congratulated the bride my father began to rummage in his brief-case and rummaged for so long that Mr Burl now addressed me, pointing backwards with an affectionately derisory thumb at him and took this opportunity to explain something I had not heard before: 'I told him all this yesterday, told him, told him! But he'll only take notice when the magistrate tells him,' and shook his head, smiling.

My father straightened himself up and holding papers extracted from his case, faced his friend and began to confess apologetically that he had other business to discuss. We were all struck silent, for had he not said earlier he 'had done with Mr Burl for today, what was there to come back to this office for after the marriage'? They both began to laugh as though each laughing at himself. Watching them and noticing the line of pale, washed-out colour round the irises of their eyes which always moves one on seeing ageing people, I felt all of a sudden strangely disturbed; it made me so aware of the long years they had known each other. The more so when I now heard my father murmur feelingly to the other, '*Ezi zizinto zokwaluphala, mfondini!*' And Mr Burl, who naturally understood the language perfectly even though he used it himself only in snatches, echoed the sentiment in Afrikaans and English, '*Ja*, this business of getting old! We are getting old, look at this girl,' looking towards me. 'Until this morning I still thought of her as small, man, a toddler playing with the toy motor cars of Mrs Tremeer's boy. Yet what about him, why Rhodes is a man now, ace photographer winning prizes, married, running his mother's second butchery. Oh man!'—here turning away from me back to my father. 'And your younger one, that buxom little one is even married to a *barrister*!' He threatened to start reminiscing again, but my father said in a suddenly businesslike tone, his mind jumping forward to the present, 'Now look here, Mr Burl, these other things I have got here to go through with you——' he who had said there was no more business to transact!

My 'new mother' and I decided to go out to the shops. I naturally stopped using her courtesy title of 'aunt', but as we walked my mind was filled with many thoughts because of my surprise on hearing myself address her by her clan name 'MamSwazi' as I now could and did. She of course had all along been able to call me by my names, 'Nontando' or the Xhosa diminutive 'Ntando', or my overseas name 'Noni' which

46

delighted even my father, the linguistic perfectionist, because of its absurd novelty; and she had been able to call me by my clan name 'MaJili', even in the masculine form, simply 'Jili', the use of which somehow elevates a woman to a more glorious state evoking as it does the patrilinear and always at once favourably disposes me towards anyone who thus addresses me; one of the subtle things I so greatly missed in my 'overseas life'. But it would have been a delicate matter for me to have called her 'MamSwazi' previously; while I had been only her possible future child for all that clan names are much substituted for real names and titles because of the soothing, softening, friendly, elevating overtones they are capable of carrying; in certain circumstances they can carry other implications. I was thinking of these things and of how everything with us in speech, address, and use of the tonality of the language reflected the ever-shifting situations and feelings between individuals and groups belonging to them and other human beings, how this factor dominated our outlook. But first before investigating the shops, we found that after all the excitements of the morning we badly wanted to relieve ourselves, and the problem was that in Alice there was only one ladies' lavatory and it was a 'Europeans Only' although strangely enough there were two for men, a Non-European as well as a European. So we had to walk to a deserted part of the town close by and squat in the short grass, overseas gloves and all!

After that we strolled back to the shops. In the main street we ran into Mr Ntloko who was to drive us back to our village. We went with him to the office to collect my father. I found the lawyer bending over an old-looking dictionary bound in red morocco, my father thrusting papers back into his brief-case.

Mr Burl said, 'Here she is! We'll ask what *she* says, she coming from overseas. How do you pronounce m-i-s-s-i-l-e?'

I pronounced it, at which he exclaimed triumphantly, 'Ah that's how *I* say it but Doctor here says it differently.'

'Oh well,' said my father, tired and putting on his hat. 'That's the way I've always pronounced it, anyhow.' There were further affectionate farewells while our feet trundled on the well-scrubbed bare boards sprinkled with the thin layer of gravel brought in by the shoes of callers. As we went out, the self-effacing employee Balfour beckoned to me and spoke anxiously in a sibilant undertone, '*IsiXhosa kodwa usasazi*, can it be that you still know Xhosa?' I laughed and said, '*Eh-weh, kakade, ompi*, but yes, of course, uncle!' He was delighted and at the same time amazed and retired into his corner muttering, '*Yo!*'

We stepped over the little fresh water furrow at the edge of the dusty pavement; a few steps more and into Mr Ntloko's waiting car. As my father closed the door of the car after he had poured himself in, Mr Ntloko started up the engine; but stout Mr Burl appeared again, his face wreathed in smiles and suffused with pleasure and he said, gesticulating, 'Either way, it's either way! It says so in the dictionary, you can pronounce it "missile" or "missle"!'—and he waved his chubby white hand; my father waved back, smiling too.

7

A Ritual Task

Now I could seriously think about my departure, of leaving 'home, *ekhaya*' for the 'home-of-marriage, *emzini*', as we say. For my father now had 'a Person, a Friend', our family had a mother.

During my last few days, those of the family who were still present turned their minds to the next ritual task that custom enjoined me, in the circumstances, to perform.

'You must go now to your sister in Uganda,' they said. 'Since she was not here to *see-for-herself*, you must go to her and act as if you had been her eyes. It is your duty to tell your mother's child everything word for word, enable her to re-live every phase of our tragedy. Let her, through you, learn to accept what has happened for it was God's Will. Let it be as if she had partaken in the gatherings of consolation that families make at such crises. It will be only if you, eldest of the umbilical cord, properly fulfil your function that your sister will find the peace that we have found through these traditional rites.'

Exhortations of this sort were repetitiously driven home to me in the formal African manner. But along with these, family and friends were prompted, too, by those inevitable prickings of nationalist aspirations of modern Africa: 'You are going North to our fellow-Africans who are so far ahead of us down here in the South. Oh, had we your eyes, you who are to see the land of the Baganda! European travellers have told how that far-off race are the most advanced people in Africa; we have read of their elaborate Kingdoms, of their culture, their high standard of living.' Here my father interrupted, pointing to a pictorial calendar he had brought back some years before from a ten-day visit he had paid to Kenya and Uganda on his way home from

49

a conference to which he had been invited in India; the picture was labelled 'His Highness the Kabaka and Nabagareka of Buganda', and he explained, ' "Kabaka" means King, "Nabagareka" Queen of Buganda. I saw them myself with my own eyes. Those Baganda? My word! I saw Africans, black fellow-Africans living in paradise, I tell you. In Uganda, black people *own land*!'

'Own land?'

'Yes!' my father said. 'Their land is theirs, by title deed, there is no alienation in that country.'

'Then indeed they are in heaven!' There were exclamations, ejaculations, transports on all sides at this and the big people went off at the familiar tangent on the theme of how we Southern Bantu have been deprived of land, living-room. And how our beloved cattle can no longer roam; not only that, but how the Law requires that we reduce their numbers to a handful each man in place of the great herds of which ritual, prestige and sheer love of the animals rendered the possession a glittering ambition. 'Natives must cull their stock,' proclaims the Boer Government, while we gaze with frustrated longing on the 'Europeans Only' areas that once were ours and where now may graze and fatten only cattle that belong to that other race. We know about soil erosion because we have been educated about it and appreciate that it is the reason we must cull stock; on the other hand, deprived of cattle and also forbidden to do the best paid work available, where then, people asked, is meat and milk to be had?

It was some time, as usual, before the big people could leave off gnawing at this everlasting bone.

Days later, the rhythm of country life being what it is, they reverted to the subject of my sister. My father called me to his study to a representative group of my mothers and fathers to be once again addressed on my duty as the elder daughter to go to my sister on my way back to Europe, 'to bind her'. Their brown eyes and much-lined faces were all turned on me while one of my uncles spoke for my father, for them all, to remind me of the duties incumbent upon me in my position in the family. I thought how with my people, you are not often left to be merely your private self; you represent others, or others represent you, so that you are ever conscious of relative status, classification, interdependent relationships.

It was not for me to reply or comment on such a speech, so I sat silent, looking at the polished floorboards. As the spokesman held forth in phrases that aroused familiar emotions, I was in fact thinking of the many practical items which would be involved in the journey being outlined. I remember thinking, in English, about the details: money, travellers' cheques, booking sleepers on the train, and how I would have to 'pass through beastly Jo'burg again'. I remember how these thoughts gave way to deeper ones, this time in Xhosa, about my real mother's other children who were no more: my young brother and the sister whom I'd never actually known because she had died as a toddler just after the 'great Influenza following the '14–18 War of the Europeans'. All I knew of her was what had been handed down to us about how she 'had adored me, the new baby' and used to toddle up and tug at the shawl with which I was secured to my nurse's back, with impatient demands that she wanted to hold me. The phrases describing us children as 'linked by the umbilical cord' threw a vivid light on her absence too, as well as my brother's; indeed this entire family gathering had seemed strangely peopled with the dead as well as those 'still with us' as we say in Xhosa, implying that they have not yet joined the ancestors whom we would all eventually join: departed children, parents, grandparents, and for the elders even my great-grandparents seemed pervasively present. Yet in a way that was not at all macabre but infused with warmth, giving a sense of continuity, strength and one-ness of the family, its quick and dead 'with us'; all due to the use of our language, whose constructions and devices successfully carry complex overtones on account of its inflected nature and alliteration.

In a haze of such thoughts I became aware that the speaker was drawing to a close, coming down to more mundane things although still using the rather elaborate Xhosa of ceremony and ritual, was now talking about the marriages I and my sister had contracted and how they had flung us so far from home.

The plan of my journey back to London by way of Uganda in East Africa took shape. I was to go by land as far as Rhodesia, to call on relations and friends there, then fly from Salisbury to East Africa. My father and I studied the huge map of South African Railways that hung on his study wall, he with a much thumbed railway time-table in hand. It was a joke with us children what a typical old-fashioned Victorian-Edwardian he was with his ready knowledge of all manner of details about travel, and how seriously he took the planning of any journey. Even by car to Alice only, he would wear his ancient brown felt hat and equally vintage mackintosh, wrapping himself against the dust and possible hazards. He was always telling us how he and his younger brothers, all now dead, had been absolutely incredulous when their other brother, my late Uncle Mac, had run to them, out of breath, and declared he had seen a 'kind of Cape cart in King William's Town' (where the Jabavus lived) 'but without horses, moving along the dust road by itself, actually *turning* in the vast square where ox-waggons turn!' in the middle of the town. 'With no horses?'—and they had all dashed off to behold the apparition. My father, when telling the story, would still make his eyes start from his head and his jaw drop just as he and his Edwardian brothers had done, and make us helpless with laughter; indeed he 'never became a true motor person' as he would say, never regarded the new kind of cart light-heartedly. In his view the horse and a man's two feet were best.

But he loved trains for long journeys. Connections, junctions, time-tables, the pros and cons of alternative routes; the European guards throughout the Cape were old friends to him, tested by thousands of miles of journeys together during which they always lingered at the door of his compartment to hail him, 'Hello, Professor!' and he would sit pipe in mouth, hand on knee and call them 'Baas So-and-so' and they would pass the time of day and talk about the drought and changing conditions in our country.

My father was to travel with me for part of the way, *andik-haphe*, as we say, as far as Bloemfontein in the Boer province of the Orange Free State which was a day and a night's journey, then return home to the Colony, to the Border.

8

The Journey Begins

So AT last I left home, at peace with myself, ritually 'bound', reconciled, accepting what had had to be, all savage, unseemly emotions of revenge and hate extirpated, happy again like all of us.

We caught that awkward train that came before breakfast. As usual the platform was thronged with Africans. We saw and exchanged a warm greeting with our pagan woman friend, Makowane, selling her prickly pears; as always on trains at home, we ran into people we knew or who knew us. And since everyone in black South Africa seems to know my father, he generally holds when he travels what seems like a levee in his compartment, receives calls from people from other parts of the train, even from other racial carriages, and calls from people at stations we pass through on the way.

At Blaney Junction where we had to get out and wait for three hours for our connection, we met a cousin of mine on the Gambu side, Governor Mjali. A forceful personality, in his middle thirties, well over six feet, with shining eyes and ringing voice. My father introduced him to me. 'This was the best student I ever had in Xhosa at Fort Hare, this cousin of yours!' —to which this *mzala* of mine gave the expected African roar of pleasure; then for my benefit he and my father 'explained' him and how he and I were related. And thereby hung a tale:

It turned out that during my years in England, a marriage had been arranged ('By the young couple themselves of course, nowadays,' my father said) between a member of his and a member of my maternal family. But it had had to be stopped because what the modern couple had not known was that a common great-great-grandmother was traced when the big people got down to the work, which must always be done when people propose to marry, of tracing genealogies to ensure that there are no blood links. This great-great-grandmother was found to have been a Makiwane who as a child had been lost because of the '*inkcitakalo yezizwe*', the 'dispersal or scattering' of tribes and families caused by the military depredations wrought by the Zulus under Tshaka and other chiefs during the eighteenth and nineteenth centuries. When fighting had abated, a Gambu search-party had set out to look for the young member of the family who, tradition said, had got lost. One can imagine the long journeys on foot across the wide open spaces of what is now called the Transkei, the calls at one *umzi*, homestead, after another, picking up hints and threads and rumours and possibilities. How many many months, even years, it would take. And at last she had been found. Such store is set on the value of the individual among the Southern Bantu, because he or she 'is a Person-of-People, *ungumntu wa bantu*' and belongs, that searches like this are not at all unusual and can be kept up over generations. The lost one, when traced, was by then a grown woman married into the Mjali family. My father and my cousin now told me how she had been a sister of a maternal ancestor of mine. So it was that when, four generations later two young people had fallen in love and been on the point of marrying, their romance had thus had to be called off. We are what the experts call 'a strictly exogamous tribe' to whom a marriage between cousins of any classification linked by a traceable drop of blood is unthinkable, repugnant even in these days. My father and my new-found *mzala* reiterated, 'It was impossible, these people are related!' Indeed so powerful are the emotions engendered by *isiko* that lovers tend to be quite overcome by the scorching blast of having almost committed incest. Desire for each other dries up, painfully and with difficulty naturally, but inexorably. Once shown beyond doubt the blood-link and convinced of it, one's feelings towards even complete strangers resolve themselves into those one entertains for siblings, kith and kin. I knew what was meant because I once had it affect me, in a lesser way: at East London I stopped to buy Kaffir beads from a ragged street vender who, when I asked him 'how he was to be praised' (to be thanked), told me to say, 'Jili, Singawothi, Masengwa' and the rest.

However, the agony of the parted lovers meant something pleasant for others of their generation; in the case of Governor and me for instance, it meant a fully forged family relation with all its implications. We afterwards kept in touch and followed each other's adventures. And months later when I was home again after visiting East Africa, I was to meet his sisters, my *mzalas*, for the first time. Handsome, gay, modern girls. We found we had much in common and were happy and proud at the enlargement of our classificatory family which had thus brought us together. And it seemed to me an example of how some of us moderns sometimes benefit from the effects of recondite things like the 'extended family' of olden days, whereas observers carelessly assert that 'Westernised blacks are but poor copies of the white man'. To this I and 'cousins' like these can scoff: 'How ignorant some observers and self-styled experts can be about "us Kaffirs"!' Indeed how can they help being so, forced as they are by the present political dispensation to observe us from a distance which distorts and throws little light on our lives as we live them?

Governor was a real find of a brother. Perhaps without realising it, a brother was what I was now looking for. My *mzala* turned out to be another of these truly 'African' raconteurs, bubbling with gusto. He and my father had a burning common interest in Bantu language, so that the entire journey from Blaney to Bloemfontein, save for interruptions for meals and bedding down in our comfortable South African sleepers, was taken up with animated discussion about the state of the orthography of South-eastern Bantu languages, Xhosa particularly; discussions about the influence of Zulu noun-class systems on our Xhosa ones in the Cape; on words appropriated from English and Afrikaans; oh, what transports of disputation they engaged in about the effect of the linguistic mingling in the gold-mining and industrial and urban areas, of the two Southern Bantu language groups Zulu-Xhosa (the 'Nguni') with the Sutho-Chwana (the 'Sutho')! They were of course referring to the mixing caused by Big Business and Industry's need for workers, and the effect this has on language trends far away, even in the quiet Reserves. Our compartment resounded with versions and new views on the perennial argument: on the one hand our two groups of languages are 'degenerating', on the other they are 'already the most pliable, flexible of Bantu languages'. They talked about the stimulus to Nguni and Sutho of Non-Bantu languages, concepts and thought patterns. They harked back to 'Ur-Bantu', that convenient specialist's term for the postulated language that must have been 'original Bantu', fountain from which all those related languages must have sprung and afterwards scattered, later each modified in the process by different influences. My father and Governor ranged over the effects of migrations on the Hamitic type of pastoral Bantu peoples who put thousands of miles between themselves and their descendants and their original source somewhere up north, up east. 'Ah, what ancestors, as they travelled with their cattle, their languages constantly being enriched by those spoken by the unknown populations they overran during those centuries of movement!' In their enthusiasm as professionals, they at times leapt to their feet, eyes shining with excitement, interrupting and cutting each other short, oblivious of me as I sat silently drinking in the scene. For me it was another of the old and intense delights in being with my people again.

An unknown man, a teacher, joined us in the compartment, drawn as by a magnet by the happy echo of voices down the corridor. He did not trouble to introduce himself, the discussion was too enjoyable to interrupt; he stood as one who would introduce himself later, meanwhile interjecting and offering!

'*Andibi, Jili*, am I right, Jili, when I agree with Mclaren in his "Xhosa Grammar"?' and he recited, modestly, from memory: ' "*That the Kaffirs intermarried to a large extent with these people is evidenced not only by the degree in which they have adopted sounds and words from their languages, but by the distinctly Hottentot features which one frequently observes among individuals of the Xhosa tribe, and by the generally lighter colour of the skin in that tribe when*

57

compared with others living farther north."' My father smacked his thigh with amusement at this display of learning by rote and cried, '*Ja!* We are Hottentots indeed!' And we all laughed. '*Kanti kunantoni ukuba'ungumSukwini?* Yet what is wrong with being a Hottentot? What if some people despise that heritage? Let them! What matters is that the Xhosa language is the most vigorous of all, thanks to such heritage. Man, if South Africa goes on developing at this rate, Xhosa will "eat up" the southern languages, it is eating them up already?'

The stranger muttered in a matter-fact way, '*Kakade*, naturally! Are not the Xhosa the vigorous ones? Wherever you find them concentrated nowadays, I mean on the Rand or in Capetown, by no means their natural habitats, there you find the Xhosas sticking to their own language like the orange peel sticks to the orange so that it is these other tribes, Shangaans, Vendas and whatnot who have to learn Xhosa. The Xhosas for their part merely take what they want from theirs, assimilate and modify it, then the speakers of the original have to re-learn the result as dictated by Xhosa usage, isn't it? I am talking about the vernacular,' he said pausing to draw breath. I noticed his 'isn't it', a common Xhosa literal translation into English; and also the typical manner in which he pronounced 'vernacular' saying 'venenkyula'. He took up his tale. 'But of course when it comes to the official languages, why even Xhosa himself, *uCira ngesiqu* (literally putting it "Cira bodily"), when in town must and learns Afrikaans and English!'

Now that remark caused tremendous enjoyment. For he was of course referring (using a collective device) to what in English might be compared to 'the fountain of honour', the sovereign of the Xhosa people for whom 'Cira' is the chiefly clan. And our laughter was tempered, as so much African laughter is tempered for those who know its gradations, by numerous considerations: such as those sensations emanating from the respect, awe, 'fear' as we call it, of the chief and his sons embodying as they did in the positions to which they were born, our people and ideas as a nation; also there was a poignant twist in that remark, with its implications that in these days our sovereign

58

concepts about life have to be rudely adapted to new patterns, that their 'bodily' representatives have themselves thus to adapt instead of statuesquely represent our own; again, there was a play of words in what he said, also poignant, because owing to our former legitimately polygynous, patrilinear society, the descendants of 'Cira bodily' as he put it are as numerous as grains of sand among us, yet however ragged an industrial worker one of them may be when you happen to meet him in some urban area, if you have occasion to 'praise, thank or hail' him by his proper, resounding clan designations you elevate his spirit as a representative of something invested with former glories; and yourself feel elevated in uttering 'his names'. Indeed, the hidden implications in the stranger's 'poetic' allusion, *ubuciko*, embraced so many things deeply embedded in the backs of our minds, how could we acknowledge them all except by the eloquent laughter we gave vent to?

My father did so acknowledge; he again smote his thigh and confirmed the man's observation, pointing at him and crying out at first in Afrikaans, '*Jy moet die Taal praat*, or else English otherwise starve! Indisputably even the most conservative, dyed-in-the-wool Xhosa fellow knows that. "When in Rome do as the Romans do", isn't that so, *andibi bafondini*?' And then suddenly serious and wiping the laughter from his face and voice, 'That is where my scholar Mjalni here is doing good work.'

For Governor was now editor of an African children's newspaper, *UmHlobo wabaNtwana*, The Children's Friend, financed by an Afrikaans publishing concern. In it Governor propagated the purest Xhosa, wrote tit-bit paragraphs, among other things in longer articles and stories, about the origin and development of words and phrases for the benefit of young people who grow up speaking 'town English, town Afrikaans, town vernaculars', slipshod hybrids.

'I am glad my boy, glad. You could hardly have been in a more suitable job had it been created specially for you.'

'Or congenial, Jili,' Governor said, to which my father cried:
'*Ancedile lama Bulu, hii?* A help these Boers have been, what?

59

I really like them for this,' and he expanded on the feature of my *mzala's* children's weekly in which he ran a column for teaching Afrikaans for beginners. 'The authorities did not teach us Die Taal when I was boy, before you people here were born. That was very wrong.'

But not all young people agree with my father in this. Many of the younger generation have become emotionally antagonistic towards Afrikaans, reciprocating the Nationalist Boer Government's policies of repression and the unfairnesses they cause in the everyday condition and prospects of everyone; especially the young fired with the ambitions of people of their age everywhere. Others of us could see the point however, when my father expressed it that 'to know Afrikaans can teach you as nothing else can the background and character of the intrinsic Boer'; we knew how desirable an accomplishment it was to be fluent in the language of those with whom you have to deal, those in power be they English or Boer. We admitted that we ought not to allow resentments bred in us by these Nationalists to cloud common sense, dull our sense of curiosity, destroy our desire to learn what was to be learnt about these people. My father said, summing up the attitude of his coevals, 'We are still learning—we, we old men: *Sisafunda tina maxhego. Ayikasiruquli tina imfundo*, Learning as such has not yet bored us!'

At Bloemfontein we parted from Governor. He lived there and was met by his wife and children, my father and I by the husband of my new mother's daughter, my father's new step son-in-law whom he already knew.

The daughter and I met for the first time; it was at her house that I was to wait four or five hours for my train to Johannesburg, and my father to stop with them for a night or two before going back to Middledrift. We regarded each other, she and her husband much younger than me and calling me by my style of 'elder sister'. They were so happy to see my father again and in that darkness (our train had come in before dawn) they bustled about their little house lighting stoves to make him comfortable. They prepared hot water for us to wash, laid out new

60

cakes of toilet soap, warm towels. Their voices were full of kindness. Neighbours and friends and relations almost immediately began to arrive because 'uJili, the Professor, Doctor, the Grand Old Man!' was here; and he too started to get excited as usual by the human contacts, his voice rising along with the other people's. Who would guess, I thought looking on and listening, that we were in a 'location', a place regarded in South Africa as only vicious? It was all warmth and gaiety in the little house. Underneath the laughter and joy of reunion, these Free Staters and us 'from The Colony', countries as different as chalk from cheese in atmosphere, we were ordinary human beings confronted with a human situation; for the relatives and friends welcoming us in this way knew everything, were feeling intensely for my father about his son and his children, about his providential remarriage, his new, ready-made family.

And as I watched the exchanges between my new sister, her husband and my father, I, for one, was beset with troublesome emotions: 'I and my sister, our husbands and children, *we* are his children!' And I was fighting to stop asking myself, 'Are these new ones also his children?' It was strange to hear them call him 'father' and to realise that they meant it 'really really, truly' as we say, and not classificatorily. I couldn't help it; I tried to suppress these twinges and wondered how they in turn felt on seeing me, this much-spoken-of, ready-made 'overseas elder sister'. They were so nice to me, behaved so spontaneously as though they thought me nice too. I was a child of his flesh; did we not all know and know that we knew we now belonged as custom enjoined? Nevertheless even custom, *isiko*, is hard put to reconcile inner complexities and this was one of those situations in which one felt thankful that 'some things should not be spoken even in whispers', as we say in Xhosa.

But the spirit of unity prevailed for the time being, although later, as I have said, our younger generation were to disintegrate, since with us the inroads of western modernity are corroding or qualitatively changing still more of what we retain in customary attitudes than they had done in our parents in their day. One realises the depth of these foundations in us,

61

since despite the inevitable corrosions and changes, I and my coevals retain as much as we do of the Southern Bantu psychology our society has handed down.

When we had eaten it was daylight but raining and bitterly cold. However, a contingent of younger people suggested taking me out to see the location, Bochabela Location. They teased me, tongue in cheek, about how, being from overseas and because of my husband, I doubtless thought 'Europeans' (meaning 'English') were best; but they would show me, they declared, how 'their Boers here *in die Oranje Vrystaat*' had really been better than 'the rooineks', as Boers call South African English; bursts of laughter at this, since it was of course a reference to the disconcerting situation we all know so well: that the Boers are not all primitive Calvinists stunted in thought as Nationalist policies and tenets of the Dutch Reformed Church imply, and the occasional Boer sadist confirms in incidents on outlying farms where a white master will sometimes spreadeagle a black employee on a waggon wheel and thrash him to death. Nor are the English on the other hand all civilised Western men as their 'overseas' inheritance would lead you to expect; with them too the occasional one will commit an atrocity. Furthermore, the English are guilty in our eyes, of a subtler, greater sin because in what we call their 'desiccated, intellectual', to themselves, 'balanced' approach to human problems they appear heartless and unfeeling; whereas the best of the Boers show signs of a warmer, more human temperament. 'They had been so long in Africa being beaten by the sun like us,' we often say, 'that they were getting to be *people*, human. But the English having come later to our land still had the northern frost and ice in their veins.' So we younger generation on leaving the house laughed at that remark about Boers having been better, as our elders laugh when confronted with some of those contradictory truths about life, underneath the laughter wrestling with them.

We went out in a closed car that a neighbourly citizen had come round to 'place at the Professor's disposal'. My father in accepting the kind offer had exercised his prerogative of age and stature by thanking the young man, yet laughingly demanding in the same sentence, speaking in SeChwana, the language of the province, 'But, my boy, is your car fit to *lend*? Is it a sedan? I don't like these jalopies with tents for hoods.'

'Oh yes, father,' the man said effacing himself. 'It's a saloon, to be sure. I sold my previous one, *that* was a tourer. And it is licensed.'

'Tyres pumped up?'

'Jili!' So there were reasons for many kinds of laughter as I was shepherded out and several of us piled into the 'sedan'.

When we came back the big people were sitting round the room on the leather settee and light-coloured dining chairs, men smoking, women's thick tasselled shawls drawn close round their shoulders against the cold. We stood at a little distance. On seeing us, they talked about their location. They were old residents who could look back on its better days, when Africans had been happy living there; people had had adequate plots of land, could build houses to their own designs—not the stereotyped matchboxes compulsory nowadays. I believed it for I had just seen many really pleasant houses, among them the double-storeyed one of my senior maternal uncle's father-in-law. In those days there wasn't the location 'supervision' (by whites) and perpetual hounding by the police. The old people were saying how Bochabela and Lady Selborne near Pretoria were examples of 'how open-handed the Boer could be when he allowed himself to be human'.

'In the old days the Boer didn't care if Africans had decent places to live in as long as *die Kaffirs* weren't mixed up among them in *their* Boer places. Ha! Not so now. The Boer has become a jealous creature, poisoned by his rancour towards the Englishman. Race-dedicated Nationalists are in charge today, destroying the qualities of their own people, filling them with hate and envy. Terrible. Yet in the old days it was better for an African to deal with a Boer than with the Englishman. What ruined the Boer was when the Englishman, having vanquished

63

and thrashed him in war, handed the whip to the loser with that 1910 Act of The Union of South Africa. What was that but incredible, desiccated, crass intellectualism? Now we Africans are paying the consequences for the inexplicable psychology!'

The time came for me to go; reminiscences tapered off. My father prepared himself with a contented smile to say goodbye. He did not refer to what was uppermost in both our minds, only pointed to a spot close to his armchair for me to approach while he made the customary little speech of thanksgiving for 'happy reunions like this one, of people of one blood surrounded by their collaterals and friends', sentiments which were accompanied by murmurs and solemn exclamations from those sitting round him, then laughter and cries of *bon voyage* in the various languages when he drew himself up to his feet commenting as he did so about the stiffening of old joints: 'Yet I can out-walk these youngsters here who don't go anywhere except in motor cars!' and lightly embraced me.

As I left accompanied by those taking me to the station, we could hear his voice, 'As I was saying——' and the other elderly voices encouraging the resumption of the tale, 'Ye-s, Jili, as you were saying!'

As my train pulled out, my coevals trotted alongside calling out to me to 'take their greetings to our sister, up there in unknown Africa!'

I sat back and looked out as my train travelled slowly through this Boer province. Approaching Thaba Nchu, I remembered: '*Eli lilizwe labaRolong*, this is the country of the Barolong', the Chwana cattle-keeping tribe from whom the Boers, fleeing from the hated English in the Western Cape, had wrested these plains. A MuRolong friend of our family, Dr Moroka, lived here practising medicine and farming; he was my father's contemporary, had been a fellow student overseas before the 1914 War. He was a descendant of the Rolong chiefs. Thanks to him a flourishing mission school and hospital had

64

been built here. Years before, my young sister and late brother had come to this school, lived with Dr Moroka and his wife acting *in loco parentis* to them so that they should learn Afrikaans and SeChwana. The Morokas had motored all the way from here to my brother's funeral and Dr Moroka had been one of the speakers at the service. I was sorry not to be able to stop and see them again; the trouble with my homeland being that it is so vast.

The Bechwana are distinct from my own people in the Eastern Cape. They appear to have absorbed the Bushmen (whom they overran on their migration) in even greater concentration than we farther south; indeed there is evidence that the huge inland territory of Bechuanaland was once heavily populated by Bushmen. Today the Bechwana are on the whole very light-skinned, a golden yellow brown. There are individuals of course who are quite dark, but they stand out in contrast to the rest. The tribe tend to have high cheek-bones and the women pronounced hips, what the experts call 'steoptygia', a legacy from the Bushmen. Round about Bloemfontein and Thaba Nchu, I saw that they seemed to have yet another legacy: Boer *genes*. There had been no Immorality Acts in the old days. You notice these ethnographic phenomena as you travel up from the Cape so that by the time you reach Bloemfontein you realise you are in another South African world. And your Nguni language gives way to the Sutho; at stations you hear Sechwana, a wonderfully energetic language with its rolled and flapped consonants which we in the Cape don't have, and its affricates. The Sutho Group (SeSutho, SeChwana, SePedi, etc.) is spoken by over three million Southerners. And because of the dispersals that I have mentioned, *inkcitakalo*, those tribal upheavals, flights and scatterings provoked by the Zulu military dictator tyrants, this language even thrust a prong away into Northern Rhodesia in Barotseland, where they speak the Sutho Lozi, or Rotse, now heavily modified. I thought of all this and of how staggering a phenomenon were those dispersals. Because of them, my own Nguni too, thrust up as far away as Nyasaland and Tanganyika; incredible distances when one remembers that it was all 'route marching and living off the land' as a modern infantryman would say, no horses, no trains, no air transport. Yet Angoni people, as they are now called, are established in those faraway places, and they trace their patrilineal descent from the Zulus of the South. Through the window of my compartment when the train was at a halt, I could hear the people speak much Afrikaans, the influence of that other dispersal, The Great Trek. '*Ons praat die taal, hierso*', I could imagine them saying gaily; a vivid hybrid slang it was too, that they were using. My ear was tickled by it.

The train pressed on to the North through flat grasslands, flat as far as the eye could see. The landscape was queer to my eyes until I realised that being Cape born and bred, I unconsciously missed the everlasting blue frieze on the skyline, of rock-topped mountains. The Free State was as smooth as a table; no sweeping shallow contours edged with distant jagged crags. Here you were on the high flat plateau that you read about in primary school Geography lessons; 'joe-graphy' as we Southerners pronounce it.

Night fell and I presented my bedding ticket to the attendant, glancing at the print on it as I did so. '*Geldig vir een ononderbroke reis as dit nie van die bedgegoedbediende se bewys afgeskeur is nie*, available for one unbroken journey if presented intact with Bedding Attendant's check.' I also read that it would not take one over 'lines of Rhodesia Railways north of Bulaway'. The South African Railways and Harbours bedclothes are green, with a special line to show that they are 'Native' and therefore even after cleaning never to be used in the European part of the train.

The attendant was Cape Coloured. This is one of their traditional jobs. And like many of them (they are famous among the blacks for this, I am sorry to say), he was unbelievably silly, filled with sex conveyed in objectionable remarks, a miserable specimen, a discredit to his people; no African girl on the train was safe from his advances and unfortunately our European guard was never at hand for us to appeal to. There were two of us sharing the compartment, and being of the

66

modern Westernised generation we had not exchanged a single word, had kept ourselves to ourselves. But this unpleasant man broke our ice and when he left, my fellow-traveller, a hospital nurse I had noticed from her luggage labels, cried out bitterly in English, 'Oh these Coloureds! Man, it will be a great day when that Verwoerd introduces his "Native attendants for Natives, European ones for Europeans, Indians for Indians" and all that. *Then* we may get some peace.' After that we relapsed into our modernistic reserve. Truly Westernised we were. Later that night I marked the contrast between our behaviour and that of the older generation when a woman old enough to be our mother opened the door of our compartment, merely to look in and question us in her old-fashioned African way.

'And who may you be, young-ladies-of-ours?' She spoke in Xhosa. My companion was by the door, nearest to her and should have replied. She did, but only eventually, and with the greatest reluctance evinced by long disobliging pauses. 'Never mind' seemed to be the motto of our elder as she waited, nothing daunted, for the answer. Now that my travelling companion spoke in the language too, I noticed she used a '*Tsefula*' version of the Nguni group, one of the more archaic, lisping, sibilant variants which are markedly soft and cautious about the so-called 'click' consonants. One could not be sure whether she was Swazi or Zulu. Perhaps Baca. However I could follow although not easily; to my Cape ears the 'Tsefula' accent only proclaimed 'some kind of a Tshaka' as we teasingly call the Zulus. This modern Tshaka young lady told our inquisitor practically nothing about herself. The old lady's disapproval was to be seen on her face; she was clearly thinking, 'What *are* these children of the electric light age coming to!' and turned to try out what I was like.

'*Wena?* And you? Who are you of?'

'I am of Jili, *mama*,' I said.

'*O?*' Her eyes lit up. '*Kwa-Jili?* Then are you related to the Professor?'

'Yes.'

67

'Then what about this "deprivation"?' (euphemisms for deaths being *de rigeur*!). 'How close is it to you?'

'It was my brother.'

'Your brother? *Brother?* Truly truly, in-the-house? *Kanye kanye, endlini?* Same mother same father?' (She had to be sure it was not an 'extended family' kind of brother.)

'Yes, mother, truly in the house. He followed-on-the-back of the sister-who-follows-on-*my*-back.' She fell silent, looking at me, and her eyes suddenly filled with compassion. Then she made the little ritual speech and I was moved because this was happening so many hundreds of miles from my own home.

'It is nothing, my child, it is nothing; the Lord will bind you. "Never are shoulders visited with a burden heavier than they can carry," ' quoting one of our proverbs, and finishing, 'Therefore He will give you the strength you need, Jili.' She went, leaving us to our Western style privacy.

It seemed a long, long journey. The train rattled rhythmically on the narrow gauge sleepers: '*Xhegwazana phek' ipapa, xhegwazana phek' ipapa, xhegwazana phek' ipapa*', just as we used to repeat after it when we were children, 'Old woman, cook the porridge, old woman cook the porridge.' Only it is not possible to reproduce the rhythm in English! We reached Jo'burg at last, that polyglottal metropolis of Southern Africa. I had to change to a train bound still further North, 'All Africa lay North,' I thought.

Jo'burg is an uncomfortable place for someone from a quiet country Reserve. The Rand area seems charged with a vitality at once stimulating, inspiring, frightening. It is like an electric field of currents, bristling with energy, violence, zest for life and progress, seems to prickle with possibilities of sudden death. Life is precious, hard-pressed, people cling to it as people do anywhere, but there it is cheap, put out like a light as we had heard at home. It is the anonymity that frightens you, indifference between black and black, white and white, and white and black; and the violence behind it all seems to vibrate

68

in the very air you breathe when you arrive there from the quiet 'Colony', the Cape.

Johannesburg people say country bumpkins can be detected a mile off, 'They look terrified and so simple, just asking to be robbed!' And robbed we often are of course, and go back to the Reserves to fill other bucolics with the terrors of that hostile city. Although I have lived for years in London, when I am home in South Africa I react like any person of the quiet Eastern Cape. I felt all these terrors and was relieved to change trains and pull out.

9

The Central African Federation

AND now I crossed the frontier into the Federation. When the British Government had passed the Bill that created a federation of the three territories, Southern and Northern Rhodesia and Nyasaland, and announced the new policy of 'Partnership' that would prevail in the land, I had greatly doubted that it would in fact, whatever the hopes, turn out differently from our *Suid-Afrikaanse baaskap*, the white domination that the whole world knows about. My doubts were based on the reputation of Southern Rhodesia, the most powerful of the countries that were to be united. Then sitting in the gallery of the House of Lords one day during the committee stages of the debate, I had seen the Government Leader resisting the attempts of the Opposition to incorporate the admirable preamble within the body of the Bill.

The preamble set out 'partnership' in a way no African could cavil at but which any Southern African supporter of white *baaskap* would naturally resist, since it forecast the end of white domination. The intention was admirable, but the refusal to incorporate the preamble so as to make it effective reminded me of those opinions at home to which I have referred, about the 'desiccated, intellectual' approach of British people towards human problems in countries such as ours peopled by various races in different stages of Westernisation. We are not convinced that you can justifiably expect fair and comfortable racial adjustments to follow the dictates of the intellect. On the contrary, we believe that in order that racial emotions should not lead to acts of communal or group hostility and unfairness to people belonging to the less influential communities, it is necessary for legislators to enact laws to enforce equality of opportunity in employment, education, freedom of movement.

70

Human beings are frail we say; therefore in order that they may do what is moral they often, regrettably, need a stronger urge than intellect alone provides for most. The British Government was refraining from incorporating in the Bill that which would so urge, and through the Leader in the House of Lords was using the dry, chilly intellectual arguments that we deprecate in a way of life we otherwise admire.

What did surprise me however in that debate was all of a sudden to hear a note of emotion, rather than the more normal British detachment; for a member resisting the incorporation of the preamble spoke of 'Rhodesians, our white kin who fought for us in the War', making me prick up my ears.

As I now, some years later, rode into the Federation on the Cape to Cairo Railway I remembered how strangely those words had sounded to me since I thought of 'Rhodesians' as being black as well as white people. As the voice had continued in tones the more telling because gentle and pleasant to listen to, and actually used the old cliché, 'flesh of our flesh', and harangued the Opposition for harbouring views 'humiliating to their own people in the Colonies' I had shuddered and asked myself as other Africans do at times like these: 'Can he mean that? Would he say it if he knew my people, my relatives in the Federation? Where do black kin come in? Are we not British subjects too just like the whites? Why should fair play towards us be regarded as a threat to our fellow whites?' And I had to force myself to guess that very likely the noble lord was one of many who was intellectually a just human being, unaware that these were emotionally racialistic sentiments, too detached to know that they might be interpreted as such by people who were not of the elect white kin.

Remembering that experience, I knew that during the next few days I would learn with especial interest what partnership was like in effect for my own kith and kin living under it, for they would naturally tell me.

At last I was riding on 'The Cape to Cairo Railway'; it had sounded so romantic in history class when I was a schoolgirl in history classes at Lovedale near my old home at Fort Hare when my father lectured there. Now twenty years on I savoured its actual romance as I chugged over mile upon mile of wooden sleepers and admired the efforts of our white settlers in linking up these far-flung countries. The railway was an idea of Cecil Rhodes. He had invited my grandfather to ride on it when it was inaugurated. It has not yet fulfilled Rhodes' dream in which the line reached as far north as Cairo; nevertheless even only to Salisbury was some two thousand miles from Capetown and I could not but be impressed, as anyone must be who makes the journey. The train pressed on bravely through bush, aloes, thorn and *mopani* trees, protea shrubs, tall grass; I noticed how Rhodesian grass seemed taller than in the Transvaal.

I was in a compartment with a handsome Coloured couple newly married at the girl's home in Capetown, bound for the bridegroom's home in the Federation. We got into conversation. The bride and I pretended to tease her husband about the appearance of his country which she and I were seeing for the first time. We said, 'What funny motor roads you have, two strips of tar along the dust track. Why, they don't compare with our National Roads in South Africa. Have you motored from Capetown to Jo'burg, a thousand miles and every inch tarred?' He touchingly defended himself and his country, 'Ah, but it takes a good driver to drive on strips. In Rhodesia we've got the best drivers in Africa.'

But we went on teasing, pretended to be unimpressed even by the vegetation and laughed at 'his' protea. 'But they're not in season just now!' he protested and we all three laughed. We were making a game out of chauvinism, an emotion which of course did not seriously appeal to me and which I doubted if it appealed to the bride. She was a quiet girl and, judging from her conversation before this, without interests outside her home, clothes and cosmetics. But she was happy and well-disposed towards the world in her new status. I think it was because we had to make the best of the fact that we really had little in common that we seized on light-hearted comparisons of our two countries; we were being patriotic in a special way, mainly for something to talk about in a friendly manner, in my case only slightly related to my deeper feelings about love of country. For that was an emotion which went too deep to tamper with on this occasion, involving as it does language, family, all things intimate. It was evil, to my mind, to charge such feelings with bellicosity; that kind of patriotism seemed to me to go hand-in-hand with 'nationalist' ideas of the Boer kind.

Then all of a sudden our harmless, rather superficial little pleasantries were violated. A Rhodesian Immigration Officer appeared at the door, a stocky short man in khaki shorts and open shirt collar with a spotted choker tucked in it. In less than two minutes this man shattered our banter with a display of the manners of some of the 'kith and kin' that the noble member of Parliament had defended years before; all because I mentioned to him that the printed conditions on his form exempted certain 'categories of persons' from filling in some items and I thought I fell into such a category, exempted from filling in everything on the questionnaire. His answer: 'I don't care what the form bloody well says,' and to my astonishment he had gone red in the face and was shouting although I was barely eighteen inches from him, '*You* are to fill 'em all up, d'you hear? Bloody well fill 'em up!' and he glared at me with loathing, like a snake about to spit poison. I was stung and instantly gave as good as I got:

'You're a thoroughly bloody little man, aren't you? Where are your manners? You're the most offensive, ill-bred creature I've ever come across, you—you "*Rhodesian*"'—and had to stop; I could not go on, my whole being seething with the political implications, injustice. I found myself trembling with rage, that my manners too had gone with the wind, no question of turning the other cheek, for a racial quarrel had been precipitated, anything might happen. Shaking, I filled in the questions, 'All of 'em', instinctively aware what 'justice' I might get if I omitted some (as I was entitled to) and consequently got involved with this man at Law. I wrote, not trusting myself to speak lest I should weep in my humiliation. Thus we both triumphed. His look conveyed that for his part, his white man's orders were being carried out by 'this munt', Rhodesian for the

South African 'kaffir'; and I knew that my tongue had lashed 'this white trash'.

He went. But shame reigned in our compartment instead of the 'joking relationship' we had managed to establish earlier, and there was bitterness. Finally the bridegroom cleared his throat and said nervously, 'You know, they are not all like that.' We girls looked at each other. A deeper note had been sounded after all. This was the young man's home-land. I knew the conflict he was suffering at that moment; how often have fellow countrymen of my own, of the type of the Immigration Officer, not hurt me as he had been hurt? We couldn't speak.

But another European loomed in our doorway. Uniformed this time, in dark blue, peak-capped, wearing long trousers instead of undignified shorts. We froze. He was an enormous man, six feet four if an inch. When he announced that he was 'South African Immigration' and would like to see our papers, we froze still more for his voice and accent declared him a Boer. He took our papers and went away leaving us silent. This time it was we two girls who were worried. Was our countryman about to humiliate us too, with that accent? We could only look out at the tall grass, at the bush, the protea, the tar strips.

Presently he came back. We turned only our eyes on him, sideways, glazed and expressionless; it was an anxious moment and there were ugly emotions in the compartment. But, incredible to relate, the man smiled. Not we, however. He sat down, handed us our papers and passports, all in one movement and at the same time addressing me, 'Miss Jabavu or Mrs *dinges* (Afrikaans for "what's it"), I see you use both names, hey? Your maiden name for reserving the sleeper. *Ja*, I suppose that's practical out here, might have to sleep along there, hey?' and he pointed in the direction of the European coaches. 'Shouldn't have married away from South Africa. Don't you know this year is the best for our rugby football prospects? South Africa's going to lick those *dinges*, man, make 'em sail back squealing. Now look, there's a query about this page in your passport,' and he spread the document open before me, turned to the page. He had electrified us and we did not utter a word, or smile. With the Nationalist Government in power, one looks on every official as representative. You hardly expect them to be civil. But the Nationalist uniform had evidently not bullied this particular Boer into acting like a bully. He was behaving like a normal human being, prepared to treat us as ordinary people too. I began to find myself responding; the frozen, protective front I had erected began to thaw. But I was far from smiling yet, wondering what the query might be, what its terrible consequences. My eyes focused at last and I read the page while he explained what was wrong. This was the incident I mentioned at the beginning of my story, when I said that my 'Entry into the Union of South Africa' had not been recorded on the night I flew into Jan Smuts airport, in the confusion caused by that nice air-hostess in asking the officials to 'do me first' because of her human feelings.

I now learnt from this other Boer that the omission was very serious. He spoke gravely. I continued to stare at the page. As I had not known, even, that it should have been stamped or otherwise recorded, I was dumbfounded. My mind instantly filled with the horrors of a broken journey, being escorted back to Johannesburg, incarceration, trials. The officer was saying in his distinctive intonation and using Afrikaans expressions, '*Yerr*, don't you see, you may be a spy for all we know. You are telling *me* you landed at Jan Smuts but there's no stamp here, nothing. Man, *yow* do we know you're telling the truth? Supposing you're telling lies, hey?' At last I looked up, about to protest my innocence. I found humorous brown eyes on my face, as though measuring my capacity for lying. They twinkled, and to my relief I became aware that he was only teasing. I heaved a sigh of relief and thought him, quite inconsequentially, an attractive, masculine type and wondered why it was that when one noticed the eyes of a nice Boer they were usually brown and when he was unpleasant they seemed icy blue. He explained the penalties for the crime I had committed, but as his voice was smiling as well as his eyes, I laughed now and said, 'But I'm leaving, isn't that okay?'

He said with mock sternness, '*Nee, dit is nie "okay" nie*, not at all! We *Y*immigration *k*arn't let you out if we dunno you came *in*.' I thought his accent was a delight after that Rhodesian man's. I explained briefly how I and my fellow passengers had been processed in rather a hurry the night we arrived therefore the officials at Jan Smuts had not seemed to be as efficient as no doubt they usually were.

To my surprise, he immediately fulminated and fumed, 'The *inefficiency* of those chaps at Jan Smuts, the whole Government service is a rotten mess but man, those chaps up there!' I was taken aback. On our side of the colour line the civil servants we were most concerned with were at the Post Offices, Railways and Buses, the Native Affairs Department, all bywords in their dilatoriness in serving us. We assumed this was out of racial spite backed by the policy of *apartheid*. His words were my first glimpse at how the civil service looks through some white eyes. 'Inefficiency, *oh Gòtt!* But what can you expect when people get jobs without proper education, qualifications? You can leave school at Standard III or IV, man, and you know you'll get a job in Government. As for at Jan Smuts, *yerr!*' and he pushed his peaked cap back from his brow. 'Drive you crazy up there, 's why I transferred to this the moment I heard I was going to be sent there,' and he pointed to the floor of the compartment.

He was being a typical post-war young man 'binding about his job'. He was not being 'political', he seemed unaware that he had revealed that his people too reacted as our own do to things like this and that there was much in common among South Africans of every colour. I thought, 'Is this why the Government frowns on the most trivial contact between the races? People get into conversations of this sort, find unexpected topics in common.'

Finding myself in the presence of a civilised compatriot, I now told him about the Rhodesian civil servant. He listened, looking out of the window. When I finished, he said, 'Aha!' tapped the crest on the cover of my British passport repeatedly, forcing me to look at it too. Then he said with a mixture of amusement and grimness, '*You* shouldn't cry to *me* with this passport of yours, man. He's yours, your British "partner", hey?'

I was reminded of that the following day. It so happened that, as the precocious young French girl Hyacinthe expressed it on communicating the news to her mentor in Elliot Paul's presentation of modern Gallic *mores*, 'A Narrow Street', it was a date in the month when it should be 'proved that I was a woman'. This is a matter that should hardly figure in one's story. But some readers may not realise the levels at which the colour bar is liable to make itself felt if you are black. I shall therefore tell how this matter affected me in Salisbury when I had to go shopping for the necessary commodity.

I was driven into town from the location; they called them Townships in Rhodesia, I noticed. As I walked along the wide sunny streets of the metropolis of The Federation I thought they looked like those of a young, overgrown country town for all their bright new skyscrapers and the long low-slung American cars that glided along them. I noticed the rather pronounced 'petit-bourgeois' aspect of most of the Europeans I saw, and their voices and accents reminded me of that immigration officer in the train, making me wince.

I stepped into a chemist's to ask the (white) 'sales-lady' for what I wanted, as a Westernised type of woman would down home in the Union whether black, white or brown. The shop assistant shot me a hostile look when I spoke. I was not perturbed by that; most Southern white assistants rather resent serving black customers, indeed, resent serving. But she followed this by suddenly throwing verbal bricks at my head. Now this was unexpected, for at home in the Union even when they resent your custom they seldom go so far as to repulse your money. She ended by calling out to another assistant, repeating the cause of her indignation: 'Whatever next! Fine thing when *Natives* wan' things like that. They'll be sayin' they're Europeans next.' And turning back to me: 'Go 'n get whatever you people use in yer own native shops, go on, get out.'

So far, I felt that the kith and kin defended in political

77

debate by the member of the House of Lords, that chamber representing the justice and balanced outlook we Cape moderate politicians so admired, had reacted with something less than balance to my type of African. My relatives and friends confirmed this impression with various experiences of their own during the years they had lived in Rhodesia. They said that the atmosphere had indeed become more acute with the coming of the post-war type of young Briton coming out to settle with the help of War gratuities. I was depressed.

However, before leaving the country I luckily had more light-hearted experiences. One was when I was invited to dine with a European missionary couple stationed many miles out in the countryside, in a bare 'wide open spaces' kind of landscape of brown grass and boulders, their house charmingly set within a lovely clump of tall Blue Gum trees. The mission was far from anywhere so that it was good to be made welcome at the end of the long drive. Before going in to dinner, the missionary's wife took me to the 'P.K.' as I noticed Europeans in Central Africa called it. Inside, I was astonished. There in the middle of the veld, far from water, electricity, modern facilities, stood a new water closet, a flush lavatory. When I came out and commented on this unexpected amenity in a not affluent mission station, my hostess explained how it was a legacy of the Archbishop of Canterbury's Tour in Central Africa. It had been felt only right to provide it for his Grace on his call on them for an hour or two; it had been built for the occasion with much digging of trenches and damming of furrows to augment the rather meagre local water supply. I was much impressed and cheered. From then on when I wanted a 'P.K.', I asked for 'The Archbishop's Room'!

10

Across the Zambesi to Kenya

IT SO happened that the day before I left Rhodesia I received a letter from my sister. Although she had so far sent only a telegram which arrived a whole week after my brother had been buried and saying only 'GOD'S WILL BE DONE REGRET UNABLE TO COME', I had been writing to her all the time. Letter after letter had gone into the void. Not a word of condolence either, from her people-in-law. Because of the letter that I now got from her out of the blue, I was more eager than ever to quit Rhodesia and could hardly contain myself through the motions of farewells to relations and friends at Belvedere Airport from where my plane to Nairobi was to fly.

A short, too short letter; sketchy comments about her little child who was nearly a year old. She did not expand even about him but went on to, of all things, the weather that I would find in Uganda.

But tucked away were two sentences: 'But I must admit, Sis, I'm getting dreadfully impatient for you to arrive here. You'll see for yourself.' Knowing her, it was those two remarks that gave me a troubled night before leaving.

At last I was climbing up the gangway of the aeroplane and turned to wave goodbye. This was the penultimate lap of my journey. I would have to stop a night in Nairobi, Kenya, for my connection to Uganda. Now I could settle back in my seat in solitude, and during the long flight ahead think about my sister.

She had come from South Africa to me in England to continue her training as a hospital nurse. On qualifying, she left for Uganda to marry her fiancé of ten years. None of us could be at her wedding because of the distance and expense, but she was given away on my father's behalf by family friends living in Kampala. She had met her young man when he was a student at Fort Hare in the days when my father lectured there. They were attached to each other for the better part of his time in the Union, during which he went on to Capetown University; before coming to South Africa he had studied in a university college in West Africa. In his own country before continuing his education in foreign lands he had studied at the well-known Uganda secondary school, King's College, Budo. Finally he read for the Bar at Gray's Inn. He was a highly educated man, the sort we could be proud of. Like all the Uganda students in South Africa, my sister's young man came from a distinguished family. He had told how his father was a Chief and was Treasurer of the Native Government of Busoga. We also learnt from him how his mother had died when he was a child and he had been brought up by his step-mother.

I thought back to how the big people had 'spoken with me' in my father's study about my duty to heal her wound as ours had been healed by being together in the ritualistic setting. I remembered the time I had become aware of my uncle's peroration descending from the lofty ritual plane to more mundane things about how we girls had married and left our old home for new ones so far away.

'You two girls are blessed on earth. *Imizi yenu*, your homes-of-marriage, are high indeed. You the eldest are married to an Englishman, *umlungu wasemanzini*, a European-of-the-water.' My uncle paused for this was the laudatory expression for a European pure and fresh from overseas, distinct from the local breed. 'You are therefore at the fountain of all the ideals that we Southerners struggle for: discipline of mind and action, decency, riches, refinements.' I could not help squirming. But I respected and was fond of them all and there was nothing to do but let him continue. 'And your younger sister is married to a Ugandan. She too is thus at the fountain of all desirable and elevated things. As for you, eldest-one, we know the people of your home-of-marriage; we see them when they first arrive in

South Africa, before they are infected of course (although indeed some never change).

'But the Baganda of your sister, we know them only from hearsay. Your father was there it is true, but only for ten days. Yet what he saw has filled him with longing. Go you now therefore and look on our behalf. And when you write, uplift us with eye-witness reports of civilised Africans, for they are said to be all that we here in the South are not.' We Africans are repetitious and given to 'speechifying'. Westerners find it hard to keep patience; which may be said of some Westernised Southern blacks as well. There was further discussion about the blessed state of Africans in Uganda, who owned their own land, had not been dislodged by incoming settlers. They enjoyed, we were told, the refinements of an ancient civilisation.

The truth was that since the yoke of the Nationalist Government descended on our shoulders we were all filled with a nostalgia for an 'independent Africa'; those of our people who were fortunate enough to be beyond the reach of racialistic Boers seemed blessed creatures indeed. So now in the plane I wondered. What did my sister mean: 'You'll see for yourself'? Then I thought back to how, towards the end of my stay at home, my father had seized one of those rare moments of private conclave with me in the Western style. With us it is seldom that individuals of different generations feel a need for it. For almost all situations there are suitable intermediaries. Moments of privacy were rare in any case because our background has different ideas from the modern European ones about 'privacy'. Our households generally swarm at all times with extended relatives. My father had seized a chance to confide in me: 'That child-of-mine does not write,' he had said gravely. I knew how he suffered, for of the three of us children, everyone accepted the fact that Alexandra was 'the apple of his eye', his especial favourite. Indeed she appealed to all because of her sweet-natured, dependent quality which seemed to draw the best out of others. As a baby she had reminded him and my mother of their late first-born; my brother and I resembled each other, but my sister had been 'the other child returned'.

81

The family legend was that I was the aggressive one. 'That child? *Pas op*, look out, a Jili type, an ox-goring-with-horns, *inkom'iya hlaba*.' My brother Tengo had grown into the proper, reflective male, kept his own counsel before acting or commenting. His manner impressed people so that they prophesied that when he became an elder, he would 'cast an awesome shadow', be a man of weighty presence. So it was good, the family said, that the middle one was by nature gentle. Our order of birth and temperaments were regarded as a dispensation of Providence and the forefathers, who had placed my sister between us because she needed siblings of mine and my brother's kind. '*Kulungile kunje nje nje*, Good it was so, so, so.' The language excelled in expressing these and similar, obscurely symmetrical aspects of the human condition, using untranslatable constructions whose effect was to 'rend the bowels'.

'She is so far from her people,' they said, but my father parried as a Westernised black Southerner felt impelled to do.

'Don't say that. The people among whom she is married are our people. They are Bantu, like us. Again like us, they are Westernised Africans. More than that, my co-parent, *umkozi wam*, is a Christian and a Chief.'

We thought in terms of our handful of modern, educated Christian hereditary chiefs. Contrasting with them are other chiefs of the blood who are traditionalists. We know that in some cases these were a handicap to their people in these times, because many traditional aspects, like polygamy, don't fit into the pattern of modern times. We therefore had our own ideas about how my sister was placed in marrying into a respected, educated, public-spirited chiefly family striving for the kind of spiritual and social disciplines we recognised.

I remembered how, therefore, the fact that my sister 'did not write' had affected the various levels of people in my family. It went largely according to generation, some earnest about the matter, others flippant. My father was distressed to feel cut off from a favourite child. Aunts and uncles were puzzled: 'Why doesn't she pass on to us the things she is learning up there of African advance and refinement? Their houses, furnishings, their farming methods must be the best in Africa. And what men they must be, not emasculated by alienation of land and pastures, holding title deeds to *square miles*, some of them as your father saw!' The younger ones: 'She's too happy to bother about us any more, why up there she's no doubt relaxing. Tea, cocktails in smart lounges, everything open to everybody, *Boers*, Coloureds, and us' (the scornful younger generation dubbed all Europeans 'Boers'!). 'Oh please, Sis Noni, tell her she must write and tell us about all that. Letters are the nearest *we'll* ever get to those East Africans and "their fathers' mansions" they used to talk about. *Ja*, mansions they called them. Can't be like these *pondokkie* tin-shacks we live in here in good ole S.A.!' This led to talk about how the East Africans must have felt when they saw our living conditions, and we thoughtfully looked at our house again.

None of us could think of it as a 'mansion' like those belonging to one or two rich Africans such as the herbalist businessman in Durban for instance. Ours was a plain, old-fashioned, 'colonial' style little house of thick stone walls, not Kimberley brick which we all knew was the best. Inside the floorboards were stained and polished and covered with carpet squares, armchairs and settees grouped about; my father's book-lined study; the rambling bedrooms filled with light and hung with family portraits of grandchildren, children, parents, grandparents, great-grandparents; old-time Victorian black ladies in billowing dresses with big sleeves and frilly lace jabots. And earnest-looking black gentlemen of the period, in stove-pipe trousers and Harrovian straw boaters. Further on in the heart of the house were the linen cupboards that my late mother used to line with dried scented twigs from our garden. Her pantries with rows of home-bottled fruits and square 'Homestead' tins in which were stored home-baked biscuits, *cookies*, cakes made from recipes she culled from *The Homestead*, a farmers' wives magazine or from the women's page in the vernacular paper, *Umteteli was Bantu*, or from that other favourite, The South

African *Farmer's Weekly*. And our kitchen, the hub of the household, with my mother's faithful stoves still there: the Dover for solid fuel, wood or coal and the four-burner paraffin cooker. The scrubbed deal table. Above it on a corner shelf our gourds for thick milk, *amasi*; alongside on a special shelf were stacked 'the oil lights', our range of Aladdins for indoors and rusty storm lamps for outdoors. And under the table, the muslin covered milk-pails which lads we engaged from the village would come to collect at sunset to milk our beloved cows for us, 'Beauty', 'Princess' and 'Savings' who had been brought from our little farm Zanyokwe, as I've said, to keep the home-kraal warm as it were, and the household in milk. Out at the back at one side of the house my mother's kitchen garden and nearby the chicken run; and beyond, the grassy part where children played on the rickety swing and see-saw next to the palm-tree, *isundu*, that we were proud of because it was an exotic in our Border country.

And from the front of the house was that perpetual, superb horizon on which we daily feasted our eyes as we say, the princely Amatola Mountains. We would look out at it from our *stoep*, the little verandah which, like all ordinary stoeps at home, is latticed with flat white laths and littered with deck chairs and canvas stools. We would drink morning coffee there and eat hot scones and butter and rock cakes. Over-eating being a South African habit, at 'eleven o'clock coffee' we would be joined by morning callers or passers-by, my father benignly teasing us from his abstemious distance in the study, declaring how it wasn't surprising that South Africans are 'killing themselves off right and left with their gourmandising; the black ones say they are dying from high blood pressure, the white ones from cardiac'. And he would add, 'Ha! New-fangled names for one thing: over-eating!' Immediately above our heads the verandah was festooned with vine which in summer would sometimes droop with fruit and, now and then, a heavy cobra.

Looking round at our country home and comparing ourselves with those East Africans it struck us that our setting was undistinguished, 'South African', drearily rustic, that our little village was a thoroughly 'one-horse' hamlet. Our house might be all right compared to most people's or to some whites' round about. But it now seemed to us terribly ordinary and stolid. No wonder the East African students had missed their homes in Uganda and spoken so much of them. Compared to their own ours was hardly an enviable country for Africans. What could you do here? Up there they were free. What couldn't some of my coevals do, they cried, with title-deeds to land such as those visitors had? We had laughed and ragged about it, over an undercurrent of speculation. As I flew on, my mind was filled with these memories.

I remembered how, during those weeks of the funeral gathering, one of my cousins suddenly said one day to a group of us standing talking next to the garage my late brother had built for the little, new motor car my father had bought him on passing his B.Sc. with distinctions and winning a competitive scholarship to read medicine up at Witwatersrand, 'Funny thing about those up-north people. All the ones who came were so *black*. Every one of 'em.' We were a little taken aback, then jumped to the defence of the East Africans. '*Oh Gott, man, moenie twak praat nie*, don't talk rubbish! Haven't we got our dark complexioned ones?' The cousin clung to his point. 'We've got them, yes. *Abantsundu*, the chocolate brown ones. What I'm saying is: those East Africans are black, like a black ox.' We protested, still not taking him seriously. But he insisted. 'You never see a South African *kaffir* that colour. Even the *ntsundu* ones, at the very least *bayakanya*, are brown with light overtones. All I'm saying is: even if we agree that among those tribes up north there are bound to be individuals darker than others, why is it the ones who come south all happen to be this black-as-sin type?' We at once stopped laughing and winced at the idiom. We were shocked to have to admit that we had all observed it. We looked at him embarrassed. This mercurial young cousin's Xhosa name was 'Hailstorm' for he had been born in the middle of that locally famous storm in 1928. He currently sported a black goatee which contrasted handsomely with his copper-coloured face. He was openly referred to as *inzwana*, handsome

85

one. He was speaking of an ugly thing, being blunt and un-ashamed about the colour prejudice that we all knew and felt. Someone made a feint at hitting him and all of us tried to laugh away the discomfort and belittle 'Hail' by parrying in Afrikaans, '*Ag, jy's stout, man*, you're naughty.' Nevertheless in the months to come I was to be astounded to find this same preference for copper-coloured complexions lurking even among the Ugandans themselves whose own deep colouring is artistic-ally complete and reminds you of the look of rich, dark fruit when the bloom is on it. These secret dissatisfactions made me wonder if there weren't more intricacies than meet the eye in the complex attitudes about colour which arouse emotions the world over.

It was in the midst of young people's flippancies then side by side with a maturer, more earnest concern that I left home. My father had written to people he knew in Kampala where my sister lived to ask them to see her and send him word. There had been no reply. The whole matter had been as if a question-mark had been flung among us. Finally a member of the older generation murmured, 'Ah, well, Noni, you will send us your report.'.

But my thoughts were interrupted by a spectacle that broke the vastness of the scene as I flew. The Zambesi River. I had not seen it flying down to South Africa. I now saw it spanning the land from horizon to horizon and felt how puny we humans were in our flight over Africa. The great river seemed to belong, was of a piece in the palette Nature held out below: the stupefy-ing extent of land and bush, over it limitless skies. It looked like a gigantic serpent, milk-chocolate in colour as though thickly sweet if one tasted of it; slow, lazy, sprawling, stretching itself across the bows of the visible earth. Away in the farthest dis-tance it seemed to splinter into huge fragments and became dotted with islands, like an archipelago. I thought of how down home legend has it that this river was the supreme obstacle in the path of our peoples as they had migrated south. Those men, according to the praise-poem histories of some clans, had to *zambesa* themselves on reaching its banks. *Uku-zambesa* is to divest yourself of clothing. They had to doff their togas of ochre-smeared ox-skins, the women their swinging skirts. Looking down I wondered how many white Southern Africans were aware of the persisting significance to some of us even nowadays of the name of the mighty river. I for one was thinking, as fellow passengers on the aircraft read their Rhodesian *Herald*, of those of our forebears who had been unable to swim and did not attempt the crossing; of those who did, and some proving unequal to the task, some were swept away, 'went with the river'; or of the strong who swam but some of their number were food for crocodiles; and what of their treasure, the cattle? Such chapters in people's histories were demonstrations of one of Nature's principles, the survival of the fittest. Dimly remembered sagas like these have, I thought, conditioned our belief that: of our migratory peoples who perpetually hived off from parent stocks in search of *lebensraum* for their cattle, only the fittest, most enterprising survived. They persuade us that our forefathers were 'truly men' in the spirit, as we say, and in the realms of the imagination. And we say the reason was because their motive was centred on something they prized above their own selves, cattle, round which they spun what they knew of poetry and artistic feeling. 'Had they been lesser men,' we say, 'they would only have pitched up at some sheltered spot, taken root, settled down and become mere cultivators.' Pastoralists, or semi-pastoralists not too attached to soil-tilling, we believe are 'masculine' tribes while cultivator tribes are 'feminine'. In Europe I had noticed that for other reasons, some nations are regarded as masculine too, compared to others: Prussians or Poles as against French or Irish, for example.

As I flew, it was the sheer size of Africa, of the skies above her, that gave me glimmerings of what Africa must have meant to my ancestors. I was able this time to give reign to the thoughts that had pressed themselves on me when I had flown from London but were pushed back by my father's cable summoning me. The engines droned as our aircraft gallantly forged its way. Yet our progress seemed to make little impression on the unending spectacle of bush below us. As the hours passed I gradually stopped thinking, could not read, just sat suspended in space, drained of energy to see Nature still so much in control over Man.

We began to lose height in order to land and refuel. I could now make out scattered hamlets of round, thatched huts among the bush. How strikingly they seemed to harmonise with the arrangement of far-flung bush and rock and marsh! They seemed like the dwellings of some natural *fauna* matching the *flora* of scrub, thorn, desolate soil. They seemed part of it, in the humble way that lizards harmonise with their surroundings when you glimpse them scampering on hot granite slabs. I thought how the creatures who inhabited those huts had bowed to the omnipotence of their setting, to the instinct to cling to bare survival. By day they had gone forth to forage, by night had cowered in the darkness, hiding their faces from the sinister, impersonal grandeur around them.

Presently we were airborne again. After awhile the captain told us he would fly low so that we might see game. So now I saw the Africa I had seen only at the films, saw the *vleis* or marshes, and waterholes with animals gathered at them. I was surprised at the excitement I felt to see the *spoor* of buffaloes, zebra, elephants. I was instantly reminded of the romance of great white hunters like Selous. We were near Lake Manyaro and saw enormous soft green marshes along which wild life careered and galloped; I saw gnu, bucks and antelopes of many kinds. The wildebeeste looked wonderful, photogenic and vicious as they stampeded heads down, tails in air.

All this lifted me out of my gloom and premonitions and feelings of anxiety and I suddenly found myself rushing from window to window taking snapshots with my box camera. Once as a child, my mother had taken us children to the zoo at Pretoria. I had shivered with alarm at the time because a black panther had recently escaped. In later years I visited the zoo in London and other cities; but these were my first wild animals in my own country.

Five hours sitting in a plane is notoriously little fun, however, but at last we landed at Nairobi. It was delightful to feel more at ease, as I did there, on getting out of the plane, than when I landed at Johannesburg. In my own country I knew how my heart would be in my mouth, adrenaline presumably pumping into my bloodstream, myself ready for some fight to occur because of possible racial reactions. The sight of South African officials would remind me how my necessary dealings with them might lead to unexpected results: inconvenience, even hardship and loss with no redress because one's colour was wrong. The atmosphere in Nairobi was utterly different, one of welcome even. It was an immense comfort, too, to arrive. For now it was only a matter of hours before I would see my sister at last.

My Sister's Country of Adoption

DAYLIGHT, and at last the final lap! My excitement and longing to see my sister and my little unknown nephew suppressed my anxieties temporarily. I was able to take time off as it were, and enjoy the short flight. It was only a couple of hours more to Entebbe, after the marathon hours I seemed to have spent travelling so far.

I looked out of the aeroplane windows and my curiosity began to function again. It was a clear sunny morning, 'visibility grand', as the aircrews so often remarked flying over Africa. Kenya spread out under us, rolling and wide, a beautiful, soft green. Parts of it were strangely reminiscent of Kent, in England; others reminded me of the high altitude plains of my own South Africa, others again were quite different, mountainous but very densely vegetated. As we approached Lake Victoria Nyanza, that great sheet of water in the heart of Africa the size of Ireland, the atmosphere became hazier, dreamier, and seemed to lose the crispness it had had over Kenya. It became humid. We were now across the Lake and flying over Uganda. All around I saw hillocks of a distinctive kind: not very high, rather flatly rounded on top, not like Southern *kopjes* with their rocky outcrops; these were worn looking, bare and brown like stone ground down over the ages into a barren sort of soil, yet from midway down the side to its shallow spread-out base each little hill was covered with very vivid green groves. I saw the drooping fronds and recognised banana trees. Before I had seen them only in the sub-tropical province of Natal; at home they do not grow in latitudes further south and to eyes accustomed to Cape vegetation, the colour of banana groves is compelling, exotic. Here in Uganda, the contrast after the other kinds of green across Kenya was even more noticeable. The impression was of a countryside cosier and tight-knit in appearance, different from the great vistas of Kenya or my Eastern Cape. Presently we flew through violent sudden rain and wind. Our plane bumped. But soon the sun shone again, the rain and wind subsided and the flight was smooth once more; but I noticed that the sky was dotted with bright white scudding clouds far from common in the Africa I was familiar with. Visibility was no longer 'grand', the vista was less grandiose, more circumscribed. As we continued to drop height nearing our destination I could see tucked away among the banana groves many isolated huts. From the plane they looked homely, cosy, inviting, nestling under the green leaves.

The spectacle of Uganda certainly was breathtaking. The greenness, the fertility seemed incredible after the thousands of square miles of dry bush and plain under my own supremely cloudless southern skies. Here was a brilliant country rich with vegetation, overhung with fleecy clouds. I remembered my father's words—'A Garden of Eden'—remembered how there was no land alienation to speak of, that it all belonged to the people of the country. My excitement mounted as we got ready to land and I caught sight of the name 'Entebbe' in large letters spelled out in stones painted white against a hill of red soil. I could hardly bear the minutes that must pass before I could be with my sister.

We clambered down the gangway, walked across the tarmac. She had been quite right in her letter, this place was hot. The warmth prickled as I stepped into the reception rooms. At last I spied her beyond the passenger barrier, holding a baby in her arms. But the sight so shocked me that at first I could see no one else and was not conscious of anyone accompanying her. My sister was as thin as a rake. Never in her life had she looked like that. 'God in Heaven, she looks like a hospital case,' I said to myself. I was at once overwhelmed by all my anxieties and fears for the unknown. The baby she held looked too heavy for her. It was as if under his weight her arms, which looked like sticks, would snap. We smiled frustratedly at each other across the barrier. Then I turned away. I was glad to get involved with filling in the inevitable Immigration forms. It gave me time. My fingers trembled as I wrote.

When I embraced her, she felt like a feather in my arms. Her baby looked at me with a momentary infant hesitation that was very appealing, the more so as when I spoke to him he responded by leaping up and down in his mother's arms laughing, so that his energy nearly overbalanced her and we laughed with him. I cried, 'So enormous at only a year old? Why, he is as big as mine was at the age of three, he must eat like a horse!' and I had quick visions of the usual infant foods that I had given my own baby years before, bone broth, spinach, bacon rinds to suck, and thought how my sister would of course dispense such things to hers in professional, hospital-nurse style whereas I had fumbled along fearsomely in between poring for hours over manuals and 'baby books'.

And now I noticed that she had a companion for he joined us in our affectionate attention to the little boy. It was her brother-in-law, William, a young man I had once met when he was down in South Africa at Fort Hare, reading science. He was a gently spoken, self-effacing person. We shook hands and he congratulated me, a Ganda convention I was later to learn, on my safe journey. He added that his heart was in South Africa. 'How can it be?' I asked. 'Your country looks beautiful! And here you can do all the science you want, can't you, with no *apartheid* to prevent you?' My brother's own passion had been for engineering, but *apartheid* had made his career medicine instead. William only smiled with me, then murmured something about being glad I had come on a Saturday which had meant his being free to come to the airport to welcome me to Uganda. I turned to my sister: 'Where is your husband?' She was busy with the infant. Her brother-in-law volunteered that I would probably see him that afternoon when we drove to Kampala and went on to explain, 'Our airport is at Entebbe. This is the town where Government Servants live. Our commercial capital is Kampala. The railway station's there. Kampala is about twenty miles from here.'

He drove us in a French car to his house nearby. William was

92

in Government Service and lived in one of the Civil Servants' houses in Entebbe. His was on the edge of the Botanical Gardens and the way to it lay across the lovely, lawn-spread Government Servants' small town with its pleasant looking white houses set in spacious gardens with hedges of the dark-leaved hibiscus or the brighter, shinier thurnbergia, hung at intervals with mauve bougainvillæa and other creepers. The whole scene was most beautiful and tropical looking. From the front of William's house I saw towering palm trees of many kinds and was reminded of our own little *isundu* in our garden at Middledrift; we were so proud of it as a stranger in our veld, amid the thorn trees and succulents, and now I was seeing its companions in its own homeland. William's houseboy had cooked a meal for us. After eating and resting we set off for Kampala. I found the climate very warm and uncomfortably humid.

As we drove, I leant forward in my seat eager to see the land now that I was at last at eye-level with it. I could not get over the greenness and now I saw grass, immensely tall and dense and thick-stemmed; elephant grass, tiger grass, even Rhodes grass which I wouldn't have recognised as the same as ours at home, *uqaqaqa*, but that my sister pointed it out to me. It was ten times as tall as our own. And now I was travelling on or skirting round one after another of the little hillocks I had seen from above, close to the banana groves on their slopes. And the mud huts that had seemed to nestle comfortably in them seemed quite overpowered by the huge clumsy green fronds; they seemed instead to cower and lurk, as if withdrawing.

And the costume of the women took my breath away. Each woman was in a long dress that literally swept the ground as she walked. It gave the impression of being wrapped in layers round the body, part of the wrapping forming a loose flap round the hips then wound round and fastened with two buttons above the left breast. The sleeves were short, above the elbow, the shoulder jutting upright. These dresses were cut to a standard pattern, with a square neck, and a wide dark sash was draped round the waist and gathered into a bow in front, its two ends swinging side by side on thighs so that you noticed the lighter coloured tassels that trimmed them at the bottom. Each woman's dress however was made from a different cotton or rayon print from anybody else's, or so it seemed at first. They were brilliant materials printed with big designs as for wallpapers for big rooms. They were in orange, red, puce, hard greens and shrieking yellows that made me blink. I was surprised, on asking my sister and William, to hear that these were not locally produced but imported from firms in England that specialised in the kind of print popular in Uganda. They contrasted with the wearers' remarkable blue-black complexions and with the extraordinarily vivid green land in which they moved and which, in my newcomer's mind, was in contrast too with the green of Kenya.

As well as those on foot we passed other black Junos seated on the pillions of many, many bicycles on the road. They rode side-saddle, looking like ritually-robed goddesses from another world. In contrast, the men who pedalled seemed less godlike for their legs stuck out somewhat comically at right angles. The standard costume for the men was a white kind of nightdress which also swept the ground as they stood or walked, but those on bicycles tucked it up in some way, at the waist. Turning my attention to this dress, I noticed that trousers were worn underneath. I was surprised for I had assumed that it was worn for coolness, on the principle that loose clothing is better suited to hot climates. When I commented however, I was told that a self-respecting gentleman here wore European-style underwear, socks, shoes, shirt, collar and tie, trousers, then the loose white nightshirt and over it the waist-coat and jacket that went with the trousers, or a tweed sports jacket; the king or Kabaka, Chiefs, all men who could afford it were well dressed in this style.

'But what is the point of the nightdress on top of all the clothes?'

My sister said gently, suppressing a chuckle, 'Honestly, you keep calling it a nightdress, it's a *kanzu*.' William added that it came from Arab dress. What a colourful, happy country to live in, I thought, my imagination fired by the mention of its contact with Arabia which for me conjured up camel caravans, incense and other exoticisms; yet although my heart warmed to hear my sister giggle in the way she always used to, I thought she was not happy if her emaciated condition meant anything.

Along the tarmac road traffic was heavy. There were lorries laden high with bananas which I now learnt were not the sort I knew at home or in Europe, the yellow dessert banana, but green plantains called *matoke* in Luganda, which have to be treated like a vegetable. My sister described how they had to be peeled with a sharp knife and well steamed before eating and that they resembled mashed potatoes and were the staple food of the people. I saw articulated petrol carriers, and many cars. Some were driven by Europeans, many by Indians who I learnt were called Asians in East Africa, but most were driven by African men: English makes, Austin, Morris, Ford, German Volkswagen, Mercedes-Benz; French Peugeot, Italian Fiat, American Chevrolet, Dodge, Pontiac. When I commented on this international array, William replied that Uganda was a signatory to The Congo Basin Treaty. I had never heard of it, I am ashamed to say; now I learnt how Uganda and other British East African countries were thus able to import from outside the sterling area.

I frequently noticed luxurious cars parked by the banana trees that drooped over pathetic looking mud buildings; these were rectangular huts, very perfunctorily thatched and obviously unfinished, for you could see the reed or elephant-grass framework poking through the red mud smeared on them for walls. I asked, 'But why, when the cars are such good quality, aren't the garages built in more permanent form? They look more suitable for sheltering farm jalopies or the worn-out Cape carts or sledges that Uncle Cecil uses for moving his mealie harvest.'

'What garages?' from my sister and her brother-in-law.

'I mean these,' I said, pointing, 'these we keep passing.'

'Those aren't garages. They are the people's houses.'

'People's *houses*?' the South African native in me was flabbergasted; I nearly fell off my seat. 'You must be joking. People can't live in those things. Why, they haven't any windows, or only those wooden shutters that are always pulled to. Besides, you can see how the plaster isn't finished off smoothly as it would be for a dwelling place. Or the thatch, it would be sewn up, not left straggling in this way.'

My sister did not answer. William did not speak either. I looked at the buildings anew and saw that what they told me was right; people were living there. I saw some sitting by them on the red ground. And there were clumps of canna lilies planted near, and petunias, poinsettias, bougainvillæa. I remembered reading how the Baganda loved flowers. But I was surprised because I had expected that the dwelling places they built would be of a piece. I was about to say so, contrasting them with pagan people's huts at home in South Africa but didn't. I was confused because I now realised I had so far seen no pagans, only 'dressed' people as we would say at home, meaning, not that pagans went naked (on the contrary they are well covered in their ochre-smeared blankets and shawls) but that people in Western-style clothing had adopted Western standards. I was too startled for the moment by the apparent confusion in standards to ask my sister and her brother-in-law to elucidate, so instead I said, 'Would you show me where the pagans live, then?' pulling my eyes away from the expensive cars and the houses they stood by.

My sister hesitated, finally murmured, 'It's—it's different here. There are no pagans as against "Westernised". Everybody "dresses", is "civilised".' I looked at her, about to demand what on earth she meant; but because she was giving me a curious imploring kind of look I bit my tongue and was silent, not knowing what to think. Questions pressed forward in my mind forcing my mouth open but I shut it again without speaking. There was a constrained atmosphere now in the car; or rather, I felt in a difficulty for I couldn't help comparing what I saw with the impressions we had received years before from the East Africans who had stayed with us. I realised I had rather expected the expensive cars I saw would be parked by 'mansions' as they had said. Were these 'dressed' people who were clearly better off than us in the South not of the class the students had come from? Yet with us at home the resources of people of the same kind were spent on the house and home first, on motor cars later.

That drive from Entebbe to Kampala was the first of the surprises to come. For, on the one hand what Southerner would not be impressed, indeed breathless at the visible signs of wealth which was on a scale I had thought Africa incapable of? Yet in this short space I already saw discrepancies that greatly disturbed me.

We drove on and climbed over the brow of another hillock and now Kampala appeared and spread before my eyes. It was a sizeable town. Its white houses were dotted over hills neighbouring one another. They had galvanised iron roofs painted red or green, some of aluminium colour gleaming in the sunshine, others were tiled. A splendid modern sight; wonderful to see it practically on the Equator in fabulous 'Darkest Africa' as I had first at Nairobi, then Entebbe, now Kampala. My spirits lifted as I contemplated what our fellow Bantu, as my father would say, were capable of.

But presently, when we had driven down the hill and were in a shallow valley on the built-up outskirts of the town, I was taken aback for we now wended our way through what was clearly an horrific slum area. I saw sad looking hovels of shops, houses, garages and beside them many abandoned rusting cars. There were no pavements but foot-walks strewn with unswept rubbish. Next to them were market stalls where I noticed meat and dried fish being sold to the crowds of Africans. On the sloping ground along the road I saw lengths of cloth spread out for sale. Close to them lay miscellaneous refuse, paper, rags, banana peel bringing flies and a smell of decay, and in the air above I was startled to see flocks of vultures circling round.

I was taken aback, for I saw that this was a location of the type that in South Africa our people are relegated to outside big towns whatever their means or ambitions as individuals. A location was the last thing I expected to see in Uganda. And this one was not like Bochabela outside Bloemfontein; it was

97

like Pimville outside Johannesburg, one of the worst which I knew of old because I had relatives there and had seen how they kept up a ceaseless struggle against dirt and disease and depression of the spirit in that area, surrounded as they are by the sewage from distant European suburbs which is conducted and released near them. To see this other Pimville after Entebbe and my glimpse of Kampala was a great shock. I looked at the Africans as they jostled one another dressed in white *kanzus* and vivid robes that swept the ground. They did not look gay. The atmosphere was morose. I was struck by this for it was a noticeable difference from location dwellers down South. There, despite slum conditions Southern Bantu have an indestructible gaiety, bubble with vitality, are infectiously cheerful in the most adverse circumstances. General Smuts once commented on this temperament as being one of the compensating factors dispensed to us by Nature in an age-long exposure to the harshness of our bare continent. The sight of the rarely smiling Baganda faces made a great impression on me, so in contrast to their fertile countryside which, unlike most of Southern Africa, seemed far indeed from being bare and harsh. Studying these reserved, indrawn expressions I felt how they reflected the terrible condition they were relegated to in their land of plenty. The faces were astonishingly dark-skinned to my unaccustomed eyes and in the mass I found them almost alarming; but I brushed that unworthy thought aside at once, for my heart was swelling with sympathy. I murmured to my sister, 'So even in Uganda it's the same old story. Here in the African's own country our people are forced to live and rot in locations.' My heart bled for them and, my murmurs petering away, I asked myself inwardly, filled with indignation, can one go anywhere in Africa without seeing our people degraded and brutalised?

My sister and her brother-in-law cut in on my thoughts correcting the remark I had made out loud. They were saying, 'This is not a location.'

'Eh?'

'It is the Africans' own town, the modern town of the Baganda.'

98

'Eh?'

'The plots are private property, title deeds, the land privately owned by Africans.' I was speechless. 'People aren't forced to live here, like this,' they went on, and William said, 'Actually, any person can live anywhere he likes in Kampala, except of course in the suburbs that the Protectorate Government sets aside for housing Civil Servants. There are localities of that kind in every town where the land was alienated under the Agreement, and Government uses it for that and other purposes.'

I recovered my tongue. 'You mean it isn't white people who have caused this place?' for I was thinking that surely my father hadn't meant this when he had talked about Africans enjoying private ownership. I looked round at them both and found my sister agonised but almost laughing as if in spite of herself. She had always been quickly amused by the ridiculous, and my facial expression must have been a study for she was clearly struggling for many reasons not to laugh at it. She said, 'No, it's not white people, Sis. You know, it's time you got this South Africa idea out of your mind! The Government here definitely does not force people to live in locations.' I now learnt that I was in the town of Katwe, a Kampala suburb. The Baganda naturally gravitated to it because it had grown up on what had for generations been their traditional tribal capital. William pointed in the direction where the present Kabaka's palace stood a few hundred yards away. Katwe was the modern commercial and residential development of the ancient Mengo.

What they told me rang several bells in my mind for I had read how Mengo was where the then Kabaka had held court when the first Europeans had arrived, and in the pages of the books they had written of those early encounters, their descriptions of the capital glowed. I now learnt that the same position prevailed now as then, in that the land here and elsewhere was held by men prominent in the politico-social organisation of the tribe. In the old days it had not been privately held by them, they had acted as representatives of Ganda Clans which were totally unlike our Xhosa ones because theirs are totem clans. But on drawing up the famous Agreement of Protection, the

99

British had misunderstood the status of these men and written them in as private land-owners, thus creating an upper-class of landed gentry. One of their descendants passed by in a chauffeur-driven shining black limousine and William pointed him out to me. My reaction as a Southerner was to ask, 'Why haven't such Africans developed the place? They rule themselves here, therefore why have they made no roads, no drains, where are the street lamps, why no proper buildings in place of squalid hovels?' My voice rose in panic.

'Well, all that will come. The Protectorate Government is trying to get something done about it.'

'What? The Protectorate Government?'

'To be truthful,' William explained in his charmingly prosy English which seemed to slow things up in my impatient ears, 'the fact remains that African landlords can get enough in rents with the place as it is so they see no reason why they should pay to improve houses or shops. That would be spending money on other people, wouldn't it? The object is to obtain money for yourself if you are a landlord, from the other people.'

I was silenced, struggling to adjust my ideas to this new angle. But remembering the standards we hold before us in South Africa and the people's efforts there to achieve them in spite of politically devised obstacles, which we had been told did not exist in a 'Black Man's Own Country', I again started to exclaim, 'But Africans at home——'

My sister burst into another of her deep-throated chuckles that at once took me back to our days as children. It was as if she could not restrain the kick she was getting out of seeing me so perturbed by these conditions. She said, 'But I keep telling you, darling, you must get South Africa out of your mind!'

I saw that I had better be silent. Nevertheless I could not put South Africa out of my mind, for was not this an example of what advanced East Africa was like, a region with money and the background of a proud civilisation that outsiders admired? Was this what people achieved in this modern age when left to their own devices?

I was shaken. I did not yet appreciate that Kampala, like

Entebbe with its modern streets, lighting, drainage, telephones, mosquito gauze and such things was Europeans' and Indians' work; so was Nairobi where I had touched down. I struggled with a whole complication of feelings as I looked at Katwe again and recalled what I'd read from H. M. Stanley's writings, something which Baganda I had met in South Africa or London had not commented on: 'WaGanda habitations (were) better and neater than *those of other African tribes.*' The italics are mine, for had I not somehow assumed that this included Southern tribes? Down South we tend to regard the Zulu 'beehive' huts as 'habitations', so Stanley would call them, greatly in need of improvement; yet they were not far removed from those I had seen on the way from Entebbe. I was staggered. And to hear how a Protectorate Government was having to persuade people to improve their town with the resources they commanded made me unable to speak. I was trying not to prejudge, too aware of how friends accuse me of having eagle eyes and realising that in a matter of minutes I had spotted things my father had not noticed. Or had he?

All I could say to myself in our own language was: wonders never cease.

12

A Southerner and Eastern Bantu

WE drove on to Naguru African Township over on the other side of Kampala. That was where, I now learnt, my sister lived, the address we had for her being naturally only the usual colonial territory Post Office Box number.

Naguru turned out to be a suburb specially built by the Protectorate Government to house workers and the poorer kinds of town dwellers. I noticed that here, as in Rhodesia, a suburb for Africans was called a 'Township'. The houses seemed decent but necessarily humble since it was a subsidised estate. I raised my eyebrows that my sister should be in such a locality. Her husband was the first ever African barrister in Kampala, scion of a distinguished and well-to-do family; hardly qualifications for living in a working-class estate.

We got out of the car, unloaded the baby along with an amount of groceries and fruit we had brought with us from William's house at Entebbe. As we did so I asked my sister, 'Why do you shop in Entebbe? There seemed to be shops in Kampala, where William says the commercial capital is.' We were struggling towards the entrance of the house with our arms full. I noticed a shade of hesitation in my sister's voice, before she answered, 'William shopped for me, before we went to meet you at the airport.' The tone of her voice caused me to say nothing. I did not wish to upset her. It had been a morning of checking myself and I stole another look at her, so desperately thin when she had always had such a graceful figure. Now she was like a post.

We stepped across a miniature cement verandah, into a small dark sitting-dining room. My sister dumped parcels and baby, and stretched across to undo the wooden shutters at the win-

dows on opposite walls. Then it became light. I exclaimed, for I
saw there were no windows at all, only shutters. 'Do you not
have windows either?' I was thinking of the houses I had seen
as we had driven along and that William's Government house
had had them, also gauze at the doors against mosquitoes.

'Don't forget we are a subsidised estate, we pay minimum
rent,' my sister said quietly, bustling about.

'But you have electric light.' I looked at the bulb in the
ceiling. 'What is the standard of housing?'

Again she hesitated slightly, then said, 'Not everyone wants
windows even if Government provides them. People usually
stuff them up.'

She walked across the room as she spoke, towards what I
could see was her kitchen; so I followed, bringing the groceries,
and saw her electric cooker. 'But why should people with
electric cookers stuff windows up?'

'Well, the cooker is our own. We put that in ourselves.'

I put the parcels down on the draining-board, and looking
for the larder to deposit the rest of the groceries, stepped into
a doorway which led to it. My so-called eagle eyes took in how
scantily provided it was; but any eyes would have done, even
a man's, for there was hardly anything. William was in the
sitting-room and my sister and I were alone, so I said in Xhosa,
'Man, don't you cook? Why only these few utensils? Where's
your household gear? And this food we've brought from
Entebbe, it's from your brother-in-law's house, isn't it? And
where is your husband? Didn't he know someone from his
in-laws was arriving?' But before I could go on she signalled in
alarm towards the sitting-room and whispered, still in our
language, 'Don't, don't! He might still be able to follow Xhosa,
he picked up a little when he was down home.'

I turned and nearly trampled on the baby who had crept
after us unnoticed, so I bent down and picked him up, glad
to escape the tension by speaking through the little chap to
William whom I now rejoined. We sat joking while my sister
made tea, I meanwhile stealing glances at the furniture. It was
not what I would have expected my sister to choose. The wood

glistened patchily because of the varnish and the edges winked with brass nails.

I looked away, out at the open to watch the people. Many women sauntered past. Their heads were shaven and glistened in the brilliant sunshine, looking rather small in contrast with their tall, voluminously robed figures. There were men in the long white shirts, others in shorts. And to my shame I couldn't help being conscious once more of the intense skin colour of the passers-by. I turned away, to William, and was aware of his now, for the first time, since you are somehow seldom aware of this in people you know as individuals. I noticed, too, a silky richness in the texture of his jet black hair, and thought, as we talked of other things, how East Africans were far better endowed in this respect than most of us Southerners; our Hottentot and Bushman connection may have enriched and elasticised our language, lightened our complexions, but the ginger-coloured peppercorns they had for hair cannot be said to have improved the fibres of our own.

William stayed quite a while keeping us company and sensitively making an occasion of the arrival of his sister-in-law's 'person-from-her-own-home', *ebukhweni*, as it would be in Xhosa for her husband and his group. Nevertheless conversation became progressively desultory. As it petered out towards sunset he rose apologetically and said he must go now and that if he saw his brother he would tell him about my safe arrival. He struck me as a kind and sensitive young man and it was obvious that he realised my sister and I had to be alone at last.

It was rapidly getting dark and the baby began to fret for food. My sister asked me to come into the bedroom with her, and to my surprise sat down and began to breastfeed him.

'Breastfeeding this huge child?' I cried. 'Why on earth isn't he weaned? No wonder you're as thin as a rake!'

She didn't speak, her mouth only set in a hard little line, and I thought, she doesn't like me to criticise her child care; but I was indignant at the unexpected sight and pressed her, 'Good God, girl, have you no sense? What is the use of all your hospital training if you are going to act like an ignorant pagan and not wean him until he's years old and running about rounding up chickens?' A tussle in words followed which it would be tedious to report; the outcome was I dragged it out of her that she was still breastfeeding because she daren't stop, there would be nothing for the baby to eat; her husband had more or less stopped giving her housekeeping money because he said other people's wives cultivated and ate the banana staple food, weaned babies on it and she could surely do the same. The young brother-in-law had been supplying her as best he could because he felt ashamed. I finally got her to admit that her husband was usually out, as today, generally with his fellow countrymen in Katwe.

I gasped. 'That place we came through, with the vultures?'

There was nothing for it but to put the baby to bed, close the shutters because long flat flies like sausages were attracted by the light. It was uncomfortably hot.

We ate a snack and sat and talked for hours; there was so much news to exchange that we hardly knew where to start and would jump from one topic to another. But I touched on everything about the family, with many halts, asides, parentheses, recapitulations, as happens when people who are intimate are reunited.

I eventually came round to her delay in acknowledging my father's telegram and not writing; how this had affected him although he had shown it as little as possible, instead continually exhorting all of us to 'be like Stoics, endure pain inwardly only'. But as I reminded her of her special position in the family as the apple of his eye, that hard little line in which her mouth seemed to be constantly setting wavered. And haltingly she told how her husband's barrister partner at his law office had been the one to open the telegram, read it, but had put it in a drawer of his desk and forgotten to pass it on or mention the message until a week later. Now I knew that the partner was also an old Fort Hare student, a former secondary school teacher at the Eton College of Uganda, who had later studied law in England and been called to the bar. He too was one of those to whom my parents had been kind and hospitable, as they unfailingly were to all foreigners away from their homes because of their feeling for 'all our people, our fellow Bantu'. So I was flabbergasted to hear that such a one had 'forgotten'. He had known my brother! My sister said quietly, 'You'd never believe how "forgetful" people are here. It's supposed to be this staple diet, makes them unable or reluctant to concentrate their attention on anything for long.'

'Is it the reason your husband did not even write to my father, either?'

My sister did not answer, and I felt I should not have said that. But I was incensed by much that I had seen and heard that day. For the moment we relapsed into silence. When we started talking again it was not about any of these things.

Eventually my brother-in-law came back to the house. I could not think of it as 'home', in a location as it was, and furnished in the way my sister had yet to explain. I greeted him affably, as one should. In the circumstances this was doubly essential, for I had secretly never cared for him but had refrained from making comments to my sister at the time as they were already in love when I met him years before. Useless to speak then. It would have endangered her relationship with me. 'One man's meat is another man's poison' and my reaction to the man of her choice was after all a personal one, I could have been wrong.

When he came in I noticed how his eyes still had the nervous, unfocusing look about them that had antagonised me when I had first met him. As before, I wondered what she saw in him and if she still felt the same. I did not know.

When we went to bed at last, my sister came in to my little room to tuck up her guest. Her eyes immediately flew to the window or rather shutters, for I had thrown them open for a breath of air. With a cry she rushed to shut them. 'Darling, you can't leave them like that in case of burglars, you'd be murdered in your bed!'

So night after night in that house I slept as she did, in a stale, airless oven. And from the next day onwards I suffered from a relaxed throat.

106

The following morning after breakfast I went into town, a distance of about two miles. My brother-in-law went before I did, in the car of some friends of his.

I walked to the main road wearing my sister's Italian straw hat against the broiling sunshine, and hitch-hiked. I found my way to his chambers. I learnt to call them his 'office'. I wanted to see what it was like where he worked, knowing how the family would want a picture of everything. I met his partner, the ex-Fort Hare ex-London barrister who had forgotten to hand on our father's death telegram. We all spoke affably to one another.

Afterwards I made my way to the bank to cash traveller's cheques, and was quite surprised by the exotic scene I found there. Bank clerks were hairy, bearded Sikhs with glowing pools of brown eyes beneath luxuriant brows, graceful eyelashes, the longest I thought I'd ever seen. On their heads were wound delicately coloured turbans of flowered and sprigged material like a girl's dress, in startling contrast with the muscular hirsute forearms. The turbans bulged with the hair and side whiskers that I later learnt that Sikhs never trim. Before this, I had seen only pictures of these handsome people, never in the flesh. They counted money out with the breath-taking agility of bank clerks anywhere.

From the bank I went on to a European importing agency where I bought pots and pans, an electric kettle and a pressure cooker for my sister; then on to a chemist to buy some proprietary baby foods to wean my nephew.

During the hot night I had lain awake thinking over what I had seen so far. I had decided to put first things first: to say nothing, only get that enormous baby off her breast; feed mother and child myself at first, obviously; in time gently ease the responsibility on to its rightful shoulders. The operation was going to take time; I did not want to cause ructions. I wondered what secret thoughts the big people at home had withheld when they had pressed me to come here.

I made my way to the Post Office to cable them that I had arrived safely, and added that my sister was well, that I would be writing. I also sent a cable to my husband to warn him that my stay was going to be prolonged so not to fix our rendezvous in Rome just yet.

Looking round at the legends indicating the types of transaction carried on at separate sections of the counter, I observed everything that went on; for to visit the bank and now the Post Office was for me to encounter East African humanity on its own ground for the first time. How different from home! I noticed the bustling Asians, not turbanned Sikh clerks as at the bank; here they were more like those of Natal, that province peopled with Indians and which to us Cape-born seemed exotic, tropical, humid. I noticed the Europeans wearing shorts, their women in flowered cotton prints and red-faced from the heat. Europeans here looked as though en route elsewhere, as if on holiday because of their clothes, not like people belonging to the place. The Africans seemed darker than ever now that I was in their midst, and I noticed they moved jerkily, awkwardly, remarkably unlike Southerners in motion; even their gestures were of another style, reminding me of those one notices among English people as against the French or Italian. And the intonation of the African languages I heard them speak was of another order too. My first impression that day was how smooth they were, flowing, mellifluous. I was intensely excited by the sounds, allied as they were to an alliterative structure I could recognise (in the manner of a faintly discernible mathematical pattern) for I suddenly realised from the absence of staccato as in Xhosa or Sesutho, that I must be at the fountain of *tsefula*, those archaic Southern forms I mentioned earlier. What a letter I would write about this to my father and to my *mzala*, Governor!

I watched as everyone jostled to be served first, as in a post office in The Reserves at home. No attempt at time-saving orderliness as in England or a town in South Africa. Most of the customers, I noticed too, did not even speak English. And when they did, they and the Asians behind the counter did not seem able to follow one another's accents easily. Then there was the smell; Africans reminded me of game, Asians of

Oriental condiments, and the Europeans in the heat of the day smelt sickly sweet. Never had I been so aware of it all and I thought perhaps it was the humidity that caused body smells to be so potent.

People gave curt commands, I noticed, did not make polite requests. I heard a young Asian customer: 'Gett me a tteleggrumm!' and saw the Asian clerk glare at him; the customer was turbanned, the clerk not. He took his time, finally raised a finger to point to where the telegram forms were pinned on a frame above the counter a few inches from the customer's nose. I afterwards learnt, apropos of the style and detail of Indian dress, that Asians in Uganda came from different religions, Hindus, Moslems, and different castes, and that there was not much social cohesion among them.

I heard an African: 'Get me a stamp twenty cents.' An Asian clerk gave him a long look, tore the required stamp out of his ledger and flung the change on the counter so that the customer had to scrabble for it. I was to learn what lack of 'rapport' there existed in Uganda as between Asians and Africans. There was something particularly noticeable when a European customer, looking as though newly out from England, 'fresh from the water' as we would say down South, requested, 'May I have twenty air-letter cards, please?' The Asian clerk scowling, said 'What?' as if not knowing what to make of so civil an approach. But another, more sunburned European banged his fist and demanded, 'Gimme ten *siringis* and get cracking,' accompanying his command with a glare; the Asian serving him sprang to it, tore off the shilling stamps with alacrity.

These and other small things added up to give me a disagreeable impression of uncouth relations between the various groups in the country, and I thought how one hated, in South Africa, to see rough local 'Europeans' in their dealings with other races. I was not to know then that before much longer in the country my sister had married into, I too alas, would be compelled to adopt the hectoring manner when dealing with 'the natives', a terrible inevitability arising out of people not

109

beginning to understand or identify themselves with one another or appreciating different habits of life.

I finally made my way back to the house in Naguru and arrived utterly whacked by the humidity, by all these impressions, to say nothing of the actions I had taken following my decisions of the previous night. When I recovered, my sister and I set to and enjoyed ourselves unpacking the new utensils. We pored over the weaning instructions, her servant 'boy' listening in amazement to the vigorous staccato language that he told my sister in Luganda he realised could not be *Lungereza*, their word for 'English'. He looked on, pop-eyed at the spectacle of his 'memsahib's' sister. Translating for me, she commented in Xhosa, 'Aha, at last they realise that I'm a person, I too have got relatives.'

Our only visitors I noticed during the next few days, was another South African girl from Capetown and her Kenya husband. I discovered among other things about my sister's in-laws that they lived near Jinja in the province of Busoga some fifty miles away; that her father-in-law came to Kampala frequently in his English saloon car to conduct his affairs, being a property owner in Kampala and that he occasionally dropped in to see her, a few yards off his route along the main road I had hitch-hiked on. My brother-in-law did not come in until after we had gone to bed during my first few days so I didn't see a great deal of him. My sister and I enjoyed each other's company. It was good to be together and she would often be convulsed with laughter as of old at familiar stories about home, or new ones like the one about my father and his old lawyer friend the day of the marriage. We cooked, weaned the baby, took little walks on the Housing Estate, and as the days passed I filled in the details about my brother. And little by little I was piecing together in my mind her situation and state of mind and heart, figuring out what I should do. For I clearly could not leave her like this and go back to my own life in Europe.

Equally clearly, I should not act hastily, only with the greatest care; for I saw she still loved her husband. To act at all must be to mend the marriage, which I knew was in keeping with the feelings of cattle-keeping families like ours down home. The former ritual of 'marriage-by-cattle' spills over into our day so that even those who marry in 'the European style', with perhaps a surreptitious exchange of cattle and horses, even saddles and bridles behind the scenes to satisfy the older classificatory relatives (hadn't my own parents been like that?), such modern people are psychologically governed by the former idea that matrimonial ruptures should be mended by group discussion and consent: the procedure incumbent on those who have exchanged daughters and cattle and thereby sealed a pact involving many, not 'two people alone, as though without people'. No wonder anthropologists dub us 'cattle-complexed'.

'By group discussion and consent'; so if one of my elders were present, the two groups would have met to discuss in order to arrive at agreement. Well, I had as yet met only the one brother-in-law of my sister's husband's 'group'. I had discovered to my astonishment that he was a half-brother. These people practised concubinage, or an odd sort of semi-polygamy, and we had not known! There had been no sign of visits from members of the family, and daily I was filled with wonder, but said nothing. I saw that I must, in decency, wait.

13

'Tillers of the Soil—Cultivators'

ONE morning during this 'waiting' period, we had been out with the baby for one of our walks, in which I carried on repetitiously as on other days, my sister tolerating me in her sweetly feminine way, about the extraordinary manner people lived in their houses. 'So primitive,' I kept exclaiming. Even the ones built for them by the European Government seemed to be treated not primarily for living in so much as shelters. 'At home,' I said, 'even the "backward" people in the Reserves, the red-ochred pagans respect their homesteads. You see them sweeping the refuse from the yard, *ibala*, don't you, darling?' As if she didn't know; she only smiled patiently and my fury rose at her long-suffering and because I was now thinking how she would evidently 'suffer' things to the point when they crushed the life out of her. What a nature! No wonder everyone at home said she had been born to be protected, by me or my brother. If only he were here to jolt her out of it. I was quivering inwardly, knowing I must say nothing of all this. I said, turning away, 'I must wash my hair when we get back.'

As it turned out, the water on the Housing Estate was not running that day, so we sent the pop-eyed boy to the tap somewhere among the houses to fetch some in a pail. While he was gone, for the usual dilatory hours as it seemed, I asked about this other thing that irritated me: men house servants instead of women as among our own families in the Cape. My sister explained how the living conditions of the agricultural tribes tied the women to their gardens, feeding their husbands and children, and it was not feasible for them to be away from home while they continued in this tradition. Men, therefore, and it was a man's country here, were free to 'go out into the world' as house servants to the Europeans. Women who did were often runaways of some sort, had somehow broken loose from the fetters. 'Ha! Tillers of the soil, *cultivators*,' I cried pejoratively, yet thinking it odd how although having read impressive accounts of these tilling tribes in books or monographs by modern European observers, I nevertheless regarded them with the disdain of our cattle-keeping background of olden days. Of course we too had cultivated a little, but only as a sideline to the main preoccupation with cattle. Tillers of the soil were really only fit to be raided and pillaged by us, more adventurous, more independent minded and aggressive lords of all we surveyed!

Then our water came. My sister decided to wash her hair too, so I did hers first, then she mine. While I dried my head, she was in the bedroom, her hair by then ready for her to start arranging. I strolled in to her and suddenly, through the large hole for a window, shutters drawn back, we saw Europeans prowling around in her yard in the lee of the house a bare few feet from the room. We stopped what we were doing and looked. My sister's gentle face set in vexation. She whispered, 'They are always doing this. They bring visitors from overseas to see Naguru Township, and to this house I'm living in because they say it's the best furnished in the Estate. As if this could be called furniture!' and she swung round waving her arm wildly, in a gesture to include the furnishings of the whole house, and the sitting-room. 'These horrible Asian-made tables and chairs that my husband bought without consulting me, just because it's not the custom here to consult your wife!'

I was electrified. Her furniture had been puzzling me all along. Yet this was not the moment to go into that. I was furious for her sake about the prowlers outside who had touched her off.

'How I *wish* they wouldn't bring people here, they keep doing it. Do you know, they come at any time. Sometimes I'm out and the Housing man lets them in with a key from the Estate Office across there. Just look at them now, examining everything.' She said this bitterly, she who endured so much, in a long-suffering silence that I was not capable of. The hurt in her voice shot through me. Snatching up a towel and flinging it round my as yet uncombed hair, I dashed out and hurled verbal bricks at the first European I ran into outside. They were a party of men, wearing those holiday looking, baggy shorts. Until I came to Uganda, I had never seen so many white people in shorts, or Africans for that matter, grown-up men at that. And for some reason the sight always added to my irritation. Totally irrational, of course. I was terribly angry and let off a tirade about their rudeness, patronising, governessy attitude in letting themselves into somebody's house when she was out to examine how she managed it, just because she was black and supposed to be backward and learning. I didn't stop there but let off all my bottled-up disgust about Europeans designing 'African' houses without windows but *shutters*, and other such details. The man, in shorts (and a tie, which stung me more) gave me a long steady look. I doubt if I was coherent. I was livid and everything I had seen so far, including my sister's silent distress, was concentrated on him, little though he knew. It was not only his manners in invading my sister's privacy, it was even the complexions of the people which had alarmed me against my will, their air of moroseness and lack of the irrepressible gaiety of my sort of African down South. Not to mention the fact of my sister living in a sub-economic 'location'; it hardly mattered that she happened to be its show-piece. All these things that I'd held back I now released on the poor man, not stopping to think how unreasonably I was act-ing. At last he began to flush slowly, perhaps beginning to follow the gist of my outburst. He started to say something but I wouldn't let him get a word in and he kept quiet a little longer, evidently seeing I was too far gone to argue with. Finally when I was out of breath, he said pacifically, like a man knowing women, 'I'm the Acting Director of African Housing, and I'm sorry we have upset you. I think in South Africa where the lady of this house comes from, the Africans are more advanced than——'

'More *advanced*? What rubbish! My sister came here to marry a man from a more advanced society than *ours*. "Housing

Director", you should know that! We are supposed to be the backward ones, we in South Africa!' I felt so desperate I was on the point of breaking down with frustration and began to stammer and stutter.

The man got his chance to speak. At first I glared at him, not listening. But gradually I realised he was apologising deeply, saying quietly that he would withdraw his sightseeing party and promising that his Department would not annoy my sister like this again. 'We hadn't realised she felt that way. We thought she had made her house so very attractive, it was a pleasure to bring overseas visitors to her place. You say you are her sister. I don't know whether you've visited other houses round here. I am very sorry indeed that we have upset her, and you.'

Back in the house I sank into a chair and tried to cool down. My sister had withdrawn once more into her faraway attitude, her eyes expressionless. The baby, gazing first at his mother then at his hot aunt, seemed to wonder what all the excitement was about and crowed. Indeed we were shaking with emotions that puzzled us as much as him. And frightened us. Then my sister said, 'You see what peculiar standards these Europeans have here. Fancy calling this an attractive house. If their own standards are so confused, can't you see now why it was hopeless for me to try and explain anything to you that day you arrived?'

After this, on some trumped-up excuse which worked, and to my surprise was submissively tolerated, I went in to see the houses of some of my sister's fellow tenants on the Estate. It was then that I perceived what had impelled the Department officials to bring overseas visitors to her house.

Later, thinking things over I felt that two basic things were at the bottom of a state of affairs discouraging to Southern onlookers like me and my sister on one hand, and British officials trying to help East Africans on the other. One was what I had already noticed, that people here had a different attitude from our own towards a house. It was not regarded as a place to live in so much as a shelter; perhaps climate affects this, and things relevant to it such as white ants which consume permanent things like woodwork. I don't know. Certainly, huts here were more flimsily built than in the Cape where we are mercifully free of this particular pest. Certainly, the changes in temperature were far more severe in the South than in Uganda; remembering our fires at home and thick shawls round women's shoulders at nights I realised that here houses could be and were, for instance, built without even a fireplace. And certainly, Africans in Uganda seemed to do everything *al fresco*, to a greater extent even than we in the South.

The second was that the standards the Government was attempting to introduce in shapes of houses, arrangement of rooms, fittings, seemed inadequately thought out in terms of the immediate background from which the people meant to live in them came from. A good deal more thought was needed. Useless for instance to provide two bedrooms for Africans since few are families of only parents and one child. What were such people to use in place of the various separate huts in which they were accustomed to accommodate the numbers of their own and extended families? Why be dismayed when they seemed to live in squalor in the Chinese match-boxes of rooms?

I thought about these and many other aspects of the problem, feeling more convinced than ever that it is impossible to introduce to other people in other circumstances those things in life that one considers desirable; such other people do better to be left alone to find out for themselves what suits them. They then adapt what they know and want, to what they gradually discover by trial and error that they do want in their new setting. Little is achieved, I saw on entering the houses on the Estate, by those who 'have' being soft-hearted and solicitous towards those who seem to 'have not'. The best things in life are learnt the hard way. And need there be unanimity about what everyone means by 'best'?

When my sister and I left the last house we visited, I remarked to her how I had noticed that where two or three people were gathered together, there was that overpowering 'pong' which I now associated with East African humanity since that visit to the Post Office and had noticed again now. She said I must not forget that people smell basically because of what they eat; these people ate the green plantain, *matoke*. They in turn couldn't stand other East African tribes who smelt because their staple food was grain and milk and meat, like us Southerners.

I spent some restless nights behind my wooden shutters thinking about fellow residents behind theirs. I had to admit that that Housing Officer had had a case in picking my sister out, although I nevertheless had to have something of the last word by consoling myself that he had been patronising and rude to her, therefore deserved my rudeness to him. However, I could not get away with this kettle calling the pot black even to myself. So I sat down to write and apologise to him. The result was that a couple of weeks later, he and I met and had a long talk, after which he and his wife gave a little 'sun-downer' cocktail party so that I might meet one or two other people working for the Protectorate Government. They very warmly invited other Africans they knew to be connected with me and my sister. My brother-in-law for one, but he didn't feel like coming; my sister, but she had nobody to leave her baby with. They invited Apollo Kironde, a MuGanda who had studied in South Africa and in England. I was interested, on meeting him, to hear him say how he was a life-long and intimate friend of my brother-in-law whom he deeply admired; I naturally wanted to be fair and get to know my sister's husband's finer points, and felt that Kironde would help me do this. He offered to take me to the party in one of his cars, but declined my host's invitation to him to come too, instead offering to return to fetch me at the end of the party lest some stranger from it might drive me back.

I began to see how it could be an arduous task for Europeans too, not only black outsiders like me and my sister, to meet East Africans socially. I especially felt the pity of this gulf as we chatted during the party, for most of us present talked from our various points of view about the progress so far, of the African

Housing programme. We tried to put a finger on where the discouraging points or the good ones in it lay. The Europeans seemed to me sincerely anxious to do the best they could, and naturally it seemed less than satisfactory that they should hear only the ideas offered by the visiting African that I was on such a subject. I myself had still met less than a handful of people at my sister's lonely little house. I compared the position with our own teeming sociability in South Africa and my heart bled for her. 'That child of mine doesn't write to us,' my father had said. How, and what, could I now write home?

However, things became brighter after this for a prospect presented itself of making social contact with the East Africans.

14

On Safari

A PUBLIC holiday fell due, a long week-end, and I was offered a vacant place in a car going on safari, that exciting East African term meaning expedition, trip, or even half a day's journey by car.

The safari was to the Western Province, towards the Congo border. There were six of us going, all Africans. We were to travel in an American car, the 'two blocks long' type, belonging to an elderly African doctor who was in charge of a large Protectorate Government medical district over in Busoga. He was trained in East Africa so his qualifications were, at that time, only valid for use in East Africa. (This was later changed by the British Medical Council.) He was spoken of as an extremely competent doctor; he had been practising for something like eighteen years. He had recently also spent a short time studying in England; although according to him, that stay in 'U.K.' had been a long-drawn-out nostalgia for his beloved plantain staple food.

The others in the party were my sister's husband and his 'brother' William, 'same father different mother'; also another Uganda-trained doctor, a young man in his twenties; and Peter Okondo, the Kenyan with the Capetown wife who had both been regular and jolly visitors to me and my sister. He had studied at Capetown University for the degree of Bachelor of Commerce and was a Protectorate Government Servant like William. Peter was a most mature young man to meet. One of the interesting things about him was that although he too was very very dark in complexion, he was strikingly handsome, with aquiline features; bright-eyed, energetic, his hands and figure slender and shapely, his mind sharp and analytic. He was neither afraid of self-criticism nor tortuous and resentful and morose. I discovered in due course that he was only part

Bantu; he was part Luo, a Nilotic people. I had begun to discover an important and disconcerting fact: that the greater admixture of other strains, Nilotic, Hamitic and others in our Bantu blood, the better physically and emotionally.

A sixth member of the arranged safari party had dropped out, so I had been lucky enough to get the vacant place and thus have the opportunity of seeing more of the country than I had expected to. We set off in high spirits. I had a corner seat at the back next to Peter, my sister's husband on his other side. In front, the elderly and jolly MuSoga doctor who owned the car, luxuriated and took his ease. He let his young fellow medical man drive, who loved being at the wheel. A couple of months afterwards this young man was killed, a head-on collision with a badly-lit lorry by night.

Before heading West, we circled about Kampala, collecting drink. I was not a little surprised to watch several bottles of Scotch together with glasses being loaded. The bottles were set up in a row in front, at the feet of the two doctors. The older one was in the middle and made himself at home in his own car, took off his shoes and socks. A start on the liquor was made there and then, whisky neat, nothing diluted. This was kept up for the entire three days. Peter Okondo and I defaulted, not much taken by the idea of the bar on wheels.

This country of my sister's was, I saw, very thickly populated for the first part of the way, as far as some miles short of Mbarara, a town of Indian merchants and European Civil Servants set in the grass and cattle district of Ankole. Until then I gazed at the everlasting banana grove, was shown the cash-crops of coffee trees and cotton bushes. There seemed to be people everywhere, walking and bicycling. Sometimes, alarmed by the honk of the horn of our car, a bicyclist complete with pillion side-saddle lady passenger would topple off into the rank undergrowth. And often, pedestrians would hop aside into the fifteen-feet-tall elephant grass then stand, gathering their dress-like *kanzu* fastidiously in one hand, and scowl as we passed. I was continuously struck by the unsmilingness of the faces of the Baganda. The people seemed reserved to the point of surliness.

I wondered if these dense banana groves, the overpowering harsh greenness of everything, the suffocating huts they dwelt in, the towering elephant grass, the swamps with their lofty papyrus did not have a claustrophobic effect on the temperament of the people. Did these things not make them feel Nature weighed them down? I had myself begun to feel crushed by the thick verdure of the countryside, although it had at first looked so lovely. I began to wonder if I would become surly and reserved myself if I lived in these surroundings; the South African in me began to need to see expanses of bare country, to long for the wide open spaces of the veld. So I was glad when we entered the district of Ankole to see the country opening out. Banana groves fell away, giving place to euphorbia candelabra trees and wide plain, *itafa*, as we say at home.

I began to get excited for the countryside was turning into the sort I was used to, with horizons receding farther and farther into the distance and the tops of the hills becoming jagged and rocky with 'outcrops', kopjes, as in the South; indeed I was told that the provincial capital we were approaching, Mbarara, was a nascent mining centre. So I realised I must be once more in the sort of terrain that harbours reefs of gold or other minerals. Mbarara (the name means 'grass') was set like a little Transvaal town in miles of open plain.

We were to stay the night with another African doctor, also East African trained. He was living in a European-built house on the grounds of the Protectorate Government hospital of which he was in charge, under the policy of Africanisation. He too was a man with many years of medical practice behind him, experienced and competent.

We arrived in the cool of the late afternoon. Our host was overjoyed to see his friends and countrymen in the 'wilderness of foreigners' (the Banyankole tribe) 'where he was stuck'. He and his wife, or rather womenfolk, despised the handsome Hamitic Bantu cattle-keeping Banyankole overlords, who equally despised the Baganda banana-eaters, classing them with the original purer Bantu cultivator peasant people whom they had conquered on over-running Ankole.

We sat on the fine lawn planted by some former Government servant, outside the house. The whisky bottles were brought from the car and everyone talked away. Since they talked in their own language, indeed had done so during the entire journey, Peter and William sensitively taking pity on the outsider and translating for me when possible, I sat back to enjoy the view and watched cattle herded by men who reminded me of Southerners. They were taller, slenderer than Baganda, copper coloured; they did not wear the *kanzu* but threw a toga-like garment round the shoulders. I was later told how these were Bahima, descendants of the pastoral, conquering Hamites who had come down to certain parts of what is now Uganda from the North-east, driving their cattle in search of veld country. How strange this resemblance to my own people, I thought. I began to be aware of affinities between some Southerners and some Easterners as well as differences. The physical type of agricultural peoples that I had seen in East Africa was something new to me, whereas to see a MuNyankole or a MuToro of the Hima type was like seeing a brother of a Xhosa man from the Cape.

The Ankole cattle they were herding were a splendid spectacle. I had never seen such enormous horns. And the queer fashion in which the herd clung together in a great tight wad, 'How do the ones in the centre,' I wondered, 'avoid being suffocated or gored?' I missed the more natural-looking scattered habit of our own cattle down South.

We sat there for two hours. I looked at my watch. The view began to pall. In any case it began to get dark. My fellow travellers were still laughing and talking in Luganda and drinking. I wanted to visit an Archbishop's room, and how I longed to wash. But none of the women of the house had appeared yet so there was nothing for it but to wait. I began to hear mosquitoes buzzing and at once remembered about my anti-insect lotion. I wished passionately that our host for the night would show us indoors to straighten ourselves and tidy up after the murram dust of the road. We sat on, drinking and laughing. But the mosquitoes seemed to become insistent as they hummed above the manly laughter and clinking of glasses and bottles. I got restless and ostentatiously and rather crossly painted my legs and arms and face right there at the impromptu bar on the soft green lawn.

The young doctor who had been driving noticed this, I chalked up a credit mark to him for it, and he said somewhat condescendingly in English and smiling, 'You are afraid to get malaria, I suppose?' I said indeed I was. He felt in his trouser pocket and offered me a dose of anti-malaria pills made by a great British chemical firm. There was no water, only whisky, so I cracked the pill a couple of times with my teeth and forced it down dry and bitter. Some of the others twitted me in English, it was nice to hear a common language at last, about my 'absurd' fear of malaria. But to my surprise the young doctor spoke up for me.

This started a long conversation between him and me, first of all shop-talk about the qualities of the particular proprietary brand he had given me, compared to other brands. Then he went on to enlarge on the question of unhygienic conditions in his country, and about the people's diet of *matoke* three times a day; about dirty habits, perfunctory hand-washing, intestinal worms and such things. The young man talked engagingly and seemed very well informed and was interesting. It was not surprising that he was deeply mourned when he died shortly afterwards. He had only recently finished his East African medical course and I could see why he was spoken of as the most brilliant medical student they had had at Makerere. He was saying in a fetching, stilted accent, 'It is the difficulty of this transition stage.'

At this point the older doctor, our host for the safari, said something to him in Luganda, clearly reproving him for the young one promptly stopped talking to me. A little silence followed, after which more was said to him in Luganda, upon which he looked towards me again but seemed to hesitate. At last he said, 'Do you want bread? And butter?'

'Why, yes, I——' I was puzzled. More Luganda followed, after which the Mbarara doctor, our host for the night, got up and weaved his way to his car which stood in the drive and made off.

I now turned to Peter who was smiling to himself. 'Look here, can't we go inside?' I said. 'It's pitch dark nearly.' He said something to the others which seemed to set off a long, long discussion. At last one of the party, glass in hand, went off, weaving too I noticed, on a reconnaissance to the house. Presently he returned and said something, upon which everybody rose and followed him back. I joined the end of the line.

We filed indoors, into darkness. When our host came back in his car to find us in the house, he exclaimed loudly. He dumped a parcel on the table, then felt in his pockets for a match-box and lit a candle. As the wavering light strengthened, I saw that the parcel, which he had placed in front of me, was loosely wrapped in newspaper and contained two loaves of white bread, a knife and fork, new and made of tin. Quite a to-do ensued. Our host clapped his hands and bellowed, upon which some cowed-looking men-servants appeared in ragged dirty *kanzus*. They were spoken to in hectoring tones and withdrew fearfully. We sat on in the gloaming. After quite a while our host lit an oil-lamp, which done he called for whisky bottle and glasses. These were placed by the nervous servants on the table next to the loaves and knife and fork. The table, I now saw, as well as the seats we sat on, was inches thick in dust. A clucking hen walked in, examined the floor then walked out again.

Whisky was poured out and drunk and I marvelled at the generosity of libations in Uganda. A 'double', I thought crossly, would evidently count as a tongue-dipper for a mere mosquito. The doctor rose, swaying, said he was going out again in his car. When he returned, it was with bottles of beer. Beer now chased whisky and empty bottles soon cluttered up the dusty floor space. All the time there was laughter and joking in Luganda. At last, a couple of hours more having passed, I absolutely had to go to the lavatory. I whispered to Peter, feeling drawn to him by now as a fellow-foreigner and sensing that his disquiet, whatever its cause, equalled mine. He hesitated slightly, then said, 'Better go out there in the dark, on the grass. It will be better.' I did as he suggested. I came back feeling a good deal more comfortable though hungry and grimy. I sat down again.

The evening wore on. I looked at my watch, twenty minutes to ten. Talk was now very animated indeed. People kept rising and gesticulating, rolling their eyes, giving one another friendly prods in the ribs with their forefingers. I leaned back and took forty winks.

When I woke up, startled and confused, it was because the conversation suddenly rang differently and, my eyes adapting themselves to the uncertain light, I saw why. Two Ganda women were standing in the doorway holding each other's hands, smiling shyly and being talked to, or rather talked at, by our safari party. Every now and then they would squeeze each other, simper and close their eyes tight as if not knowing where to look. These were the 'wives', so I was told, of our host, the Makerere graduate. They had been summoned from the kitchen 'to look at the foreign madam' who was travelling with the friends of their lord and master. They looked at me. Steeling themselves to it, they gazed and gazed, continuing to hold hands, then dissolved into subdued giggles. Their husband addressed them peremptorily, well exhilarated by now by this reunion with old friends. 'Come to the foreign madam and greet her!' Obediently they approached me, the braver of the two pulling the other, their flamboyant costumes sweeping the cement floor that was caked with dust and soil. When they came level, they turned to hide their faces behind their fingers. The masculine party roared with laughter. Finally their husband tired of the interlude and dismissed them, whereupon they swept out, almost tripping over a contingent of children under five who had followed their mothers. I noticed that their clothes did not seem to have been clean for some time, that they had the pinkish coloured hair, rather wet noses and prominent stomachs I had remarked in so many children since my arrival in the country.

125

At ten minutes to midnight there was a hurry and scurry. A place was being cleared on the table amid the drink, for food was ready. It was brought by the wives, steaming banana mash heaped high on enamel dishes that looked like wash basins. A cooked fowl followed in another enamel basin filled with a curry-coloured liquid. Then came the cowed servants, each armed with another enamel basin and an opened bottle of beer. I watched them kneel at the feet of each of us, hold out the basin, tilt the beer bottle. I saw that the drill was to hold your right hand under the bottle which had been filled with cold water, and rub the fingers of that hand under the drops without bringing the left hand into play. So when the servant came round to me, I did the same. Then we ate. I saw how the *matoke* was eaten with the fingers of the 'washed' hand; it dripped wet still, towels not having been offered. I began to see what the young doctor had had in mind when he talked of hygiene.

I too helped myself to a spoonful or two of the plantain for I had not yet eaten any in Uganda. However, I found that the taste for it, as for many national foods, was hardly to be acquired in five minutes. So my host pushed towards me the two loaves of bread and the butter, still in their newspaper wrappers, and with a friendly flourish he held out to me the knife and fork he had bought with the bread. The light dawned on me. So this was what some of the Luganda conversation had been about during the afternoon when he had shot off in his car to the shops.

I was not offered any of the chicken and, thinking this was an oversight, I happily announced, pleased not to be too difficult a guest, that I did at least eat that. I asked for a piece. The bird was handed to me and while I tried to cut it, I noticed a sudden silence. An angel passing over, I thought, ignored it and went on trying to cut. I found it frustratingly tough. Had I not fasted so long, I would have remembered of course that no matter how some travellers glow about noble tribal hospitality, tough meat is the order of the day among those peoples in Africa whose cuisine extols flesh that is passed through water rather than actually boiled in it, or quickly singed in smoke and ashes than roasted on clean live coals; I knew this full well from many a meal eaten with pagan relatives at home. Also, not many of my sort of African go in for exciting spices which may possibly tenderise the meat. I can only say that Southern and Eastern Bantu don't 'like their food' in the 'civilised' sense. They only like it to be familiar, and absolutely filling. In any case the fowl the doctor's ladies put before us, before they withdrew, was the usual hardy, self-sustained by subsistence-scratching species, endemic through vast stretches of the continent. I afterwards discovered too, that among the Baganda chicken is traditionally taboo to women. It had therefore not crossed the minds of my medical hosts to offer me some. Hence the silence.

In the end I was glad of those loaves and the butter. And I noted the contrast with the equivalent class of my own people at home in South Africa, in the social position of women.

It was half-past one o'clock before the meal was over, after which followed further discussion. It appeared that because a foreign lady had descended out of the blue as from Mars, it had to be thought how to get hold of a bed. Finally it was arranged that the men-servants should be sent to bring one over from a spare ward of the Protectorate Government hospital a few steps away, of which our host was in charge. Next problem: blankets. More discussion. Eventually they were also sent for from the hospital. And then horror of horrors, what about sheets? Each time one or other of these unthought-of items had been mentioned by my sister's gentle brother-in-law or Peter the Kenyan, our doctor host looked staggered. He would blink, as if finding it needed care to assemble his thoughts amid the dust, beer chasers and banana mash. Then, struck by an idea, his eye would brighten. When the item of sheets came up he went through the process of cerebration, finally swayed and turned to order the servants, 'Go to the hospital, fetch sheets.' They shuffled off looking like sleepy serfs by now so that I felt for them. Almost before he had finished the sentence they went. But the doctor was advised to follow them since they naturally had not the least idea what it was they had been sent to do. And so a bed materialised and at last we retired.

I lay thinking hard in that hot sitting-dining room, wooden shutters of course drawn tight against mosquitoes, robbers, spirits, ghosts, also against lions, for Ankole was lion-country, they had said.

In the morning we had planned to depart very early so as to catch sight of some lions when they went for their early morning drink in the Queen Elizabeth Game Reserve. But the performance of getting up, eating breakfast, *matoke* for everyone and bread and butter for me, meant that we did not in fact leave until after midday.

When I woke I went to the lavatory. It was then that I saw what Peter had meant when he said the evening before, 'Go out on the grass in the dark, it will be better.' The lavatory was an Oriental-style hole in the cement floor. But the coverless hole was surrounded, as I imagine it isn't in the Orient where the people have known for countless generations how to use it, by piles of *faeces*. I forced myself to gaze so as to be sure afterwards that I had not been dreaming. I looked about and saw that the door was made of planks of wood that did not fit efficiently, so that flies were buzzing in and out without hindrance: house-flies, green bottles, blue bottles, horse-flies. There was a partition between this and what I saw must be the bathroom, also Oriental-style; it had a sloping cement floor for water to run off into a hole in the corner. It had no bath, a tap stuck out from the wall. I saw enamel hand basins like the ones the food had been served in the night before, heaped in one corner beneath a coat hook. A man's tie was draped on it so I assumed that was where you hung your clothes while you took your bath. The basins and the walls had not lately been cleaned with abrasive to remove the grease.

I turned away, and in doing so beheld, five steps from this bathroom and lavatory suite, the kitchen. I saw the doctor's womenfolk peeling a small mountain of the green bananas they were to cook for breakfast. It was a somewhat breath-taking sight for, dressed as they were in their brilliant, flowing robes they looked like Gauguin figures incongruous next to the heap of banana peel. I noticed that the peel, and nobody can call the banana a tidy plant I thought, looking on, was not afterwards cleared away; for the fresh peelings were being tossed on to the pile at hand which had obviously lain for some time. The decay and the flies made a startling contrast with a clump of handsome, rich canna lilies growing next to it. The whole and the beautiful ladies reminded me of a composition by yet another artist, Dali, and I now realised his angle on life was not due to the workings of a sensationalist imagination; it was true to life, only not so familiar perhaps in the Eastern Cape and Western Europe that I happened to know. The Ganda women were unperturbed; they peeled away while their toddlers waddled about beside them among the lilies. I remembered again that piece I had read about how the Baganda loved refined and beautiful things, especially flowers.

I walked slowly back to the house, the words of the youngest of the doctors echoing in my mind, 'Ours is the difficulty of this transition stage.' At breakfast later when I watched my companions eat their *matoke*, my stomach felt a little delicate.

At last we departed, but too late to see *simba*, lion, who is an early riser. Sitting in my corner of the car and looking out at the candelabra euphorbias and umbrella acacias, I reflected on 'the difficulties of this transition stage'.

No MuGanda I had met before coming here had mentioned its existence. This young doctor, so soon to die, had been the first to do so. I had assumed that such people, unlike my own, had been spared a transition since they were reported to have been already 'refined, clean, cultured' when the Westerners had discovered them. They had flocked *en masse* to adopt the Western Christian way of life. But where was the effort to bridge the gap, since some were aware there was one, as this young doctor had shown that he was in his heart of hearts?

I was reminded of the accounts handed down to us young ones by the big people of mine and other families back in the Cape, about the religious zeal of their fathers and grandfathers to adapt themselves when the 'transition' first hit us in the

South; how those earlier generations had made conscious and constant efforts to measure up to the new requirements, the higher standards of life; to stretch the intellect to try and meet the new ideas. We young people in the forties and fifties of this century listen and shudder to think how unbearable life must have been in such a hive of puritanism, of perpetual endeavour. We catch glimpses of the earnestness that must have accompanied it when, nowadays, our elders associate to 'fight Demon Alcohol' under the banners and badges of 'The International Order of True Templars', for example. Someone later wrote of the contemporary scene in China under the Communists, a state of social upheaval which I felt one could contrast with what was happening in parts of Africa without at all advocating or condoning Communism and brain-washings.* I asked myself: Where in this part of Africa were the equivalent of our Southern frenzied or earnest, 'pierced' people, *amagqoboka*, who, in our language, were pierced with something of the urge to triumph over the slough caused by the former way of African life being broken and made invalid in the present era? And who hoped to triumph by adopting the disciplines of the West? I had seen examples here of the use to which the wealth was being put which the British had introduced, but why had I not yet heard of the 'urge', even if I might have been unlucky during this short visit in not having come across it? In South Africa it was ever present, almost to excess, if you happened to be temperamentally inclined to whisky chased by beer.

We had of course no sooner got into our limousine than my fellow travellers started 'to make with' the whisky. And looking

* 'Two facts emerge . . . First, the majority of Chinese are enthusiastically engaged in a campaign to transform their society. The nightmare trains with their interminable, nagging loudspeakers, the omnipresent sweepers glowering at a dropped cigarette end, the triumphant fly-killings, the meetings, the notices, the Boy Scout sentiments, all the fuss and frenzy which would drive the average Briton mad in a week—these things make the Chinese swell with pride, not cower with fear. Is it arguable, then, that a materially backward people *can* only triumph over dirt, disease and illiteracy by temporarily infecting themselves with a sort of quasi-religious madness?' (DAVID HAWKES, reviewing *Visa for Peking* by A. de Segonzac, *New Statesman & Nation*, 13/10/56.)

on as they refreshed themselves, made merry and talked in Luganda, I was reminded of another group of their countrymen of the same vintage but other professions. They had been, in addition, political leaders, and had gathered to meet a British politician passing through Kampala on his way elsewhere. I happened to be there, and while the visitor went to telephone from another room about his flight bookings, I and the Ganda leaders waited round a table on the hotel verandah. I had watched how merrily they had drunk too, flashed their eyes and laughed, until the traveller rejoined us; then they had closed up like clams, dignified outwardly but seeming to me, who had seen them a moment before, to quiver inwardly with something that looked like lack of self-assurance.

I saw more of this underlying lack of confidence when we halted on this safari at the Kichwamba hotel to have lunch. Normally one would have drawn up at the front door of the hotel. There was a perfectly glorious view, too, from there, across the wide, wide plain below. It was dotted with thorn-trees and gaunt euphorbias. The waters of Lake Edward and Lake George snaked their way in the distance, and beyond, the Mountains of the Moon were shrouded in cloud and snow. I was taken aback however to be rushed past this vista and to see that we were driving past the front door, round to the back.

Pulling my eyes from the wonderful landscape, I realised that the merriment in the car had evaporated. The faces of my companions had withdrawn. Except for Peter whose eyes shone with mischief, the others had become unsmiling. 'Dignified,' I thought, crossly quoting the usual epithet. However, as our long car came to an uncertain halt at the back door, I caught sight of a sign, 'Ladies', through a purple bougainvillæa bush. It momentarily drove everything else out of my mind. I positively dashed to it. And after the one at the doctor's ménage, this one at Kichwamba was delightful. No running water but sensible, antiseptic with clean hand basin, spotless towels and bars of toilet soap.

By the time I emerged my party had disappeared, although the limousine was still there, grand and somewhat forlorn all alone by the back door. So I walked round stretching my legs, enjoying the view and admiring the superb site of the hotel poised on the escarpment. And then I came upon my friends, sitting on the grass a few feet from a little outdoor cocktail bar attended by a sophisticated-looking black barman or, rather, copper-coloured black. For I discovered he was a Cormorean, an island I had never heard of, I'm ashamed to say, although it is near Madagascar not so very far from my own coast. On high stools before him were two Europeans in white shorts, a European girl in a candy-striped frock which was refreshing to look at. My safari party looked strangely dejected. Each held a pint of beer in his hands and glowered at it. I asked them about the lunch. I was pretty interested in the prospect after my meals of bread and butter in newspapers.

'Lunch? Colour bar!'

'What? But there's no colour bar in Uganda!' I exclaimed.

Peter said, smiling, 'Well, the lady said that to our host, "You can't have lunch here, you didn't book." She also said, "I can give you sandwiches, and you'll be more comfortable if you sit under the trees over there and eat them." '

'Goodness, are you *sure*?' I said. We tried to figure out what she meant. Peter said, 'Mind you, she is right. There's no doubt we should have booked. After all, this weekend is a public holiday. Anyway, she did offer us sandwiches. They are cutting them now at the back.' As he spoke the others shot him uneasy looks and muttered in their language. So I asked the older doctor, 'Well, didn't you have it out with her?' He had been to 'U.K.', as they called it, was a man of the world. I said, 'Perhaps she only meant that we could take the sandwiches with us for picnicking, her remark about "under the trees", I mean. We are on the road, aren't we? She needn't necessarily have been trying to "colour-bar" us from the dining-room.'

He did not reply. A morose silence prevailed. But eventually the spirits of the elder doctor revived a little and he spoke and said, 'Me, I don't like to talk to these Europeans,' and shrugged his thick-set shoulders in the large check sports jacket he wore. His eyes were very red with feeling.

I turned away from him to Peter, 'Well, you could have had it out with her, couldn't you?' I felt confident in him about this for I had seen enough to realise he was the same species of 'foreigner' as myself, from a settler country and like many such, not afraid of merely speaking to a white-skinned person as though to a creature from an unknown planet. But the elderly doctor intervened before Peter could open his mouth.

'No! I told Peter not. I don't want.'

Ah well, the man was host, was senior; we were travelling in his car. The sandwiches came. Very nice they were too. As I munched them I reflected on what seemed to me like hyper-sensitivity and on the frequently erroneous British interpretation of 'politeness' or 'dignity'. As a Southerner however, I was in-clined sometimes to give it a different interpretation and think of the name, as my *Concise Oxford Dictionary* had it, of 'the colour between green and orange in the spectrum coloured like buttercup or primrose or lemon'.

Yet, remembering how gay they were among themselves and how their laughter in the car had sometimes infected me too, in spite of my being in the dark because of language, it seemed unfriendly of me to be inclined to apportion blame. If not actively doing evil and only acting according to their lights, were people not blameless after all? A hankering thought.

15

Hamites and Others

WE left the hotel, and the road dropped down and down until we were on the plain where it was again noticeably humid. We saw plenty of buffalo and buck. And elephants, dark grey and stationary in the distance. We crossed the Kazinga Channel that joined the two lakes, then after a long discussion in Luganda, it was decided not to go to Katwe, the settlement of time immemorial, where we would have seen the ancient salt lakes where natives have worked the salt and used it for barter for probably hundreds of years.

We turned right instead, towards Fort Portal, the capital of Toro district. We had now left Ankole behind. The Game Reserve was rather dull because we had started late in the day and animals were by then resting, mostly out of sight in shade and crevices.

We called at Tufmac, the Protectorate Government industrial concern where Uganda's fish supplies from the lake are frozen and cured and dispatched. But it was a public holiday, so the commendable idea of taking time off from the whisky glasses in the car to see the factory came to nothing because everything was closed. All we saw there were the Marabou storks which stand about the edges of this lakeside project, hundreds of them, looking formal in black with their pink necks and faces rather like a lot of solemn gentlemen attending an anti-liquor meeting.

We reached Fort Portal early in the evening, about the same time we had reached Mbarara. And now our party positively ran round in circles. I gathered that the jolly, elderly doctor had months before left it to my sister's husband to arrange accommodation for this trip. He was now amused to find my brother-in-law had neglected the task. Laughter and conversation grew more animated as glasses were topped up all round. Someone suggested going to the Omukama of Toro, the 'Kabaka' of this kingdom, but nothing came of it, although we did drive around in the rank vegetation in a little valley looking for an unspecified 'Princess of Toro'. When at last we located her house, she was not in, only dopey-looking servants who couldn't help us.

We finally went to another colleague of our host's who was also African in Charge of a Protectorate Government Hospital. The scene was a repetition of the night before at the other doctor's, almost in detail, and I wondered at the amalgam of Western and African influences in this part of the continent, that such effects should result. However, the presence of William and Peter, whose outlook was also affected presumably by the same influences, helped to put this adventurous safari into some sort of proportion for me. Otherwise my over-all impression would probably have been distorted. Again I must not blame, I told myself.

We had another late night. Whisky, gin, bottles of beer; *matoke*. William had thoughtfully brought what was left of my bread and butter, not forgetting the implements that had been bought along with them. So I ate my Staff of Life. When bedtime came, this doctor at any rate had a spare iron bedstead of his own. But I made my two brothers-in-law work on my behalf, find an enamel wash basin, rub off the accumulated grease with sand, get me hot water and a towel; I was tired of being polite, therefore no longer prepared to endure the clogging of my every pore with the dust of the road. In the morning we were served with the tardy *matoke*. I made my brothers-in-law ask for tea for me. This took ages. There were receptacles, a china service the doctor had bought a long time before in a spasm of Westernisation, and had afterwards locked up in a cupboard in the dining-sitting room. It now took some time to locate the key, further time for his womenfolk to figure how to operate the tea set. They had to consult their lord and master, sending nervous messages by children who became terrified because he glared at them as they spoke, interrupting the whisky session which was already in full swing when I emerged from my bedroom to find empty

135

bottles, cigarette stubs and chicken bones still on the floor and table from the midnight meal.

Presently the main members of our party, the older and younger doctors and my sister's husband, went off in the car, taking our Fort Portal host with them. William and Peter and I were left, sitting on hard chairs in the room. After a while a decrepit car labelled 'P.H.M.V.', (private hire motor vehicle), a taxi, drew up at the door and out stepped a very stout, middle-aged black lady. She wore a blindingly pink, staggeringly tight dress of shiny rayon material. Her vast bosom hung down in outline. The driver got out and preceded her as she walked in to the three of us. He announced that this was the princess, 'Omukama's sister'. Her hair was thick and grey, brushed back attractively severe, swept from her forehead and brought to a neat bun at the nape of the neck. I thought she could not speak English for she was silent, the taxi-driver doing all the talking and William or Peter translating for me. She had a woman attendant, also silent, who dropped down on the dirty cement floor and drew her feet adroitly to one side, a statue beside her shiningly pink-clad mistress.

Peter and William did the honours in Luganda, intoned the charming, repetitious 'greetings' the formula of which I had learnt from my sister. First William recited it to the visitor and she made the ritual replies. Then she recited it to him, and he ritually replied. It was a long-drawn-out process most beautiful to listen to. Next she turned to Peter and went through it again word for word. It was not good manners in *kiganda* custom to assume that everyone in a party has heard; one goes through the performance with each individual, except that women travelling with their lord and master are expected and themselves expect to be silent while the man speaks on their behalf. The background of concubinage and serfdom has its ways of bequeathing a sense of 'woman's place'.

The greetings over, it was then explained about my being a traveller from South Africa. Hearing this, the princess looked at me with curiosity. Then, seeming to gird herself to the effort, she courteously started the greetings to me in Luganda, or

136

it may have been Lutoro. Peter and William intervened to explain about my stumbling pronunciation and faulty pitch of tones, how I did not know the language. At that her jaw dropped; she was flabbergasted at the news, stared and stared, then suddenly deserted by her royal breeding, burst out laughing, and the reaction lasted for some time. Finally she had to wipe moisture from her eyes, and sweat off her face, she had laughed so much.

Gradually she controlled herself however, and then a mighty silence reigned. We looked at one another or into space. For minutes on end, twenty minutes, half an hour. But this was not the first of those hours I have spent in this kind of social communion in the African way of life. I knew it in the South, had met it in Rhodesia, now in East Africa it was something familiar to me. Amid much that was disconcerting and strange it was comforting to share the African acceptance of silence as another way, besides talking, of sharing one another's company. I was able to pursue my own thoughts about many things: the room we sat communing in, which was bare but for the littered table and floor; how there were no books, no pictures to look at, no decorations; the aspect of the sparse Asian-carpentered Western furniture, its angularity hurtful not only to the body but to the eyes; the absence of ornaments of local native crafts such as the small reed mats or carved animals with which, I had seen, foreigners living here decorated their houses. What could people think about or *do* in this barrenness? Was it surprising that in the disturbance of physical, seasonal and social rhythms caused by the amalgams of new and old in Africa, inner adjustments of sensibility and soul were also disturbed? There was no way of telling what such adjustments had been like formerly. I could only think how in the present era at any rate, under my very nose, they had not yet been achieved. Was this why sexual intrigue, for instance, played so prominent and spiritually destructive a part in present day African life? Or preoccupation with the circular arguments on tribal politics, so lacking in direction in the Western sense that they are incapable of transference, as they stand, to a platform of national politics? And glancing at the beer, gin and whisky bottles on the table, I thought how the original 'beer culture' of our societies has been described, even extolled by those who have studied us and traced the interaction of ceremonials with the ritual drinking or pouring of libations of native beers that marked the achievement of recognised gradations in the rhythm of group or individual life, things like harvest-gathering, rain-making, war, ox-racing, male circumcision; and I thought 'What would become of those gradations, how would the substitution of bottles of seventy-proof Western distillations finally blend, in the emerging ways of life, with the original place of nutritive beers in olden days?'

As if echoing my thoughts, the elderly princess pointed at the litter of bottles and gave what sounded like an order to Peter. He murmured something that sounded like an apology, then got up and went to the cupboard where the tea-set had been locked away, gave it a quick search and came back empty-handed. Our visitor said something peremptorily, pointed firmly to the used glasses on the table. Peter looked at her in obvious surprise, but she went on pointing and urging. So I saw him open a new beer bottle, fill a used glass, and hand it to her. She knocked it back while he ambled to his chair. He had no sooner started to pull up the knees of his grey flannels to sit down than, smacking her lips, she called to him again. This time she pointed to the whisky. She pressed Peter to fill it nearly as full as it had been with beer, then sat back, took her ease, held the glass in both hands and said, to my great surprise in English:

'I was not home when you came to my house. I was drunk last night.'

Before I had digested that, she reverted to Luganda which William and Peter presently translated: the princess was saying she was now going to the *Rukurato*, the Toro 'parliament', equivalent to the Ganda *Lukiko*. There was to be an installation of *Gombolola* (sub-county) Chiefs. She emptied her glass, licked her lips, rose and left us.

When the others of our party came back, we told them about

this installation and it was agreed that we should go and watch the pageantry. However, it took us time. We had first to motor here, there, everywhere, collecting drink for the remainder of the safari. We aimed to get back to Kampala that night. It was now midday.

When we finally got to the *Rukurato*, the ceremony was over and the crowds were dispersing for the monarch, The *Omukama*, tall splendid figure of Hima manhood and aristocracy had departed. Even so I was thrilled to see what I did, everything so colourful and immensely exotic in my eyes. There were people in snowy *kanzus*, in filthy rags; there were the maimed and mis-shapen, others whole in body and limb but unbelievably ugly peasant types. They milled shoulder to shoulder with some breathtakingly lovely specimens who looked exactly like African types I had seen in a film years before, in London, called *Dark Rapture*, about the famous seven feet tall Batutsi or Watussi, Hamitic Africans of Ruanda-Urundi on the Belgian Congo border not far from where we were. In the crush of people I spotted a party of five of these women, with jet skins so smooth they looked like ebony, and the finest imaginable aquiline features; large doe-like eyes above which the brows swept in an arch so faultless and meticulous one had to look again and again to be certain it was natural, not artificial. And as they clasped the toga-like length of cloth draped in folds from the shoulder, I saw that their hands and wrists were divine, long, tapering, delicate, out of this world. I'm afraid I stared my eyes out at them. I noticed how one or two had not the usual tight African hair; theirs was loose, the curl big, sweeping, bubbly. And it glistened. I had not seen hair like that in the South. These people looked like Ethiopians. They seemed a little group apart. I asked and was told they were members of the highest ruling class, they might be Banyankole, Batoro, Banyaraunda, anyway they were of the Bahima stock, and the older doctors said with scorn, 'They think themselves purest Bahima.' Myself, I found it a pleasure to see these examples of the approximately purest form of the foreign blood that had improved local African physique. Ancestral Bahima were pure

Hamites, but on arriving and subjugating the Bantu people they found in Ankole or Toro, to name two localities, blood inevitably mingled despite the strict social gulf between the cattle overlords and the tiller peasants. Nowadays peasants not lucky enough to have inherited some 'Hima' element are at once noticeable: stocky, broad-nosed, glowering of brow, and the handsomer the individual MuHima, usually the less Bantu blood in his veins. In these Western Provinces I had noticed a good deal more of the element than among the Baganda and Basoga; east of the latter the 'Bantu' were redeemed by the infusion of Nilotic *genes* as in Peter's tribe, *Jaluo*, to name one.

Many months afterwards I met the visiting King of the Batutsi, the late Mwami of Ruanda Urundi. It was an afternoon and evening at the Kabaka of Buganda's country palace at Bamuwanika. He was many inches over six feet, six feet nine I believe and therefore not over tall among his subjects: 'the little chap', as an English guards officer of perhaps six feet four would say of a brother officer of five feet eleven inches. By that time I knew Prince Baddru Kakungulu, the influential classificatory uncle of the Kabaka and he introduced me. I had to rustle up all the French I could remember, so pleased was the Hima monarch to meet a stranger who knew 'his' language. After an hour and a half of this, my head aching from the linguistic strain, he rose to take me to meet his retinue of Batutsi chiefs who, although in attendance sat removed in a room by themselves, not with their king. This and their deferential attitudes as he addressed them struck me so in contrast with our Southern tradition. Some of these Hamites were taller still, over seven feet. In the conversation, much of it about '*les vaches*', since unlike me whose cult was of Cattle as such, leaning if anything towards the Bull, theirs was of the Cow, I gathered that they too on first coming to Uganda were deeply impressed by the unheard-of wealth demonstrated by the number of Africans owning motor cars, and amazed by the preponderance of the Bantu peasant physical type. '*Bahutu pe!*' as a MuToro aristocrat presently whispered to me pejoratively.

But standing outside the *Rukurato* watching the milling crowds, our older doctor suddenly remembered that he knew the *Katikkiro*, Prime Minister, of Toro; so we started to walk up, full of whisky as some of us already were, to the Omukama's palace. It was superbly situated, at the very top of a sharp hill commanding grand views. As we came closer to the tall reed fence surrounding it, the crowd grew thicker and out of it appeared a young man, this time a friend of our younger doctor, someone who had trained with him at Makerere College, a non-MuGanda who happened to be in Toro on holiday. They greeted each other joyously and I was surprised that they hailed each other in English. It afterwards transpired that they only had English in common. Our young doctor asked his friend in loud tones, 'Is that butcher of a European medical officer still working at —— Hospital?' He was passionately interested in his science, and the two talked at the tops of their voices above the crowds, all about 'convoluted bowels' and what 'that European butcher' used to do about that condition. Dreadful things apparently.

It seemed that the Katikkiro could not be got hold of, so we turned back to walk down the hill again. Our plans seemed to be going off at half cock yet again, I thought. The crowd was growing dense and now that we were walking against it we had to work hard, being pushed and counter-pushed; the smell of humanity was overpowering. We met a little procession climbing up, a drum being carried and played in front of a heavy ebony French Empire arm-chair decorated with gilt and borne by two sweating blacks; and behind it, an ancient-looking Egyptian kind of harp with horse tails tossing at its curved corners was being played by an incredibly ugly old man. I eagerly asked what this was all about, but none of my party could enlighten me and I felt vexed. They had known precious little all along, I felt, had seemed to care less about the places we had travelled through. Indeed, they looked on the doings of *this* place, as they kept calling it, as beneath their notice. Peter knew more, but as he said, he was a foreigner and in a foreign land you try to find out things.

At last we got back into the car. The engine started up, the

141

shoes and socks of some of us came off, the whisky glasses clinked and we were off. We were to go back to Kampala by the Mubende road, thus completing a circle. As we left Fort Portal, the capital of the province, we motored through bare, veld-like country sparsely populated. I saw some white settler farms. The few settlers there were in Uganda were in this area and I could see why—this part had the best climate so far, was fresher, less humid, wonderfully open. A man's country, instead of being suffocated by banana. On the road much later on, very twisty and beautiful in parts, we passed a huge dead snake slung by the tail from a tree, its crushed head dangling down over a milestone. It looked about fifteen or twenty feet long, so I yelled and begged to be allowed to see it properly and take a snapshot. Peter got out with me and we found a note by the head of it: '*Roger, I killed this with my bare hands! Stan.*' We told the others about it on getting back in the car, but with the whisky bottle passing round, the anecdote failed to arouse interest.

We arrived back in Kampala that night, and the car drew up to deposit me first. Our host slipped on his shoes and got out to bid me goodbye. I shook hands and thanked him formally, in African style as well as informally in modern style, for having taken me along. He acknowledged this with an engaging smile which quite transformed his very dark face; he delivered himself of a charming, courteous, very 'African' speech about his pleasure in having temporarily assumed responsibility for a guest in their country, his happiness at returning me safe and sound.

I was assailed by feelings of guilt for having regarded him and his friends with analytical eyes and suddenly warmed towards him and remembered his bouts of laughter and gaiety on the road, wondering if I should not suppress the memory of the other things. But next, he said as he gathered himself to go, that he was now pressing on, late though it was, to Busoga Province for he missed his family, his little children; he was not to know it, but this instantly jerked me back to reality, for I knew that 'family' for him meant three women. I thought of those others in Gauguin colours and their children, in their Dali setting.

The warming process in my heart froze. As I watched him climb into his car, I stood thinking how the price of that Western commodity would keep such infants supplied till puberty with the proteins that the pinkish hair, wet noses and pot bellies showed they lacked, stave off the widespread deficiency disease called *kwashiokor*. The price of the chromium fittings alone I thought, since it was a showy American car and I saw them wink under the street light, would keep them in toilet soap until they grew up.

I waved goodbye.

16

Adjusting

WHEN I got back it seemed the time had come to act, before I should lose my restraint. One of the upshots of the safari was that my sister's husband and I were no longer on speaking terms. On the last leg of the journey, I remarked, speaking in general terms, I thought, on the astonishing number of unhealthy people one saw in Uganda: deformed, misshapen, flat-footed, with noses eaten away (by syphilis, so the two doctors explained), dragging startling elephantiases around, with goitres, red eyes, knock-knees. My brother-in-law took this as a personal affront and made a half-hearted rejoinder denying it. His bosom friend the younger doctor however, who could not resist talking medical shop, immediately affirmed that it was so. 'The health of the people is terrible,' he said, and went into a monologue about what he had learnt at Makerere about malnutrition, how this was a matter of ignorance since the various necessary foods were available in plenty. He talked about the pink-haired children:

'They grow into these clumsy, awkward, flat-footed adults,' he continued, earnestly waving a hand above the steering wheel. 'And these are the end-products of protein deficiency during infancy. Don't you know that, my friend? You should. It's a fact. And all of us have had this *kwashiokor*, all of us here in the car have had this malnutrition. Our mothers don't know what it is. They think Nature gives all infants this pinkish hair. As for malaria, these bloodshot eyes, all of us have got malaria! I could stop here, take the blood of the five of us, insert the slide under the microscope and you'd see those things. We shouldn't have got annoyed yesterday when the *mukyala* (lady) here applied her mosquito repellent and took those pills. We should do something about it, but do we? Yet that disease is dangerous, we are lucky to be alive! And lucky we are not deformed, that's all. This is a tropical country, disease and malignant organisms proliferate. People are ignorant. And ignorance spells disease and death, my friend.'

His realism sounded positively indecent in the charged atmosphere that made itself felt at his words. I could see it was shocking for such things to be said outright and it was tactless of me to have broken the rule of avoidance. However, four of my companions got over it and the previous atmosphere of merriment reasserted itself. They reluctantly accepted his strictures; after all he was one of them and everyone knew how irrepressible he was about his medicine. When I parted from them, it was all affability.

But my brother-in-law remained tense. There were too many unspoken matters between him and me and the disloyal speech I had provoked from his countryman had touched them off. So back in Kampala I turned the new situation over in my mind. I had my own ideas about this marriage. But mine was a personal reaction which had no place in the repairs that had to be effected. My sister must still love him. In any case, with the wishes of the family steering me, the whole thing was a matter for patient, joint discussion.

I sat down and composed a friendly letter to my sister's father-in-law, addressing him, African style, as 'my' father. I wrote how I had been sent as envoy to my sister on the matter of our only brother's death; that having come, I had, being a woman, noticed that certain things concerning his son and daughter and grandchild were in need of adjustment; that since, in my country, an older sister shares the responsibility with senior members of families joined by a marriage to adjust matters if possible when they go awry in the link between them, so I was therefore approaching him as head of his side, in my capacity as envoy and representative, to ask him, although I was indeed only a child, to come and hold council.

The old man came promptly. And I was glad, for his immediate response fitted in with 'the Bantu way' of our own Southern background: the immense Bantu concern for 'the humanities'. An aspect that I knew from home, imbibing the atmosphere from the days at one's mother's knee, was more important than punctuality, privacy, money; a fact of life which calls for continual juggling in order that ideas of 'progress' may fit into the Southern Bantu scheme of living in Western terms. Not easy, as I well knew. But I had been surprised, even taken aback, however irrationally, to see how Eastern Bantu 'juggling' differed from ours down South; and had seen enough to realise that the epithet 'Bantu' was largely made nonsense of by the geographical qualifiers: Eastern, Southern.

I had already been surprised to notice that our East African family by marriage kept so much out of sight of my sister's house; I told myself that this might be a difference in standards only, perhaps not sinister. Perhaps I was misinterpreting various aspects; were not anthropological observers always talking about this or that African 'culture' in the dispassionate terms in which they spoke of other ancient or contemporary 'cultures'? Then why did my first real contact with another dismay me? I felt I had a lot to learn.

And my lessons began the day 'my' father-in-law arrived and I watched him manœuvre his elderly limbs stiffly out of his long black English saloon car, much as my own father might have done. But this was a much smaller man, shorter, very much darker. He had a shaven head, was meticulously dressed in a dark suit and felt hat like a business man. The young man at the wheel also stepped out and was introduced as his son. I noticed he didn't look much like either of his two brothers, and guessed with a fleeting sense of despair that he was probably by yet a different mother.

They stepped indoors, and as my brother-in-law was absent, we had only an affable preliminary exchange of greetings. I gave the father the news he eagerly said he longed for of his 'old old friend, that great man The Professor Jabavu', noticing he pronounced the 'j' more like a 'dya'.

They had, oddly enough, first met many years before, in Jerusalem, at a missionary conference. It was the year my brother had been born, as a matter of fact. My sister's father-in-law had gone as a dignitary of the Church of England; indeed, it had been the very month of my brother's birth and I now told my father's 'old friend' how my father had brought home a medicine bottle filled with water from the River of Jordan for my late brother to be specially christened with.

I felt sure this wasn't the first time our old father-in-law had heard the story because he and my father had met once more since those days, during that fleeting visit to East Africa on his return from India before my sister got married. But repetition in Africa oils the wheels of human contact, so he listened with obvious delight. From there, he asked about my brother and listened in pain, but insisted on the details. I was surprised to see how deeply he felt about it, and to hear him describe his grief for his 'old friend', since neither he nor any of his had written to console; but this was a thought to be suppressed at that moment, for I knew he must be sizing me up, feeling me out with the Bantu antennae that I knew to be so delicately adapted for the purpose, that of adjusting human relationships between two groups.

My own feelers were operating too, and inwardly advised me that: despite his unexpectedly elementary command of our common language, English; despite the presence of his friendly son which reminded me of their concubinage; despite all these things he was clearly a nice old man, a sort one would be able to discuss matters with. A multitude of differences, of contradictory as well as sympathetic approaches to life, lay before us to be sorted out somehow. A relief therefore to sense during this preliminary encounter that the ground was being trodden in a spirit of co-operation.

It was a short first encounter. He and his son drank the beer my sister had offered them, to my amazement, since back in our own home men of his circle and age, my father's, are staunch teetotallers; so puritanical that when in their company it never even crosses the minds of us young to want a cigarette or a drink let alone have them. Then the old man rose to depart, saying he would be with us again; he gave the date, which instantly reminded me of my own father's little Victorian habits. The

147

unexpected little similarity between these elderly and so different Africans threw me into confusion. He announced he was now going to find my sister's husband to tell him to attend on that date. He also mentioned the names of others connected with 'the case', among them my sister's erstwhile guardian who had acted *in loco parentis* and given her away when she came to be married. He was an East African who had been South, met and revered and loved my father, had married a South African and was father-in-law to the Kabaka of Buganda.

And so the council sittings began, our father-in-law resolutely driving fifty miles each time, bringing chosen members of his family as helpers and supporters. And we too, far from home as we were, had our little complement, Peter and his South African wife who had been our main visitors so far.

Every angle and aspect of the marriage was scrutinised a hundred times, in the African style. The old man preferred not to rely on his English and everything was formally interpreted from Luganda to English, English to Luganda. The spirit of friendliness, the desire to negotiate and conciliate was supreme.

Things went well. My brother-in-law listened in an attitude of humility and co-operation, so that even when I was forced to look away from him because the nervous manner of his eyes and speech irritated me, I was bound to admit that he too respected the shadow cast by his big people. In spite of myself, I felt for him in his predicament. I saw how his big people were castigating him for 'not living like an educated man, he who had married a daughter of a supremely educated man whose way of life he had seen with his own eyes'. Yet I could also see that something impelled them to expect him to live not too differently from the ways they themselves were used to.

This was indeed a predicament, since the life they told themselves they'd like to live, bearing in mind their positions as Church dignitaries and leaders in present society, was clearly in conflict with what they'd been brought up to, which was naturally still deep in them. To realise this vividly, I had only to rest my eyes, in turning away from my brother-in-law, on these 'brothers' of his wearing neat suits and ties, and think of their mothers in the background in those huts among the bananas even as our council was going on.

I realised the difference between my own big people who were a third and fourth generation of more or less gentle-paced 'Bantu-ised' Westernisation, and these who were a first generation confronted by a more sudden pace. It struck me as I listened that their position was more complicated and confusing than my great-great-grandfathers' had been. Men like this father-in-law had known a world in which 'the West' had not been heard of, yet in the same stride from beholding the face of the first *Bazungu*, Europeans, they drove saloon cars; the sort my father and his coevals down South still thought of as 'sedans' in their out-of-date fashion reeking of the earlier covered waggon and the Cape cart.

Our Westernisation had been gentle-paced; more or less: I am not forgetting our hundred years 'Kaffir Wars' in South Africa against the encroaching Europeans. But here in East Africa the business had been sudden and recent, the encounter faster, without conflict; more or less: I'm not forgetting the religious sectarian wars that broke out among the encroaching Westerners in front of the doubtless astonished natives.

I wondered if our initially resisting the incoming culture hadn't in a sense simplified matters for us; given us time to clear the decks as it were, compared with the more immediate acceptance of it here in the East. Individuals involved seemed more confused, to have made less of a clean break with the past. Although 'clean break' also tends to be an over-simplification. While the translations into the two languages continued, in the family council, I saw how it was no such thing even for my own family down South. We too lived against a psychological background of so much that was handed down from our past. In the handing, ideas were undergoing a qualitative change. The *mores* that I was used to were neither purely Western nor purely Bantu. We were not 'black Europeans', yet I saw how we were not 'white Bantu' either. At home I had seen a dramatic presentation of these things because of a death that had gathered us together. Here I was seeing them again because a marriage

149

had similarly gathered another group of us; crises which could spotlight what held good in us, show the kind of people we were. But I found it hard to know what that was, what it all added up to; perhaps we were all only blameless Aethiopes, as the gods might say.

What it seemed to add up to at that moment however, was that the young couple were persuaded to agree to a 'regimen' of life which was to be 'an educated life'. The father-in-law now and again touchingly burst into English in his concern, exclaiming, 'Educated pipple, yet mismanage their house affairs!' My brother-in-law undertook to 'support and feed' his wife and child in 'this Western way' to which he had seen she was accustomed when he had taken her; was to eschew the custom of his own people whereby the wife tilled her banana grove, supported and fed the husband and weaned her babies straight on to the banana food; also eschew their custom of concubinage, 'having the other ladies', as it was expressed. Many other injunctions. Having reached this satisfactory point, the council also laid down that the elder sister should now move away from her sister's home, continue to visit elsewhere near by, so that the couple might start afresh alone, in the manner of 'the privacy that was evidently so essential to the Western way of marrying'.

I therefore went to stay with friends in Kampala, and bliss it was physically to be out of Naguru and in a house with proper windows; my relaxed throat improved at once.

It was also agreed that, African style, 'mental and spiritual guidance' should be given from now on by one of the senior Ganda counsellors; he was to make weekly or twice-weekly visits to supervise. And my sister's father-in-law was also to send someone, unspecified, from his homestead in Busoga to hold a watching brief as it were on how things went on.

One of the things that had startled the father-in-law at these councils was to hear about 'the sexual inadequacies of South African women', who it was said were not like East African women, 'were too European, lacked the knowledge of techniques and tricks expected by men of East Africa'. The old man digested this for a long time, finally said, re-emphasising in his own English after the translation had been given of his view about where the cure would lie, 'Old family person can teach these young pipple if they marry not knowing how to do.' It seemed, from the amount of cogitation he had to apply to the problem that this state of affairs was almost unprecedented.

My sister and I had been thunderstruck at the proposed 'cure', indeed at the allegation, giving us as it did a blinding glimpse of how differently the sexual act was regarded in this community from our own at home. I managed to suppress my feelings and, in order to meet their side halfway and not be intractable, urged my sister in our home language, 'Let us wait for God's sake, and see if in fact any such teacher is sent. It may never happen.'

At the council sittings, I came to understand for the first time what my sister's husband had really meant years before when he had told my family how in his country, 'Young people are given their own house to live in as soon as they are adult enough.' We had imagined small-scale ordinary houses, had imagined the young being thoughtfully allowed to practise house-keeping, to use paraffin cookers, keep accounts of groceries and how to measure and buy stuffs for curtains, cushion covers and such things. Now I found that the young adults did not live in their separate 'houses'; they only slept there. I found furthermore, that in them these adolescents were expected to live a vigorous sex life which traditionally ought to be pursued away from the shadow of the grown-ups, out of 'respect'. They must sleep in houses apart, that they might receive their sexual partners at any time of the night. If in the same house with the parents, they might collide and compete with the sex life of the father when he 'had his ladies'. The wife (or wives, if true polygamists) and concubines (in both sorts of matrimony) were supposed to acquiesce, and they did.

How on earth was I going to write that letter home? How could they believe the existence of a tradition whereby adolescent girls were flung to men or boys? For was not girlhood in Southern tradition, despite the thousands who fall, the 'precious

151

vessel of a family's honour'? Was not that why the 'family who took her in marriage compensated her people and affirmed respect for their daughter by giving in return the equally precious cattle'? Had not everything revolved round that? Was not even the beauty of the land in the spring or after the rain that broke the drought likened unto a girl?

Our tradition was that nubile girls slept in a hut accompanied by a chaperone, an older woman to guard them from being got at and 'getting spoilt'. But in Ganda tradition, in these 'houses of the young people' the purpose was to remove them from surveillance and protection; here the custom was different. Indeed, I learnt that in Buganda and Busoga girls who became unmarried mothers were almost more readily marriageable than those whom Southerners would regard as 'unspoilt, beautiful vessels of honour', for they had demonstrated that they could produce children. What sense would my maternal uncles and aunts and my father's side make of this?

Months afterwards when I was back in South Africa and trying to tell my own people the customs of some of our 'fellow Bantu', I learnt from my classificatory cousin Governor Mjali, the one who had travelled in the train with me and my father as far as Bloemfontein talking linguistics, that some years before, while I had been at school in England, his sister Elvira was courted by a Muganda student at Fort Hare as my sister had been. But Mjali *père*, a church minister, had totally refused consent, declaring that no child of his would be handed to '*iintlanga*, foreigners in unknown lands'. At the time, Governor said, the younger generation had thought her father brutal. But I now happened to fill in the picture for them, because without knowing about the episode I came to know the former suitor while I was in Uganda, had seen the way he lived and his family background. My Mjali relatives were aghast. They cried, '*Kanti ixhego lalisazi, l'ev'emantunjini!* So the old man knew, felt it in the bowels!'

At another of these marriage councils, something else had been raised: about some part of my sister's anatomy. 'Not

Having Been Pulled', as according to their ideas it should have been.

She and I were puzzled. And during the whole of my visit this item was not clarified for us. Since it was clear that we had no inkling of what was meant, it appeared that it was extremely difficult to explain. I could only extract when I got the chance to prod the people concerned diplomatically, something about how their great Chief and *Katikkiro* of the beginning of the century, Sir Apolo Kagwa, had written a book about the customs of the Baganda in which recondite matters of this kind were explained. But the work was in Luganda only, so I could not enlighten myself. Furthermore I was told that 'the missionaries' considered it 'a bad book', indecent, that it would in future be brought out in an expurgated edition. Anyway the mystery was said to be a hindrance to this marriage, my sister at fault on account of it. The old father-in-law repeated that he would send another 'old person' to investigate and help, along with the other of the watching brief. He would send them in his big saloon car. Having said that, he shook his small shaven head, gazed dolefully at the floor and at the well-polished shoes peeping out from his *kanzu* which he wore for these formal sittings. The whole thing made him exceedingly disconsolate. He had spent money on the education of some of his sons.

These councils uncovered for a Southerner in a way perhaps nothing else could have done the layers of the social structure of an exotic land, an 'Interlacustrine Bantu Kingdom' as experts like to say in their dispassionate terminology. The family spokesmen painstakingly explained their traditions of concubinage for example. The knowledge seemed terrible to me and my sister. To experts it would be acceptable, as that of another culture, Greek, Inca, what you will. To the Interlacustrines it seemed natural. Their traditions spilled over, as ours did, into 'these days of education', or 'of electric light' as big people at home lightheartedly say sometimes. We were thus told about 'woman's place', how here a modern man, even if a member of the Christian Church and therefore presumably straining after different ideals, might have a 'ring wife' (the one he married at the altar), along with 'other wives' and concubines. He would also have 'other ladies' (as Luganda has it, a supremely gracious language) whom he could if I may put it Scripturally, 'go in unto' at any time the mood seized him. And it seemed to us Southerners that in the prevailing social climate in which no opprobrium attached to such ideas, to say nothing of the sweaty geographical climate, such moods tended to seize a man at any time. It was no doubt a reflection on the conditioning my sister and I had been subjected to that we should be particularly startled in this respect to learn that work at the office of a morning was not sacrosanct and could be interrupted for such seizures; and a reflection on the conditioning of so many of the women that they should appear to accept the fact as one expects the sun to rise and set each day. We heard how 'Men have very great *amaddu*, lust', as they might have five digits to each hand or two lips to the mouth. But more of this 'conditioning' by and by.

The discussions, conducted as they were emphatically in a spirit of friendliness and effort to reconcile, lit up not merely the lives of individuals, which perhaps could be unimportant though distressing, but attitudes of society. Against them, our views stemming from a South African family were regarded in the main as odd. The senior generation of Easterners taking part tried patiently to guide us. It had to be pointed out to us, among other things, how 'Kabaka also, and other educated modern high people' lived life 'according to custom'. Here they referred to it as *kiganda*. As I gradually realised its equivalence to my own Southern *isiko*, I appreciated their regard for the observances a society evolves and which pin-point, as it were, its 'criticism of life'. Accordingly, *kiganda* as with *isiko* could emotionally and socially be ignored only by the exceptional individual. I saw how it was not for me to label it shocking or bad, I should see it simply as 'different'. I tried for example to look at the attitudes to incest in this light: I saw that here it was inherited *kiganda* for a man capriciously to 'go in unto' his wife's sisters, utterly unthinkable in Xhosa life where once a man marries, his sisters-in-law are to him as his own flesh and blood. In this respect, the point was raised about how 'Kabaka also practised the custom' as all Uganda knew, therefore the world, in their eyes. The divergence in the Kabaka's case was that he had taken his wife's *elder* sister. And as the elucidation progressed, I became aware that because this was an elder, not a younger sister-in-law, Baganda felt a horror towards it analogous to the feeling I, a Xhosa, would feel at the thought of a man taking any of his sisters-in-law.

At the risk of being tedious, I must explain here that the concept of 'incest' is a little different in the eyes of English, Xhosa, as well as Ganda people: English people think sexual commerce between brother and sister, mother and son, father and daughter, incestuous. My own Xhosa people share this view, but in addition, with us cousins of all degrees count as brothers and sisters; furthermore, each girl or boy has more than one father or mother, those classificatory parents whom we regard as real parents to all intents and purposes. Therefore because of the net cast by our 'extended family' system, our definition of incestuous covers what English people would regard as merely immoral. But of course in our case, the epithet 'mere' in this context arouses the shudders, goose-flesh from head to toe; it is totally impossible for us to look on any traceable blood relative as a sexual partner, as I showed in the case of my Mjali and Makiwane relatives; also, one's brothers- or sisters-in-law become *ipso facto* one's blood relatives. I am not pleading a case, it is just 'one of those things'.

Ganda people appeared, from what they told me and my sister, to have yet a different code; and the things they accepted, which an Englishman would call 'only immoral', were to her and me incestuous. In Ganda eyes, their Kabaka might acceptably have taken a younger sister of his legal wife, or 'Ring Wife' as they call wives wed in Church, or by Western laws. But it was the fact of its being the older one, popular and most gracious and charming though this sister was said to be by everyone. Because of this view, the Ganda totem clan system had been shocked to the marrow of its bones, since a Sovereign's sexual irregularities were believed to call down bad magic or misfortune on the Baganda as a whole. The collective instinct had been to get rid of Mutesa and select as Kabaka one of his brothers-by-concubinage. And this would have been according to tradition. Later however, the shock and upheaval was modified when the British Governor banished Mutesa, thus 'insulting the nation which Kabaka personifies'. The premier clan ritually concerned, along with the entire tribe, swung right round and, as it was explained to me and my sister, accepted and 'swallowed His Highness's mismanagement of his house affairs'.

Here I marked another of those latter-day, adventitious modifications of a people's *mores*, something a Southerner could follow. The swallowing had not been easy. It had grated. But it is in such ways when cultures clash that national emotions are sometimes fanned into flames which can scorch unexpected patterns into a people's character, affecting their potential adjustments to other nations as they come into contact with them. And I thought, 'Oh, this transition stage!' remembering the dedicated young doctor.

17

Easterners and Southerners

WEEKS passed. The senior Ganda counsellor did not in fact carry out the duty of 'calling on the couple and supervising'. Neither was 'the old person' brought to investigate and instruct on 'the sexual deficiencies'. As I had thought, and hoped, 'it never happened'.

However, my brother-in-law appeared to be 'pulling himself together', as Southerners would have expressed it. I was beginning to feel self-conscious because at one point during the councils the Easterners had said how in their opinion, various Southern expressions were not what they expected of 'Bantu', seemed 'too tainted with Western ideas'. My sister aroused less disapproval because of her quieter temperament; the responsibilities devolving on me no doubt made me too vocal on her behalf. But 'tainted'!

However, they misjudged my sister. She was long suffering, yes; the sort that inevitably has to be bailed out by someone in the family. And always is, because they value her sort of personality, of an appealing dependence and gentleness that brings out the best in them and quite rightly diverts their doubtless too aggressive energies. Were our clan names and praises not *Jili*, *Masengwa*—right on to *Mandeluhlwini*? And as I've said earlier we naturally admired, being a patrilinear society, Jili women like my old classificatory aunt who showed those characteristics. (Even to the point of forgiving those who inherited the 'slim hips and thin tapering legs, *ingcondo*' that the men of this clan are praised for, in startling contrast to 'the rounded, adipose female shape proper to a mare and mother', the ideal Southern Venus!) My sister, while not a mare to look at, was softly feminine, had turned out from childhood more trusting, less self-reliant in temperament than an idealised Jili, therefore especially precious, especially loved by them. But she was no less 'tainted' than I or other Southerners of our kind. Her Eastern Bantu people misinterpreted her outward aspect. Because she was subdued throughout their contact with her so far, they were attached to her and said so. Her demeanour fitted into their sense of a woman's place and they thought her natural, her manner preferable. Mine didn't, though God knows I'm no feminist. And I knew it would in any case have been useless to describe her real nature. Misconstructions had, as usual in human relationships, to go hand in hand with attempts at understanding one another. Anyway I felt I'd done what our people at home would expect me to do in the circumstances.

Now I began to feel I should be on my way to my husband who had, over the years, come so much to understand the conflicts in a wife like myself; and shared my view that the backgrounds we had inherited were not really at loggerheads but enriching. His family and mine had known one another across the Atlantic since the days of our grandfathers, representing not very different Liberal attitudes in the old Cape Colony and the then Britain; and both linked by a certain conservatism of feeling, allied not to a necessarily consistently reasoned system of thought, but the 'muddle through' policy. I felt I had muddled through somehow satisfactorily and needed to be with him more than ever and must soon go.

Yet I felt none too happy about my sister's prospects but was compelled to write home and report as best I could. I wrote nothing about the details, nothing about the society as compared to our own; for how could they make sense of it without experiencing it for themselves? My sister herself had been unable to write and tell them. I could only recommend them not to worry, and to mark time.

While composing these difficult epistles home, I had to plan flights and arrange a rendezvous with my husband for our holiday in Italy. He had suggested, when putting me on the plane from London to South Africa after the cable about my brother, that on my return we should meet in Rome and he would take me to our favourite Tuscany where I could indulge in the pastime of gazing at the landscape so wonderfully fashioned by Man as much as by Nature, unlike Africa. So I seemed to almost live at the Post Office. Luckily it wasn't a long walk from my friends' house in Kampala. I didn't have to hitch-hike. I trotted in and out sending cables that cost a small fortune.

Along with all this I hurried to squeeze in what I could into a programme of sightseeing and meeting personalities. At that moment I did not expect to come this way again, too expensive; I did not like to think how long it might be before I could afford to return to my sister. No doubt it was the pressure of the circumstances and the peculiar intimacy of my sister's being 'married to this place' that forced my eyes and ears open, sensitised them as it were, to some of the subtler things one tends to miss when visiting foreign countries as an average tourist with no personal tics.

One morning I went to Kasubi in the Mengo area whose capital, Katwe, had so struck me on the day I arrived.

Kasubi is where the mansions of the royal graves of the Baganda are traditionally maintained. I saw the royal 'widows'. Each of them inherits the situation through a system in the totem clan structure. Each woman takes up her abode at Kasubi, sits on the grass matted floor. She has nothing to do, only gaze at the enlarged photographic prints of the present Kabaka's father and grandfather. These women are statutory widows representing the real ones long since dead. They must remain chaste until they die. The mansion of remembrance really is a mansion; a huge domed, beautifully reeded and thatched hall. It would be totally misleading to call it a big hut, though it is made of mud. I saw how these ceremonial buildings are something the Baganda do know how to construct for they are ranking architectural art, proportioned, imposing.

I looked at the widows, thought of them gazing into space hour by hour, day in day out, year by year, life passing them by, awaiting their own deaths, upon which other women would be honoured by being chosen to step into their shoes; 'be granted the living', as it were. As a visitor you are expected to tip them, and I was told that the Kabaka traditionally supports them. It was an impressive scene. I reflected how to the Baganda it would not appear, as to me, like a genius for the macabre.

Another day I was taken to the Mosque by a friend who was born a Moslem but had become emancipated. It is a building on one of the many hills of Kampala and so compelling in its pristine whiteness and with its onion dome and turrets that I thought it not surprising that many Africans here were attracted to Islam. I saw the stone laid by His Serene Highness the Prince Aly Khan. My friend and guide approached the African keeper who wore a fez and *kanzu*, and told him in Swahili and speaking as a co-religionist that I was an *ingreza*, English, explaining in an aside to me that otherwise I'd be regarded as a woman, and therefore unlikely to be permitted inside, Moslem women themselves only allowed on sufferance. As it was, the keeper could of course see that I was a woman, but accepted otherwise. He shuffled off for the keys and on coming back, muttered. My guide whispered that he was saying, 'The *ingreza* must afterwards tip me. English infidel women aren't going to see this Mosque for nothing.'

There was a masculine gathering under a dense mango tree within a few feet of the white walls. True believers were holding a feast on goat's meat, big mouthfuls skewered on long sticks. They sat on Ganda grass mats the pleasing colours of natural dyes. A fringe of small boys in miniature fezes and *kanzus* stood in a respectful ring round them, watching. There wasn't a woman in sight, not even a little girl among the young onlookers. And they seemed absolutely black, their complexions setting off their embroidered skull caps. They wore snowy, voluminous *kanzus* and drew them up in their hands as they walked or changed their crouching positions. Highly polished leather shoes glistened at the hem, and sometimes navy or parti-coloured woollen socks came to view. Some wore red fezes, others white caps with eyelet holes worked all round in gold thread. A huge fat man drove up in a large and cavernous old American car, shambled up the tiled path leading to the Mosque. His arms were akimbo and he pulled his *kanzu* right up as if there were water underfoot. He wore a large, floppy red turban tied Arab-style, slung aggressively carelessly so that it somehow looked particularly masculine. A man following him I noticed wore a burnous.

We slipped off our shoes. The keeper tried his keys, turned round to put a query to my companion, obviously about me, for he gave me a searching look as he spoke. Then he went away. While we again waited, I asked my friend what had been said about me and what was happening now. He said the keeper had gone to look for another set of keys, the first hadn't worked. 'If you must know,' he went on, 'he asked if you were menstruating. He has to be told because on their impure days, women must on no account set foot around here.'

I felt myself blush all over but recovered and said, 'Well, you didn't even ask me.'

He laughed, 'What if I had and you'd said you were? You wouldn't have completed your sightseeing of Kampala in that case.' Then he told me a story about the only other time he had been up to this Mosque; it was to a wedding, and the bride sat out there on the steps all through the ceremony. 'Seems she was having "the curse", so of course she couldn't enter the holy place.'

'But how do you know she was?' I asked, startled by the colloquialism which he must have picked up at his English university, and incredulous, feeling I seemed fated to keep coming up against this harmless phenomenon, first in white Rhodesia now in black Islam.

'How did I know? How do you think? The reason was broadcast, given out at the time. Everybody had to be told.'

'What? Oh, no! Given out baldly? How awful!'

'The kind of thing that makes you sweat in this religion.'

'But,' I said, 'fancy picking that day to get married.'

He said, 'Moslems, I'm telling you. The date was fixed, everything planned without consulting her. "Woman mustn't talk"!' I got a feeling of what it must be like to be a no-account creature, a sort of insect in a world of men.

The keeper returned and let us in. It was a large hall,

attractively bare and spartan, a garish splash of colour at one end, if anything emphasising a rough masculinity about this exotic place of worship. But, again man-like, I thought, as I noticed the red cement floor under our bare feet was disfigured by spots of cream paint that hadn't been scraped off when the building was finished. We went up the spiral stairs, and from a turret at the top, Kampala looked lovely. We gazed down the hillside on the estates belonging to the African head of the Moslem community, the handsome, and magnetic Prince Baddru Kakungulu.

Before we left, the keeper demanded his tip, and my friend gave it, but there were more mutterings as before. My friend smiled, explaining that the keeper refused to consider that my tip was included in the one just given, he had to see that it came from me and was saying I must give it to my friend to pass to him since he felt unable to take it from my hand since I was, truly speaking, a woman. I did as asked!

We motored down through the African settlement on the hillside, Kibule. It was much like Mengo, only many foreign immigrant tribes lived there who came to work in Kampala, the Jo'burg of Uganda. I saw women dressed in bright filmy, flowing robes draped over their heads and shoulders and reaching to the ground. They reminded me of old-fashioned coloured plates in illustrated Bibles. They had gold ornaments stuck into their noses. I was told these were mostly Nubi tribeswomen of the Sudan. They were even darker than the Baganda, but tall and willowy of body. I saw shops selling arrays of groceries, cooked sweetmeats attracting flies, little heaps of charcoal, sticks of sugar cane, small piles of cassava laid out on the ground, stacks of small sized braziers for cooking on, and of course the ubiquitous bundles of *matoke*. I saw men busily making bicycle pillion seats, carpenters planing beds and cots out of unseasoned white wood. And many three-walled structures of elephant-grass canes smeared with red murram mud caking off, labelled in English, 'Hotel' or 'Bar'.

Now we drove through banana groves to a Ganda homestead where we stopped to visit, for my friend was acquainted with the *omwami*, the gentleman. However; we found his women-folk all sitting on a patch of ground by the house. The *omwami* was out, and as he locked the house and took the key away when he went, the women used either the lean-to they cooked in or sat about outside until he returned. The house was sealed with the usual wooden shutters. All round banana trees drooped over it and cassava bushes grew alongside. The owner was a local businessman, member of the Chamber of Commerce. I had met him in Kampala wearing a dark suit and starched white collar.

We tried another household. Flower borders had been made along the sun-baked path leading to the door and there were poinsettias, giant salvia, St John's Thorn. Here the man was home. Inside were seven cane armchairs ranged round the rectangular room. Between two of them was squeezed his bicycle. On another there was a large heap of clothes waiting to be washed. On the murram and elephant grass walls hung pictures of the Kabaka's wedding. There were two wooden tables that had not lately been dusted. The *omwami* recited greetings with my companion. A woman of about my age came in, was not introduced, took a seat and sat in silence, as I did, for our entire visit. The man had in his hand a volume entitled *Co-Education* written by the Hon. Dennis Herbert who, I remembered, was a former Principal of Budo College since returned to England and had become a member of the House of Lords. Our host turned over the pages studiously as he talked. All the time, at the outside edge of the doorway, I was aware of a pair of solemn eyes looking in at us, bulging like hard-boiled eggs. They belonged to a teenage schoolboy in white shirt and shorts, who scuttled out of the way when we left.

My companion then told me how the talk had been politics, about getting rid of the *bazunga*, and how the whole country would be ruled by Baganda. 'Of course he is a MuGanda,' he said.

The next afternoon I was taken by two young Makerere students from the Province of Bunyoro to meet an elderly princess of their country living in Mengo. They told me how theirs is the oldest and senior of the Interlacustrine Kingdoms, that the Baganda stemmed from theirs although now the most powerful because the British had helped them in war and stolen part of their territory and handed it to the Baganda. The Kabaka, they said, journeys to pay ritual homage to their monarch whereas the Omukama of Toro, the Omugabe of Ankole and the Kyabazinga of Busoga all travel to Mengo to pay theirs to the Kabaka.

They told me that the BaNyoro were really a cattle-keeping tribe, not peasants. They pronounced it charmingly, 'pee-zents'. They said all their cattle however had been finished by 'the Breetsh Government' some thirty years before, when the Protectorate 'had pretended to inoculate their herds against disease but the vaccine had really been for killing'. I was startled, but glad to be on cattle; common ground with them, I thought. Having contemplated society based on the banana, my mind was by now filled with ideas about societies and their links with vegetable or animal: my own people's cattle-complex as it is called, the Arabs and their camel, even the British (or 'Breetsh') and their dogs and horses. I had in mind the emotional or artistic impulses revolving round such animal fixations, or *matoke*. On a visit I had paid to the museum in Kampala, what I had seen there of the tribal arts of the regions had given me more food for thought.

The young men went on however from the anecdote about the decimation of their cattle while I was thinking how to put my ideas to them, and before I felt I'd grasped all there was to the mishap of the vaccine. I realised they were now talking about extraction of bottom front teeth. Of course, I had noticed many individuals whose lower jaw had been so treated. Now I was learning that various tribes practised the custom.

'We BaNyoro like to do it too.'

I asked why, for it seemed a pity to disfigure handsome faces in this way.

'But you see, it must be. I am telling how it comes from our cattle. If you don't tak' out those teethes at bottom, nobody can marry you.'

Naturally I now stole a look, noticed that in their bottom jaws these students had artificial teeth.

164

'Comes from *cattle*?' For me this was a new variant of the 'complex'. 'And nobody can marry you? What do you mean?'

'Girl don't want boy wit' teethes in bottom front.'

'Why not?'

'Is custom. And boy, he too don't want girl wit' bottom front teethes.'

'Why not?' You often had to prod people.

'Oh, you see, is custom.'

I tried another angle. 'When are the teethes—I mean the teeth—taken out? When a person is young, or when?'

'*When?* Oh, when he get big.'

'Why——?' But he cut me short, unexpectedly going on voluntarily:

'If you not tak' them out when you get big, then you just look like go't. And nobody wants that,' he said emphatically.

'Look like "go't"? What is that?'

They looked at me in surprise, the way some people are surprised when strangers don't know what is well-known to themselves. Then the one who was doing the talking began to cast about, how to explain and murmured aloud, 'Go't, go't, what can I say for *embuzzi?*'

Ah! I was glad of Bantu etymology for I recognised the root of a word now archaic in my own language, *imbuzi*, supplanted nowadays by a more streamlined assimilation from the Afrikaans, for 'goat'.

'Oh, *goat*, you mean!' added hastily, 'Yes, quite right, go't.'

'Yes!' he smiled, glad.

'Goodness, so you mean,' I said, picking up the thread, 'if you retain your bottom front teeth as an adult you look like a goat, and nobody wants you?'

'Oh no, they don't. No! Is bad to look like go't, is ugly!'

'Well, what when you take them out?'

'Ah, then is good. They marry you then.'

'What do you then look like?'

Again that look of puzzled surprise at me. 'Why, then you look like a cow.'

165

18

No Longer a Visitor

So at last I caught the plane for Italy. But because of seeing my sister standing watching, forlorn as we taxied out, when I met my husband at Ciampino Airport at Rome he found himself listening, phlegmatically of course in his English way, to my pleas that by hook or by crook we must go and live in Uganda to be near her.

Months later we went. We lived about two miles from her, my husband working for the Protectorate Government. I now sampled a new kind of life as wife of one of the expatriate Civil Servants, the *bazungu* towards whom the people of the country had ambivalent feelings as I had seen on my visit. Meanwhile, with my little nephew well and truly weaned, my sister had taken a job, in addition to running her home at Naguru, as a Sister at Mulago African Hospital which was on one of Kampala's many hills and some three miles from her house by road. She daily travelled in somehow, sometimes picked up by me in my car, sometimes by other people, other times by the dilatory bus. But it did her good to work, meet people, fill her days this way.

I settled down to see what the country and people were like to someone living among them. The background was the happy one of the Kabaka of the Baganda having been restored to his people and throne after banishment and exile. Various older expatriate Civil Servants of many years employment in Uganda had previously suggested to me that much of the anti-British sentiment I had found was due to the banishment of the Kabaka by the British; that before, for instance at the time of my father's fleeting visit, Uganda had been a contented, insular country, little affected because situated deep inland, by political tremors shaking West, North and Southern Africa, even Kenya, Tanganyika or Somaliland and Aden nearer at hand. Uganda was cut off and apart from what happened in the outside world, for which reason observers felt justified in using the epithet 'insular'.

The banishment of the monarch of this richest, most advanced Province changed all that. But now for his return. This was how it was described by *Punch* magazine in England, and now that I was a resident in the country I realised that the description had not been meant purely humorously; it had been a pretty factual report:

RESTORATION COMEDY

It has been a week of cheering in Buganda, because the Kabaka whom the Governor summarily deposed and exiled two years ago has returned to ride in triumph under an archway inscribed 'Welcome from the Protectorate Government'. Crowds are quick to sense a change in the balance of power.

Whether they are quick to acknowledge the symbolic value of the accompanying political clergymen, members of the Africa Bureau, teacher-peers, women Labour M.P.s, ex-officers of the Guards, lawyers, dentists, theatrical designers and guests even more glamorous is open to doubt. Are these bored visitors, yawning in the palm-lounge of the Imperial Hotel, really to be identified as the force that smashed the defences of the Colonial Office and restored the Merry Monarch to his throne? Are these the kingmakers?

True, the more favoured among them are occasionally invited to the Palace, where they are regaled with whisky and tonic water, and have to be careful not to tread on any of His Highness's subjects who, of whatever degree, crouch low in his presence. It is disconcerting at first. There comes a loud knock at the door, and round it, but only a few inches above the floor, peers a bearded face. This belongs to the Lord High Treasurer, who is not playing at bears but is anxious to acquaint his sovereign, as a matter of form, with the Budget proposals. We are now living under a constitutional monarchy.

His Highness does not really like whisky and tonic, especially when it is served in sherry glasses. 'These glasses are too small,' he sighs; but no one, not even the A.D.C., straight from the Grenadier Guards, seems able to do anything about it. Prince Henry, the sovereign's half-brother, is sent to have a look at the pantry, but returns to say he has forgotten the nature of his mission. 'Scatter-brained Henry!' says a crouching courtier affectionately.

But the Palace itself is a real credit to the Public Works Department. One palace, Kabaka, for the use of. It is a District Commissioner's bungalow adorned with a cupola. Some such special distinction is necessary, because in an ordinary P.W.D. bungalow one is not liable to meet a Hereditary Strangler on all-fours.

Politics, in the middle of all this Black Mischief, keeps breaking in. The European friends are forbidden, by a monarch finding his new constitutional feet, to attend a cocktail party given in their honour by the Uganda National Congress. They hurriedly find previous engagements elsewhere, in Kampala's only other hotel.

The Kabaka goes forth in his glory, icily indifferent to Sir Andrew Cohen's ungainly attempts to placate him. He has no longer anything to fear from the Protectorate Government, but the Uganda National Congress are another matter. He shudders a little as he drives under the arch they erect in his honour, like Louis XVI accepting the tricolour cockade at the Paris town hall. The inscription demands immediate elections for the whole of Uganda, and is not a tribute to feudalism.

Farther on, however, there is a more pleasing arch, erected by the Sudanese Association. It bears the simple legend: 'Be happy; good morning.' Apparently it is still the honeymoon, and not yet time to write *Bonjour Tristesse*.

I saw how the *bonjour tristesse* aspect asserted itself afterwards, as the kingdom prepared for self-government. This was no new departure, but the approaching fulfilment of the Colonial Office's long-agreed policy. The historical background to this, and condition for the Kabaka's restoration, hinged on the sovereign being changed from a despot and feudal ruler to a constitutional monarch modelled on that of the British. It hinged on Africanising the Civil Service and on appointing Africans as Ministers and to other posts in the Protectorate Government. Also, the Government was accelerating the programme of education so that there should be qualified Africans when self-government came. The date, by mutual agreement, had not yet been fixed, but the matter was not in doubt. The Government had, too, among other things, increased the powers of African Local Governments in several areas, Buganda, Busoga, Ankole, Toro and the others. Many activities flowed from this policy, or at any rate plans for them. I couldn't help wondering whether some of these things might never happen; a legacy of my experience of some of the activities planned, but not carried out, at the councils on my sister's marriage.

Nevertheless, the background and developments were all so different from my own country that I recaptured some of the enthusiasm my father had imparted to us at home when telling us how Uganda was 'an African's own country', everything done for the people's benefit, and how they had only to say what they needed for ways and means to be sought to arrange it.

I got a flavour of how the social aspect of life was affected by the people's traditional political set-up. I pressed to arrange this before things should change too much with all these innovations. So one day Apollo Kironde, my brother-in-law's friend, arranged for me to visit the Baganda's *Lukiko*, traditional parliament, or as it is now, African Local Government. The A.L.G.'s as they are called, are perhaps like county councils. In those days the *Lukiko* buildings were in the Palace Grounds, which are called the *Lubiri*. Now they are concentrated in a splendid new hall that cost a quarter of a million pounds, erected at the end of the long avenue leading from the palace. It was designed by an English architect and carried out by Asian contractors, the gardens landscaped and planted by a Kenya settler, the Baganda providing the money.

As things turned out, I thought afterwards that I had seen

how the traditional feudal background influenced people, as much in watching Apollo make the arrangement as in visiting the parliament.

He rang up one of the king's men at the *Lukiko* from his law office which was always thronged outside by prospective litigants; they did not show that they minded when I jumped the queue and prolonged their long wait. I could follow the language by this time and heard his reference to '*omwala wa Professor Dyabavu*' and to something about a '*muzungu*', which I guessed, correctly, Kironde later confirmed, was about the odd fact of this *omwala* being married to one of those ——.

I was particularly interested to notice his, to my Southern ears, tones of self-obliteration in addressing someone in high office. Kironde was himself a landed aristocrat. He spoke so deferentially that I wriggled. Every other word seemed to be the silky, long-drawn-out '*Eh-h-h*', and '*Ss-e-bo*', the latter usually translated into English as 'Sir' but in context more deferential than that, more like 'Sire' in Elizabethan plays. Yet this tone could change when the individual spoke to inferiors and be masterful, stern, curt, hectoring—at any rate to my Southern and Western ears. The impression struck home for I had listened to Apollo in his other rôle. Such things seemed to come naturally to a MuGanda, 'juggling' in 'this transition stage'; I was thinking how, as an aristocrat in their unusually class conscious society so unlike other Bantu, he always carried in the back of his car a silent, full-grown able-bodied manservant who would sit like a statue, gazing into space until given orders by his master. The spectacle constantly reminded me of the background of slavery between Arab and African, African and African in this part of the world, especially to see how when the master spoke, servant trembled, perspired, was abject, unmanned in his deference. As two aristocrats now spoke to each other, I was reminded of our Xhosa tradition which holds that 'a man is a man, can look his superiors by blood or position straight in the eye, requires to cringe to no-one not even his Chief, since any man's "place" is an honourable one secured by hereditary primogeniture'. In that system there was no feeling of insecurity for nobody could be elevated to god-like status one day, next day dashed to that of a crab as they could under despots like the Zulu Tshaka, for example; nobody might treat with a man as though he were less *or more* than a man.

The difference between our own and the attitude I saw among the Baganda struck me so much that when I got back to my house after leaving the *Lukiko*, I pulled down from the shelf my copy of H. M. Stanley's *Life and Manners in Uganda*, and felt that the despotic social fabric he had seen in Victorian days was not vastly different from what I was seeing decades after. Stanley wrote:

'Imagine a young British subaltern despatched by the Queen's command, specially chosen by the Queen for special service. How the young heart palpitates and the nerves tingle with delight! He spurns the ground, and his head aspires to the stars!

'If a young British officer feels so joyful at a *constitutional* sovereign's choice, what must the elect of a despotic autocrat like the Emperor of Uganda feel? No sooner has he left the imperial presence with the proud command ringing in his ears than his head seems to swell, and almost burst from delirious vertigo. His back, hitherto bent through long, servile dread, has suddenly become rigid and straight as the staff of his spear, and an unusual sternness of face has somehow replaced the bland smiles which hitherto decked it.

'For is he not "Kabaka" while on the Emperor's errand? Do not his soldiers respond to him when summoned with awful alacrity, saying "Kabaka (Emperor), behold us"?

'. . . "*Like father, like son*", and equally true would be the saying: "*Like king, like people*". The conduct of the chiefs proves that in Uganda at least it is true, for, like the Emperor, they adopt a despotic style, and require to be served by their inferiors with abject servility and promptitude. Among themselves (the Waganda) recognise only might, and Mutesa could have been pardoned for exercising greater severity than

171

he does.' (This was Stanley's reference to Kabaka Mutesa I, great-grandfather of the present one, Mutesa II.)

'For this fierce people requires to be governed with the almost unexampled severity of might and power which Kabaka Suna so cruelly employed.'

With national life getting back to normal, it began to transpire that those who had been rash enough to believe that the Kabaka was never to return, which was what the British Government had given out, and had therefore advised their compatriots to plan for the future minus a Kabaka, were now called his 'enemies'. His 'friends' including those who had kept their mouths shut waiting to see which way the wind would blow now demonstrated loyalty. They got busy currying favour with the fountain of authority and honour, Kabaka, not fully grasping the difference between a traditional Ganda despot and a 1955 Agreement constitutional monarch. Their method was to attack and beat up the 'enemies' bodily. During that period, I saw what was meant by 'primitive mob action', an established factor in Ganda social reaction, in the tradition of their organised political state. I saw men set upon by a crowd of Baganda, beaten so that their *kanzus* were drenched with blood. I saw how the spectacle roused the usually morose and taciturn people so that men yelled, women ululated. They jumped for joy, were exhilarated; bloodshot eyes flashed, well-formed teeth gleamed against the coal black, sweating faces.

I shuddered and looked away. So this was the Africa my sister was married to, our 'fellow Bantu' people. How often I was forced to look away, swallowing, particularly when I saw grown men fling themselves on the floor or on the ground before their Kabaka. I had never seen social reactions of this kind. I looked on as they writhed in the dust, hobbled on knees and rolled on the carpet. I saw the Kabaka robed, design by the then head of the East African University College Art Department at Makerere, a European lady. I saw him wearing his State Crown 'of gold and rubies presented by His Britannic Majesty' on the young Kabaka's coronation, saw him walk in snow-white *kanzu* under 'the ceremonial umbrella'; I saw the handing over of the *Damula*, traditional sceptre of *Katikkiro*-ship; saw the traditional stance of loyalty in grasping imaginary spear and shield that Ganda despotism required in olden days should be struck before the Kabaka; I saw the pomp and panoply.

I asked myself, 'What in heaven's name is "advanced" about all this?' feeling that I and other Southerners had been fooled by European onlookers who swooned with delight at such exoticisms. They had described the spectacle of the Interlacustrine monarchs' splendour: drummer, fifers, courtiers, body-guards, standard-bearers and others making up the processions who either followed or preceded the kings wherever they went; and the similar but lesser processions that accompanied their chiefs and lesser elect, so on down the social scale. But now that I saw for myself, it no longer struck a romantic note. The spectacle was contrary to my inherited Xhosa feelings. With us such servility would be unthinkable, along with its contempt for the individual's personality.

As time passed I saw how the tradition, as tradition with us at home, had a continued hold, an 'ethnic' continuity. If a MuGanda held a job as clerk in a Government Department for instance, he did not dream of carrying a typewriter from one office to another; a slave-like 'boy', often a greybeard, did that for him.

I studied the position of the Chiefs. They were picked at the caprice of the Kabaka, and it was accepted by society that a man, thus elevated to pomp and glory and riches, for chiefs traditionally reckoned to fatten off the land and people under them, must make the most of his moment. Capriciously elevated, so might he later be dashed to the ground to make way for some other favourite. Dr Ingham, Professor of History at Makerere College, has written:

'The supreme executive power was in his (Kabaka's) hands; so too was the judicial power though some of his authority in this latter field was leased to the Kabaka's chief minister, the Katikkiro. Legislation was the will of the ruler, not, as in

173

many other East African tribes, the custom of the people expounded by the elders . . .

'The complete and willing surrender of all individual rights, even the power of life and death, to an arbitrary ruler suggests a whole-hearted acceptance of the Kabaka as the personification of Buganda and of the Baganda, and the view is supported by the character of the nicknames given to him. The whole theme of those titles is that of the uncontrollable power of the Kabaka. He was said to have long teeth which ate all the animals in the neighbourhood, for such was his power over the lives of men. He was likened to the queen white-ant which can devour any of the other ants. Or he was like the blacksmith's charcoal which melts iron and moulds it into shape.'

Well, well! As Southerners, the nearest we had come to such a state of affairs was when the Zulus threw up a Tshaka, who altered their tribal political organisation and, as dictator, forged them not so much into a nation as a military camp for the purpose of plunder and spoliation; or a Mzilikazi, thrown up by the same historical 'sport' so to speak, who did the same with the (Rhodesian) MaNdebele, a hived-off section of the Zulus. My own tribal political background, not being a Zulu, was that of the ordinary pastoral Southerner whose political organisation, and flowing there-from social and individual psychology, was more like these 'other tribes' referred to by Dr Ingham, whose life was governed not by despots but by 'custom of the people expounded by the elders'.

When I saw the physical and social expressions of this other tradition, persisting in these 'constitutional' days in Uganda, I asked myself again and again, 'What was "advanced" about it? How could men think, let alone think straight or act in a way that made sense to them in such a mentally pulverising setting?' For with us, degraded as we were according to Western standards (which if one rejects, what is there to offer instead?), at least our ethic was, 'A Chief is a chief by the people', which meant he was the mouthpiece of the people's feelings on given matters. And those feelings were obviously regulated by past experience and adapting precedents when contingencies arose. A faulty 'mouthpiece' in the sense of incompetent, half-witted or unmindful of the people's wishes, could be removed; political devices existed for such an emergency. They were used, after open discussion and with the concurrence of every man. A would-be dictator or despot would wake up to find himself without followers, all gone away to another more normal expression of chieftainship. Our tradition was antipathetic to such things as had happened to the Zulu people. Politically we despise Zulus for having allowed themselves to be manipulated by a dictator, letting their 'personalities as men' be extinguished.

Zulus, like the Baganda, are great favourites with outsiders. Yet Southern blacks themselves generally deplore the characteristics noticeable in their social aspects: servility, fawning, degenerate effects, Xhosa in particular say, of military 'discipline'. These are offset by bullying tendencies. 'In this you see what happens,' we Xhosa declare, 'when a Tshaka or Mzilikazi rises up amongst a people and institutes a despotism which cares for no man's son or daughter.'

I could only suppose, on seeing for myself, that British visitors to East Africa in the early days were liable to be impressed by the glory and pomp because they, too, came from a kingdom of such. But they seem to have overlooked the many other ingredients in the evolution of the pompous and glorious kingdoms of the West, and tended to despise tribes in Africa who lacked these spectacular attributes, lacked 'ancient tradition'.

Indeed one does not deny that we tribes lacking pomp and circumstance are simple people; nevertheless, the more thoughtful of us nowadays generally feel that this lack of 'ancient tradition', fossilised claptrap we call it, is an advantage because it makes cleaner slates of our minds as it were; leaves us more ready to take to new techniques and new attitudes which come, at any rate in Southern Africa, with the arrival of industrialisation, Western standards of living and philosophical heritage. We have accepted all that; what does it matter that 'Poor Whites', negrophobes and other undesirable types also arrive at the same time? Seldom that anything comes without flaws. What counts are the ideals and whether they are worth striving for. Gazing at the effulgence of ancient tradition as I saw it for the first time, in a country largely removed in content and time from ideas that animate the Western world, I began to doubt whether people subject to it were willing or able to empty their minds of this particular kind of past, or adapt and transfer it to the twentieth century Western era. We in the South liked to think that our days of savagery had been 'noble', glorious; but did we not face the fact that they'd been filled with crudities too? We felt we might be better men even than we had been in the past, for being able now to adapt, and fix our eyes on new ideals. True they may prove unattainable and therefore all vanity, as some of my friends in England sometimes say to me. Myself, I rather believe in the art of life being a perpetual straining after the unattainable; what would you do if you suddenly got it, found you'd done all you wanted to do?

It was against this background and awareness of contrasts that I felt I now saw my sister more clearly. Had it not been that she had married into this colourful setting, I would perhaps only have looked on as a detached sojourner. As it was, I spent my spare time in soaking up the atmosphere in this way and seeing not as much of her as I would like, in order not to interfere.

19

Ganda and Xhosa

THE months went by. My sister still seemed far from what she used to be in the old days. Her sweet expression was strained, preoccupied, brave; I could only hope for the best. We talked mainly about her job at the Hospital and then she would light up. The work interested her immensely; there were one or two fellow South Africans nursing there as well as a girl who had trained with her in London. Everyone liked my sister, as they always do. We would meet for lunch sometimes and I would drive her to Naguru at the end of her day's duty and we'd play with my nephew.

Her husband gradually became conspicuous in the house by his long absences. It was tacitly realised that Mengo and Katwe were sucking him back. He became a member of the Legislative Council as the Protectorate Government was being gradually Africanised according to the new constitution on the Kabaka's restoration.

I went to its sittings occasionally and listened to the debates, taking affable teas during the interval in the marquee on the lawn with him, Kironde and other local people I came to know. Kironde had been appointed by the Governor as a Minister, was no longer in legal practice, had moved from his landed estates in Mengo to an expatriate Civil Service house at Entebbe. When the African members spoke in these debates and I listened to the historical backgrounds they quoted or precedents they cited, compared these with what would come into my own mind in the circumstances, I saw how the geographical situation of each African country and the contacts it consequently made affected it and moulded the character of its people. I was a Southerner and they Easterners in behaviour and outlook because of these things, none of us Africans just because we were born such. And I saw how the tribes of the various provinces of Uganda regarded themselves in comparison with one another. I saw the effects on them, and on me, of varying African climates and types of vegetation. This began to take importance in my mind. I came to see it as a profound influence on a nation or people. Another revelation was how linguistic links, Bantu and others, had no more unifying effect than similar links in Europe. I remembered the ambivalent feelings existing between average Englishmen and Germans for instance, despite the Saxon basis of English. Or between Poles and Russians although they speak 'Slavonic' languages.

I realised I should have known all these things, in fact found I did know, whenever I checked. However, the effect of what I saw as I moved round Kampala and went on many more safaris was to make me understand how true it is that 'none of our knowledge can transcend experience'.

All the same life in my temporary homeland had to go on, as life always has to. However much I cogitated and inwardly reeled because of new experiences, there was the usual social round to get on with: I was invited to or gave sundowners, went to meetings or lectures at the Uganda Society; there was shopping, the house, to say nothing of landscaping and tending my brand new garden. And I went on safaris and on exploratory trips.

When my teenage daughter flew out from England for her school holidays, we often swam at the pool at Government House, thankful to be asked, since pools on my fellow expatriates' Protectorate Government estates or clubs near by were colour-barred, not by Government but by the British Civil Servants themselves. My husband was welcome since he was white and English, but I and my daughter made things awkward. *Civis Britannicus Sum*, I thought, but didn't bother to mention this to the then Governor, Sir Andrew Cohen; I liked him immensely; there were so many urgent ideas about politics and policies in Africa to thrash out with him, much as we often disagreed, that I accepted his and his wife's invitation to us to go whenever we liked and swim and talk. It was prompted by friendliness, nothing more.

However, this business of the expatriate English and their noticeable proneness to colour kept coming up even after this unusually progressively minded governor had left, having done all he could in his admirable intellectual way to pave the path for 'Western civilisation'. An example from one of my experiences: once, some friends of mine, Continental Europeans, fellow Civil Servants, got involved in one of those storm-in-a-teacup disputes after having entertained my husband and me as guests at their club on a Protectorate Research Station, a dispute that mounted to the usual Englishmen's 'secret ballot'; all of which seemed to show me and the Continentals that, for insularity, the British and the Baganda were hard to beat and it was sometimes a case of the blind leading the blind.

Anyway these were the hazards of life for a 'Westernised' or 'civilised' African like me in this country of my sister's. When my daughter came she experienced others, one of which especially rather surprised her. To begin with, I allowed her to mix with children of Ganda families. One of these told her how she possessed brothers and sisters, indeed pointed these siblings out, born to her 'aunties' because when aunties came to visit, some of them her mummy's real sisters, same mother same father, the said aunties often 'slept in Daddy's room, with Daddy'. My teenager, with her background of Britain and the Eastern Cape, put this kernel of knowledge on my lap for me to chew over for her as best I could. Upon which I'm afraid I put the local playmates out of bounds.

Yet I kept on trying to come to terms with this exotic background which was beginning to grate. But try as I would things came to a pass that when I was compelled to leave my house to go shopping or visit people, I found I was averting my eyes so as not to *see* 'the Natives' who embodied and represented it. I looked right through them as though they did not exist.

Such conflict between common sense, emotion, human values inculcated during one's childhood—would it not tear a person

179

to pieces? I was being so torn and therefore tried all the harder to think, since the attempt to think things out was another of those habits inculcated during the formative years. I tried to analyse the position of finding that I felt and acted like a prejudiced person.

This whole business of feeling impelled to try to 'like' and 'be nice to those natives I knew' was a dilemma. To my dismay I saw I was now in the same boat as those whom we Southerners call slightingly 'liberals', meaning white people whose brain and sense, education or conviction tell them there's no reason not to like us blacks; but whose emotions are rooted, as evidently mine were too, in an instinctive revulsion from a way of life more primitive than their own. Instead of sorting individuals out as friends according to interests and habits in common, such liberals (with a small 'l') tried to like 'blacks' but couldn't quite make it. For how can you like people because you cerebrate about it in an emotional vacuum? Is it true that one only begins to like or love, even merely tolerate perhaps, primarily if one's emotions are free from the effects of shock or hurt or 'fear of the unknown'—as much where groups are concerned as where it's a question of individuals?

Just as I would be making a stupendous effort to overlook some of the things that startled, shocked or hurt me, my stomach would suddenly heave: as it did on an enlightening occasion at the sight of another of those Dali scenes, this time a dignified Ganda lady sitting bang on the dusty pavement along the main street of Kampala, surrounded by a pool of her gorgeous flamboyant robe, right beside a stinking refuse bin.

I refer to this as an enlightening incident because it was what showed me with sudden clarity that what I was suffering from was not a sort of race prejudice, black though they were indeed, compared to my own people, but their disparate social observances and manners, the attitude to incest. Such things, I realised at that moment, had filled me with 'fear of the unknown' in the people, and that therefore I had got into this state of recoil. I found myself wondering acutely as I tripped past, doubtless with nose arrogantly wrinkled up in distaste, how unnerving she would very likely find it to be in my company when I had such idiotic reactions to normal things like flies and smells near dustbins and rotting heaps of *matoke* peel.

But alongside my own experiences, my sister's continued and it became progressively clear that things were disintegrating in her *ménage*. Her father-in-law was kind, well-meaning, obviously at a loss and deeply hurt by the marriage representing conflict directly under his parental aegis as it were, between different backgrounds and sets of values.

And he was so nice and friendly an old man within that astonishing social setting of Church and concubinage that, for my sister's sake when I talked to him, I would follow their Ganda custom in which a woman sinks and kneels on the ground in talking to a man. I forced myself because I liked him as a person and wanted, cerebrating away, to express in terms that would be intelligible to him, my own and my family's appreciation of his efforts to reconcile his son and my sister, his efforts to join the apparently unjoinable ways of life.

As the marriage deteriorated then, my sister and I became much thrown in with other ladies as we say, for they rallied round, tried to guide and help her to see things through their East African eyes. What continued to 'ravage my bowels' as we say in our language was, in looking at things through their eyes, to see the resigned cynicism of this particular group of educated Interlacustrine women. It brought back to my mind the whole question of mental conditioning which I had noticed on my safari during my first visit. They seemed to be adjusted to a doubtless justifiably 'twisted' feminine distrust and contempt of men as they knew them in their social fabric. For example: one young wife, who had studied in England and elsewhere abroad, trying to be helpful in my sister's predicament in a way that we appreciated very much, offered advice to us ignorant foreigners. She said when she came to tea one afternoon, 'I will bring you a waist band of beads. Wear it at night, next to your body, your skin. Your husband is sure to like that. We Baganda ladies find that these men like it.' 'These men'!

I had looked at those 'waist bands' at the Museum in

Kampala, unseeingly, like a tourist. I had not emotionally absorbed their erotic use. They had seemed quaint symbols of an exotic primitive culture. Yet this girl now related them to a husband who seemed, like herself, of the modern world.

Another day, a different Ganda woman friend asked on coming out of the bathroom-cum-lavatory what was the purpose of the tube she saw there of depilatory cream. When we told her she fixed a long look on my sister, sucked her lips thoughtfully. Finally she said, 'It is not good to take away your underarm hair when your husband is on safari. You should not. Perhaps that is the reason he needs our East African ladies.' We looked blank. My sister said, 'But I don't use it only when he's on safari. Of course, he happens to be on safari at the moment, but it's for any time. What has he got to do with it?' But our friend was silent of a sudden. We could make nothing of it.

Months later I stumbled on the answer. Re-reading Roscoe's account of the Baganda, I found the explanation: propitiatory customs to do with secreting or preserving hair-shavings, nail parings in connection with sex-life, sorcery, and on undertaking enterprises such as journeys. Another of those things I had known really, having read of it in anthropological monographs here and there; but experience now told me more, enabled me to link 'such enterprises as journeys' with those 'safaris'. Tradition over again, hovering over people even today, I thought, feeling what a pity it was that my family had not had a copy of this particular book when my sister was being courted; though perhaps we might not have read or taken it in, you don't usually read to check up on people while you look on them as individuals. I had bought my copy of Roscoe in London after that first visit to my sister, when I'd got back from Italy and was packing and preparing to return to be near her in her crisis. It had cost me six pounds second-hand!

A further *t* was crossed and *i* dotted in connection with her marriage, when I was presently back home in South Africa recuperating from my domicile in the tropics.

It was after I'd tried to describe the wonders I had seen and heard during my sojourn in Uganda, that a friend directed me

to read a copy of Krige's *Realm of the Rain Queen*, an anthropological study of one of the most primitive and faraway tribes on
the northern edge of South Africa. I nearly fell off the verandah,
for what should I find but an answer to that mystery about
'pulling' some part of the anatomy which our relatives-by-
marriage had complained hadn't been done to my sister, the
mysterious rites of which we had been told no more than that
they were described in Sir Apolo Kagwa's book in Luganda.
I now read how at nights, the Lovedu women and nubile girls
sit in their unchaperoned 'special houses' (shades of Basoga and
Baganda), and carry out a tribal custom of pulling one another's
clitoris to ensure that it should grow long and hang down, a
special attraction to the male partner in sexual intercourse. I
drew a deep breath. Quite apart from vocabulary difficulties
in translating during the family councils, it must have been
obvious to them that my sister and I were not within a million
miles of comprehending; was it surprising that friendly disposed
Ganda women had given up trying to help and fallen silent?

As for when I read Roscoe's account of how, traditionally in
Ganda society, offenders would be fined 'so many women, so
many cowrie shells' or other currency, I saw what a gulf there
had been between our backgrounds. I thought I saw the root
of that feminine distrust, contempt, resentment going hand-in-
hand with conditioned acceptance of subjugation. Woman
humbly sank down and knelt, yet inwardly despised 'these men'
in the very act of humouring them. The difference I saw was
that in the South, even before Western philosophy was introduced, our ethics regarding the personality of the individual
were not of this order, though indeed left much to be desired.
What man's daughter among the Xhosa people could be
thought of as 'an object' to pay a fine with, or to curry favour
with by titillating the proclivities of a superior from whom a
father hoped to extract largesse? I could just imagine the reactions of even a blanketed pagan at home: 'What, a person's
daughter? *Intombi yomntu?* The beautiful vessel of the family's
honour, whom the land resembles when the rain has come?'
Oh my, the thing was inconceivable!

20

'The Order of Release'

OUR family in South Africa finally re-called my sister and she and my little nephew flew home. The marriage had been given another try and had failed. My sister could not, just could not, become emotionally or sexually one of a particular type of East African group.

Neither could her husband sustain the inspiration he spasmodically showed himself subject to, in the matter of forging a different life. His own people wanted him to do so, seeing the ambition less clearly than he could. But their society engulfed them equally. All this was understandable although so painful.

The marriage would have been possible if my sister could have discarded her 'Westernised Southern-ness', that 'taint', and accepted Ganda *mores*; otherwise South could not live with East, the cultures in this day and age too diverse, whatever the original common source of fellow Bantu-ness. Her father-in-law helped her to the last, sent one of his womenfolk as his representative to see her off at Entebbe airport, entrusted her with 'Shillings Fifty' as they say in East Africa, to give to my sister as 'travelling money to buy groundnuts on the way'.

The day she left, he wrote me a letter from his home fifty miles away and described his feelings at this dashing of his hopes, saying: 'For I thought the marriage of an East African with a South African, especially the daughter of a so great man, Professor Jabavu, would be like gold and show how people could educate their children together to raise up. I am too much hurt in my heart.' When I got the letter a few days later, even I was not so flint-hearted as to be immune. I was immensely relieved that my sister, 'my mother's only other child left' had been saved, yet I shared this old man's hurt.

Finally, more months later, the Protectorate Government

184

Court of Justice heard my sister's divorce petition which she had had to fly back to Uganda to present. And the judge said, among other things, in giving judgement:

'At a family council the respondent had declared his intention to pursue the KiGanda way of life and saw no reason, whatever her background, why his wife should not eat *matoke*, the staple food for a MuGanda. I believe the petitioner when she says that she was kept on short rations and was not provided with the wherewithal to maintain herself and her child. Rather had the respondent taken the lofty and untenable attitude that his wife should embrace the KiGanda way of life. It is little wonder that the petitioner, whom I considered to be of a very refined and sensitive nature, felt humiliated, suffered such mental torture as to be likely to make inroads into her health. I give the petitioner the custody of the child—the respondent's habits are not conducive to the well-being of the child.' *

That was a great day for my sister and me. We were no longer related to this part of the world, were free to be outsiders. Physically, this was 'The Order of Release'!

That night she and I talked until the small hours about our late mother and brother, tears of relief not far from either of us that they had been spared the things we had lived to see of the 'Africa' of which they had entertained such hopes when they were alive. As we all had indeed, when we had not known the facts. We puzzled with each other why our father had seen so little of the things that struck us; finally concluded that the fact of being a man, much as we loved and honoured him, would militate against his noticing the significant details. Also his had been a short visit during which everyone he met had put on their best bib and tucker to meet a distinguished person. But most important factor that must have blinded him to all else, we remembered, was that in Buganda 'Africans owned land'. It was this that had made the country seem to

* District Court of Kampala, Cause No. 17 of 1956, Divorce Jurisdiction. Before Judge Jeffreys Jones.

a land-starved Southerner, a man at that, 'a heaven on earth'. Nobody was to blame.

The following day my sister returned home to South Africa for good, back to our own. And that was how her story ended.

After the dissolution of that link, after that release, I gradually became aware of the consequence of being the outsider and foreigner that I was among the people of the land; it's perhaps been noticeable from the story already, how the rot was setting in.

Things got no better once the marriage link was cut. For example, I had occasion one day for the services of a Public Works Department 'fundi' (East African term for craftsman, usually Asian or African), at the Civil Servant house we lived in; I was amazed and chastened to catch myself thinking, before the poor African man had even started on the job, 'Huh, alleged craftsman!' A few moments later I was chastened again to catch myself giving the man and his ragged, high-smelling assistants that cold glittering look of hostility that a settler gives 'a native'. I had seen white Southerners giving me that look; my own expression I caught only by chance, stepping past a big looking-glass on the wall. In that instant I realised that the difference between me and an 'abominable settler' type of creature was only that I had become aware of what was happening to me; there was therefore hope, perhaps, in my case. I tried to take a grip on myself, to re-establish common sense and decency.

But to upset my equanimity, it would take only a stray 'local' meandering across my private garden the way they seemed to do in Uganda, using it as a short-cut. 'No Southern native, no civilised person would do this sort of thing,' I'd mutter unreasonably, shaking with vexation, and turn away, knowing from experience how futile it was to remonstrate.

But one day, it happened! A fellow taking a short-cut wheeled his bicycle right across my bed of seedlings. Before I could think, I shrieked from the iron bars of my window, demanded what in the world he thought he was doing. For

186

once the trespasser turned out to be an English speaker and answered loftily:

'Don't care what saying you. Me, me don't care. Not your country.'

At which I found myself shrieking again but more desperately:

'Just do it again and I'll send for the Police, you—you Interlacustrine Savage!'

Well, well, how things had changed. I turned from the window limp and trembling, my hand utterly damp, scarcely able to light the cigarette I badly needed. Had I not now finally cut myself off from the 'fellow Bantu' my father had taught us to look on as our people too?

But to repudiate what has guided thought and feeling during one's life brings its own anguish. I came to realise that the depressed state I was in was due to my having built more on to the concept 'Bantu' than it warranted. I was to blame, not my Eastern or even Interlacustrine fellows. They were not tainted by ideas about ethnic links that some of us, especially down South, derive from the Western language we speak in common with one another along with our own, and which disseminates philosophies about cultures being related through language, religion, myths and such things. These fellow Bantu thought in their own way; one tribe felt no link with the next, as of olden days. Why should they feel I was one of them when I wasn't? They had seen it first, my fault for having taken so long.

Other, more experienced fellow civil servants tried to comfort me. 'Your second Tour will be far easier. You won't expect too much of the people next time. You'll guard against those maddening procrastinations of theirs that seem so important to you just now, promises seldom kept; you'll know the old blighters too well. And keep inside the herd of fellow foreigners where you know where you are; makes life easier all round. You've got End-of-Tour blues, there's hardly an expatriate who doesn't get them. And you've not respected this deceptive climate, out in that garden working all hours like

187

a black instead of letting that "boy" get on with it by himself.'

Expatriate *malaise*! But now that I had my dose, it was probably more acute than in fellow outsiders for I had not originally thought myself a foreigner. My disillusionment was profound.

I longed to see my fellow Southerners again on their march forward to Westernisation. With all its shortcomings, tiresome *tsotsi* teddyboys, gangsters, this way of life seemed infinitely desirable. I wanted to go home and see once more how people sweat blood as they progress; how they gain experience in co-operation and cohesion as they pass through those steel tempering ordeals of Treason accusations, women's anti-Pass campaigns, bus-boycotts, banishings, imprisonments, floggings for political 'offences'.

All these things seemed to me to be, if one remembers that it is the long view that counts in Africa, why our lovely South Africa was a significant country. I couldn't see the relevance of the 'primarily African' State in East Africa.

When I expressed myself on such lines to fellow expatriates, they shook their heads, looked at one another and at my husband, finally said, 'Look, this girl had better go back to her own country for a three-months' "Home Leave" although you haven't finished your Tour of Duty yet.' And to me, 'Go, for goodness' sake and come back refreshed, a new person, and not fret. You'll settle down in future to look after Number One, as most of us find we have to in the end. Give us a bit of peace by letting the problems of "your Africa" well alone.'

I longed to go but couldn't altogether believe I was right to yield and do it. Nevertheless my flight to Durban was booked, not by me; one is forced to give up sometimes and let others act.

Just before I went, I ran into an anthropologist friend from the University College with whom I had had many arguments about 'Africa' and 'The African', usually disagreeing tremendously, he maintaining that my impressions were unfair, I that his were unrealistic. On this occasion I said, joking—if you could call it 'joking' to make the barbed cracks of the turmoil

I was in, 'I am off to South Africa, home, "to be doctored after having been in foreign parts, to be cleansed by my own tribe" and all that—*you* know!'

His blue eyes momentarily lit up, ready for yet another discussion. But something warned him, so he told me months later, that for once he had better hold his tongue; I had clearly had enough!

It was wonderful to motor out of 'The Lake—"The Inter-lacustrine"—Region'! to climb out of the warm-bath-on-a-hot-day atmosphere of the banana kingdoms, up the escarpments, on into the crisp 'champagne' air of Kenya.

And when I flew over the Zambesi once again, then the Limpopo River and into Union Territory in a clear blue sky and saw the wide open spaces of high, high veld; and presently the ridges of the mighty Drakensburg range, that familiar frieze of distant jagged peaks on the horizon; then the rolling plains of the Transkei Native Reserve, *EmaXhoseni*, dotted with herds of black and white (Friesland type) and brown (Afrikander) strains of cattle, 'marbled breeds' as we say, I trembled, hardly able to contain my feelings. Even the cattle, scattered as they grazed, were a sight for my sore eyes. Don't ask me why, but it was wonderful to see individual oxen and cows ambling freely as I had always known cattle to do, not tightly bunched together like the lion-fearing Ankole herds I had seen in Western Uganda.

Next, how my heart leapt when I spotted the typical Transkei flotilla of African men and women on horseback, not far from Lusikisiki! How I had missed Africans, in non-equestrian Uganda, paying calls on horse-back, the young people of the household running to unsaddle and rub down and water the visitor's mount, as we used to do for my classificatory uncle, one of my childhood's dearest memories.

But my heart swelled almost to bursting when at last the plane touched down outside East London once again and, as we taxied, I could see the 'long low' Cadillac of my classificatory kinsman—Sonny Mahlangeni. When I got out, I found that Sonny hadn't come himself, was at work in one of his surgeries down town, but had sent yet another classificatory kinsman of his own to fetch me for this last lap of my journey.

As we smiled and greeted each other exchanging clan names —'Majili!' and 'Kuboni!'—glittering eyes of Nationalistic 'European' types looking at us were filled with the familiar racial looks: explosive, granite hard, resentful, jealous as we know of old because we presented the spectacle of 'Natives' who fully embraced 'the Western way of life'. Such looks aroused my usual, also explosive South African racial responses. But this time, instead of glowering and snarling back I smiled all the more joyously with my kinsman's kinsman, saying to myself, 'So what? To blazes with them!' I had been 'abroad' in Africa now, had seen these antagonisms in perspective. Had my stay in the geographically cut-off tropical Lake region not shown how it was this very clash, the coming explosion being built up here in the South that was precipitating me and mine into the twentieth century world? And which of my real countrymen didn't want to be in step? *Alles sal reg kom*, we say in Afrikaans among ourselves, all will come right!

What mattered at that moment as we stood in the cold dry wintry air was the intense joy of being home again; being where I knew what was what, whether in its crudest white-versus-black forms, or its subtlest and most heartwarming manifestation of family and friends, language, familiar scenes, inspiring landscapes proclaiming our history; where one was no longer an exile among people with whom one had no common ground.

Heaven on earth that day, to tread the soil of my lovely, lovely homeland.

21

The Calves to the Kraal

A DAY or two later, coming back from the graves of my brother and my mother and from calling on people in the village, I gazed at the verandah of our stone-built 'antique' house flanked by its euphorbia trees and Birds of Paradise shrubs. An antique house in this Eastern Cape 'Border Country' we say, harking back proudly to the hundred years' war with the Europeans encroaching on our 'Kaffraria or Kaffir Land' from their Western Cape across the karoo; it had been built as long ago as 1860. Its owner had been an early European in these parts. More than ever now that I was back again, I loved my squat single-storied old home; its thick stone walls which my father had recently had washed white, our water tanks at the corners; its green, newly painted zinc roof. And inside the ever open front door, I loved the rooms in their assorted shapes and sizes with their plain ceilings of white matchboards, here and there a sky-light boxed in above one that was awkwardly placed and would otherwise have no light or air. The whole so 'colonial', rugged and rambling.

I loved the polished floors that my own mother had strewn with rugs. My new mother had replaced some items, 'Thrown out our old things', was my initial reaction. But on looking round I was reassured; some old rugs were still where they used to be, well worn and frayed at the edges; and in the corners of the sitting-room were familiar bowls of yellow lilies and of my own mother's favourite plumbago sprigs with their pale blue flowers, *umthi ka Maqoma*, 'the bush of Maqoma', whose descendant the present Chief of the area where our small town Alice stood was my late brother's liege lord. That very morning over my breakfast of dark brown millet followed by thick sour milk out of an elderly gourd that glistened with use as though polished (I was back at my own staple foods!), my father, telling me the local news had recited once more the 'praises' that Chief Maqoma had composed in honour of my brother on being born in his area; and had reminded me of what the old chief had said on hearing the news that Jo'burg gangsters up in the Transvaal a thousand miles away had capriciously shot my brother: '*Ezizigebenga zindibulelel' umntan 'am*, these terrorists have-for-me-killed my child,' putting the verb in one of its astonishingly versatile Bantu inflexions impossible to translate into English, conveying in this particular context a piercing poignancy. Using too, the 'my child', which by custom is the relationship of every man to his Chief; a phrase alluding to the concept that Xhosa chiefs represented their subjects, never owned them as despots do. But when 'Ndabemfene' Maqoma thus 'threw his blanket' over my new-born brother, he was paying a special tribute to the achievements of my father and his fathers: one with complicated background. Firstly, in the modern era Chiefs don't count. And secondly, in it Jabavus had worked for the progress of Africans in South Africa, not only Xhosas in the Eastern Cape. Maqoma was acknowledging the acceptance of national rather than tribal or regional ideas in the manner of a scion of Xhosa royal blood who was at the same time a Westernised man. Thirdly, Jabavus were not really his people at all. We were not Xhosa even by descent. Our Jili and other Ntlangwini clans were Fingo, Zulu offshoots scattered by those *iinkcitakalo*, dispersals of long ago and settled among the Xhosa for generations. Our antecedents had thus arrived near what is now Alice and Fort Hare, 'the land of the AmaJingqi', Xhosa clan ruled by Maqoma, ancestor of the one in question and a primogenital heir of the Xhosas but of The Right Hand House, had therefore hived off from the territory in the Transkei of the heir of The Great House and crossed the river with his followers and cattle to people a new area. Jabavus and many other Fingos had long since absorbed Xhosa custom, *isiko*, to say nothing of language, adopting theirs in place of our own archaic, soft *tsefula* tongue. And——

But these are very long stories and I have touched on them

earlier; they made up the fabric of the life my sister and I had known long before going so far away: to England and marrying, to East Africa and marrying. Now home again at Middledrift I refingered the fabric. I knew the stories inside out. But I must say once again that with us, repetition oils the wheels of life. My father went over all such things again, as he had done for my sister when she had arrived back sometime before. He and the other big people of my family realised her need and mine for reassurance, the need for this 'doctoring by our own tribe after having been away among the unknown'. I was feeling doctored already, it was good to be home.

Although my father and my new mother and I talked of my brother, of my late mother and others who were 'no longer here', we exchanged reminiscences about them happily, in acceptance. My father was full of his old vitality, histrionics, jokes. I kept remembering the formal ritual utterance that had rung round the house at the time of my brother's funeral, on the lips of all who had been present: '*Akukhonto, Jili*, it is nothing, Jili, the Lord will bind you and your life will go on'; and so it had proved to be, I now thought. Custom, the ethnic continuity implicit even in the qualitative changes that it was undergoing, had exerted its curative influence. Even when I had told the long story of the things I had seen 'up in East', my father and his contemporaries listened in the Southern Bantu custom: making no comment, offering no comparisons or judgement at the immediate moment. They withheld their surprise or pain. I was allowed during each of the days that went by, to 'Speak and cast out of the system that which had disturbed'. An audience would gather, usually on the verandah: relatives, collaterals, friends, our servants, passers-by halting on their way past our house. They heard what I had to say, judiciously interjecting the monosyllable, phrase, or syntactic echo, which 'encourages' the story teller or pleader of a case. Then they would adjourn, and thoughts arising from the revelations would be left hanging in the air. The rhythm of life in our country Reserve pursued its own old gentle pace. We would disperse, my father, now retired from the university, ambling to his study and further work on another edition of a Xhosa book, the rest of us to other occupations. Comment, it was tacitly understood, would be made later, at one of those informal, partly ritual gatherings, in the form of the customary 'speech'.

The weekend came and with it, among the people 'of-here' or 'of-ours', came one of my classificatory girl cousins to keep me company, since there were no agemates or contemporaries of mine in the house; my sister and my little nephew, who now walked and spoke fluent Xhosa I was told, had gone on a long visit to our uncle at the Makiwane farm. As the eldest son, our uncle had inherited land in foreign tribal territory which his great-grandfather had been given by the British for fighting on their side during one of the regional wars. Our ancestor had without doubt been a quisling, we young ones liked to say! The farm was called Confluence Farm, at the meeting point of two rivers. It was set in gorgeous scenery: mountains, shallow valleys, wide sweeping landscapes interspersed with tall pointed hills of a particular kind of geological formation in that part of the country. It was our 'maternal home'; as children we had always gone there 'to be indulged, fed on fresh liver by the mother's people', treatment you traditionally don't get from our paternal people, who are supposed to discipline you and make you worthy of your line and clan.

On this Sunday morning my cousin and I were indoors in the sitting-room chatting and laughing. By now I was no longer over-excited and on edge, only quietly aware of the reassurance and pleasure of being in our house that had no iron bars, no wooden shutters. Through the open windows and front doorway, the bright southern sun was shining. The air was crisp and dry, light diffused by the roof that sloped over the long verandah outside.

My father sat underneath it on a lounging wicker chair but bolt upright, his yellowing panama hat tilted incongruously jauntily over his face. A few feet from him in the garden, next to the wire fence sat his old friend, also bolt upright. This seemed to be the way elderly Africans of their type sat here at home, I thought, as I looked at everything with new eyes. He

194

was on a dining-room chair that had been placed for him under a shade tree.

My cousin and I talked desultorily, in low voices not to disturb the big people. She and I were so glad to be together again, we could enjoy sitting silent for minutes on end. Here at home silent contact meant something positive for you were filled with the same thoughts as your companion; you were not in an isolated world of your own, as I had found elsewhere on my safaris. We had hardly slept, our night taken up with stories: hers about her job of teaching Arithmetic and Grammar to children in primary school 'in their mother tongue instead of English', the recent clock-reversing dispensation of the Nationalist Government. All teachers had also to learn Afrikaans now, the official language ousting English. Many of us Border people didn't speak it, ours never having been Boer country. 'Man, those Free State and Transvaal Kaffirs are in heaven these days, some of them from babyhood have done nothing but *praat die taal*!' she laughed, telling side-splittingly funny anecdotes about the struggles she and other rustic teachers went through, especially those afflicted with heavy 'vernacular' accents. In between, I told her about the Bantu up East. She exclaimed, at times yelled out loud at my stories as I did at hers.

But this morning we were more collected, behaved properly, in the recognised subdued manner out of respect for our elders outside. Somehow they both seemed to me greyer than when I'd last seen them, decidedly ageing. We listened to them. When not talking, they just sat. We knew that their eyes were resting on the frieze of Cape mountains across the distant horizon in front of our house, across the valley dotted with stunted thorn trees, across the bare contour line of intermediate hills beyond it where the *kloofs*, the apron folds of the sides of the mountains begin. My father and his friend were serene. In their old age they preferred to 'leave politics to the younger generation'. They had done what they could in their day. Their vote in the Cape had been taken away by General Smuts in 1936. After that their 'moderate' tactics based on British gradualism had got them nowhere. Now they were old, younger people were trying other moves. Themselves, they could sit quietly on such a Sunday morning, in no hurry to go anywhere. They were in their Sunday clothes, navy serge suits bleached to a coppery tint by the suns of many years. They wore their Edwardian boots of every day. Watch-chains dangled from their waistcoats. Having sat and enjoyed the shade, they looked forward to a gentle walk to the morning service in the church round the bend of the same shallow hill on which our house was built, the church from which we had buried my mother, then my brother. Our elder under the tree was saying, as if to himself, 'Doctors? African doctors? My word, they are coining money.' My father replied gently, '*U-tsho?* You say so?' but only to 'encourage' his friend to chat as he clearly wished to do, about views which he and we young ones indoors naturally knew of old. I felt how conversations of this sort among the big people seemed to portray aspects of those qualitative changes that are taking place in our outlook and customs; we younger people tend to be impatient, for ever glancing at our wrist-watches, thinking of the insignificant activities that awaited us. Yet the big people, like these outside, were not so old-fashioned and out of touch as we liked to say they were. Didn't watch-chains dangle from their waistcoats? My father even wore a wrist-watch as well, an Oyster, treasured memento of one of his official visits to America; the turnip watch had belonged to his father. But where his skill in exchanging ideas with contemporaries and older people lay was in his patience, his refusal to let the latter-day sense of time clash with the ancient African sense of it which, like other 'ancient' things, spills over even into these 'civilised' days; patience born of a profound happiness in and acceptance of those aspects of 'African' life that had been handed down. He and his friend spoke in Xhosa.

'Doctors? Coining money!'

'*U-tsho?*'

'Coining it, man. And what's more, the public waste no time. The moment such a one opens his surgery, they flock there. As if they've waited for just that moment to kick away that white thing they've been going to for years, suffering his *apartheid*,

196

enduring his bare open-space-out-in-the-weather of a waiting-room.'

'*Ja.* Supposed to be a waiting-room, that patch of *apartheid* ground trodden hard and dusty by feet upon feet there at the side of his surgery; no cover, no shade. When the sun is such as to roast *u-boboyi*, a hoopoe, alive. Or the rain is such as to drown a crab. Continue!'

'Yes, a crab. You have it exactly. Where you may not sit on the verandah because if you do it will smell of Kaffirs, of ochre.'

'*Nants'* into, the very thing! You see, my friend, the African doctor on the other hand says to himself, "The money that will issue from that ochre, *it* won't smell of ochre, oh no, not it!" Those white fellows used to do well of course, eat their fill because black patients had nowhere else to go for Western treatment. So it never entered their heads how they need do differently for their clients, need study their human needs. Such is the impatience of these whites. Although there were the exceptions, not so?'

'One or two, one or two,' the other grudgingly conceded. 'Oh indeed there are always the one or two in these things. But when the African one comes along, now *he* knows what it's like. For when he was a light-weight child, his own mother sat out on that bare open space with him on her back, they-both baking in the sun. So the *first* thing he does is to make the clients comfortable, welcome, to make them feel that he has a *feeling* for them, a *feeling* for their sufferings: that he isn't impatient with them: that to him they are human beings: who come long distances on empty stomachs: who must be welcomed. Well, he does that then!'

'He does that.'

'Does it, does it.'

'Does it.'

'Um-mh!'

'Um-mh. Does it, you say.'

'That's what he does. That's it, that's it.'

The conversation would see-saw like that for ages. My cousin and I looked at each other and smiled. The old people weren't really discussing, only bringing out for re-inspection ideas lodged in their heads from experience, since the days when they too, had been at their mothers' knees. That was before the end of the last century, when the notion of professional black men trained as whites were trained scarcely occurred to anyone. They were telling each other nothing that the other did not know. It was just pleasant to review the past along with the changes, ruminate and draw on memory while the sunlight fell on the stones and wild flowers and the land around them in its peaceful way. It shone with morning brilliance on the beds of horizontal creeping cactus by the wire fence that kept goats and sheep from the tempting green leaves of our garden. It picked out the creeper's bulbous leafy cushions, shone on the flowers they bore, enormous trumpets of pale colouring with petals arranged in collars that intersected, the throats of the trumpet-shaped flowers themselves deep like a delicate gorge, long white powdery stamens reaching from within them to the open air. Being large and bright, these flowers caught the eye. But my elders were indifferent to the presence of such dramatic plants of the veld, too used to them. Instead their eyes scanned the distances, habitually looking for signs of rain. What was pleasant to savour was the sitting in the shade with one's felt hat on, or on the verandah sucking one's pipe, sharing thoughts, waiting for that short walk to church. Effortlessly they touched off the see-saw of talk again.

'Yes, that's what the black one does nowadays. Next, he knows of something else, even more important that he must do in order that "Like a hunter collecting his pelts" as the pagans still say, he may collect his nucleus of cured patients, partisans who will swear by him even if he has failures too.'

' "*Amafele*, the pelts of the hunt"!' the other smiled at the pleasantry.

'*Ja*. And to secure the collection, that doctor "must explain the sufferer to the sufferer's satisfaction, *Kufuneka elo gqira limc-h-a-ze umntu*," ex-plai-n a person!' The words were drawn out for emphasis on a long high note, like a chant. They provoked a burst of laughter from my father who cried out in applause, 'Oh say that again, say it out loud!'

'*Ja! Limchaze!* What's more, explain artistically, poetically, properly, beautifully, in detail! I don't care whether the sufferer is an educated person or a raw pagan, there is N-O person alive, if he is black, who is not satisfied only by being thoroughly explained, my friend' and to underline the observation, he threw in the little idiom 'Yes, no!' then went on in a new pitch of voice, '*Nam*, I too, am satisfied with only that, only that!'

'*Hek-eh!* Aha! *Utsho! Nawe*, you too?'

'Indeed, *I*! Look at me! You see, I went to a European doctor for years. He died. His son took over the practice. Right there, at-ours. I kept it up, going to this young slip of a boy. *But!* I heard that a young black had arrived and opened a surgery some distance away. Eight miles. What? Did I waste time? I went at once. Leapt on my horse! Went!'

'Which slip of an African was that one, now?' my father asked. The other paused to explain the young man's family and as usual to go into the known genealogy of it. Presently he returned to his story.

'And when I got there, such kindness did I find, such *feeling*, *ubuntu obabulapho*, the humanity that was there! And at last, I was able to discover what my trouble really was.'

'*O?*' My father gave that short sharp expression of interrogation. 'And you were able to understand it?'

'Well, even if I shouldn't perhaps say I understand, at least this youngster tells me something that I *can hear*.'

'Oho, aw, aw. Something that you can hear. What does he say?'

'This is what he says: this complaint of mine, this pain that pierces me over here on this side,' straining forward now and drawing his right arm across his body indicating a large area below and to the left of the heart. 'It appears, it is indeed clear, it is in the spleen.'

'The spleen? Continue!' My father spurred him on, again using the echoing inflexional style. But he was more than only conventionally interested now. The talk had gone into its next phase; generalities were over, the details to illustrate promised to be new, not known to him before. I was aware that the form and pace of the exchange, the reactions it produced in teller and listener were according to a pattern; pleasurable because linking the familiar with the unfamiliar. My father's face like his friend's, began to furrow at the drama that was unfolding. His friend reiterated:

'The spleen! Yes! *Eh-weh-h! Ja!*' So important, the confirmation had to come in all languages. 'And did he trumpet me, trumpet me, trumpet me?'

'Is that so? He trumpets properly that one, does he?'

'Yes no! Indeed! What's more, he takes his time. That other youngster of a European, why, all he did was to trumpet you perfunctorily, once, twice on the chest. Very rarely on the back. And all done in a minute. Imagine it! And without a word. In silence. Thin white lips drawn tight together. Bushy yellow brows twisted. But this other one, why, he makes you take off your shirt and your vest! Trumpets you right on yourself, on the flesh. And many times over. All the while explaining, explaining, explaining. That's what satisfies me about him. Ho, he trumpets that one!'

'I hear you. Continue.'

'Well now, the medicine he gives me, it is already accomplishing *plenty*!'

'What, already?'

'Already, I say. Listen!' And now unfolded a long story with all its physiological details. My father listened patiently, following every phase with serious sympathy, however indelicate. At times my cousin and I looked at each other, hardly able to suppress our laughter, even distaste, since the older generation of simpler people seldom shrank from being positively Elizabethan in their frankness even if we modern younger ones did. Yet we knew that the only way to keep in touch with the people was to travel with them all the way when they spoke, for much of the frankness which we found unseemly is based on a different outlook on life and use of language; a good deal else is, according to custom, wrapped in discretion, for example those complicated adjustments between individuals which as we say 'may not be spoken aloud even in whispers' during the time while misunderstandings are being solved in order to restore an equilibrium. I again felt my old admiration for my father's ability as I listened to him quietly juggling with such old, even threadbare ideas, in the process implanting something of the new. Wherever he went among the people they felt satisfied because he talked with them properly. And when my cousin whispered to me in English, her eyes twinkling, 'Gosh, Cousie, a proper old people's session!' I was reminded how my father usually said he had formed such habits from listening to his own father in his youth, when the old man had juggled in the same way; and how that grandfather of mine and my mother's father had listened to our great-grandfathers in days when the going was harder, the nostalgia for the past still strong, the people still inwardly quivering from defeat by the incoming whites and the subsequent upheavals physical and spiritual.

My father's contemporary was going on with his story, 'And then, would you believe it, when——'

But my father suddenly cried out, 'Friend, please hold hard a moment, wait!' And we saw that his whole attention was centred on two small calves that were toddling along the path beyond our garden fence. His neck was stretched, his eyes bright. 'Wait!' and soothed the jarring interruption by throwing in his friend's clan name. 'Wait, *Nzaba*, let me not interrupt you. But I want you not to miss this. Do you see these calves passing by?'

The other turned round in his chair with difficulty, with the deliberate movements of old age. 'I see them.' The calves trotted past, very young, one brown, 'red' as we say, the other black and white. They swung their little heads from side to side as if imitating the way they had seen older cows and oxen walk. My father said proudly, 'Those are ours, calves-of-here-at-home'; he might have been referring to the 'children-of-here-at-home'. His friend was full of admiration and muttered while both men's eyes followed the young animals tenderly until they were out of sight, together with their small herd-boy who looked as young as they, the sun glistening on his legs which were well anointed for Sunday, with Vaseline.

'Now that red one is the offspring of T-H-A-T cow that I bought when What's-his-name was selling that pedigree stock at Healdtown, remember?'

'Well do I remember!'

'This is the grandchild. You see, that cow had a calf. The children of the home here christened that calf "Savings". Now it is Savings who is the mother of the little red one you have just seen. And what milk we are getting from just this one mother, ho, any amount of milk!'

'You don't say? But that's what I like about pedigree cows. *Ama-Afrika* won't understand that with a single pedigree cow you can feed a whole family. No, *they* must see numbers, no matter how thin and dry-uddered. Miserable things from which, however you sweat and pull, you can only draw a cupful of milk.'

My father could hardly wait to endorse this, his eyes shining even more brightly with excitement. 'Even if an animal has just a trace of the marble, *ibastile* (bastard), it is better than a dusty little native cow. Of course, on the other hand, if too pure-bred, that has its drawbacks. For there is then the question of its special feed. No, let it be pedigree but a little marbled. Then it has all the advantages of the native animal. Can forage for itself and so on. But on top of that it has milk. I have another one here at home, *i-Feslande*, a Friesland. But I had bad luck with her this time. You know, I sent her to be climbed but the bull missed her out.'

'Missed her out?'

'Missed her out.'

'My! Bulls have a way of being troublesome about this thing. Now at other times they want to climb every cow in sight.'

'Missed her out.'

'So then that one is childless?'

'That's right. However, on the other hand, if she had been rightly done by and not missed out, the quantity of milk here at home would very nearly have put me in a quandary. As things are, I am having to *give* it away!'

'Oh, what a help is milk! You know, at home at-ours, because of this drought we have reaped hardly anything to speak of this year. That we are alive is because of my marbled cow at this very moment. I'm telling you, we are existing thanks to her! Eating thick milk day after day. My working son in Jo'burg has seen to it that our kraal has no more of these dusty natives any more. Over the years he has been weeding my stock out, sending money to improve it. Today what I possess is really good. A handful only, mind you. But pedigree marbles.'

My father opened his eyes wider in appreciation and said:

'Doubtless others pity and despise you then, with your handful; consider you a poor man!'

'Yes, poor! But are those men themselves rich for their dusty native bags of bones?' his friend cried rhetorically. My father capped him:

'Don't they see your thick milk?'

' "Don't they see it?", you ask! Ha! Are they not also eating it?'

They laughed heartily at this point. The sentiment was one close to their hearts as both were well-known progressive small farmers; they were partly enjoying the linguistic by-play impossible to convey in English. And they were partly harping on the hidden factor, that enlightened householders such as they would often find themselves having to feed not only their own and extended families but kinship claimants too, some of whom can be mighty conservative about things like improving their stock.

And now followed another digression which we who were listening quite expected: all about the everlasting attachment of our people to the idea of cattle, how no home was a home without its kraal, even a token one such as ours at the back of this very house at Middledrift; how a marriage was hardly a marriage even these days, without that passage of cattle from one family to the other; about the small herd one of my uncles had reared and guarded on behalf of my late brother from little calves he had been given when he had been born, by relatives and well-wishers. My father compared our 'complex', as experts call it, with things that other nations and cultures held sacred, reminding his attentive friend how all peoples at some stage or other held *something* precious, be it horses, buffaloes, camels, dogs, deer. Here his friend exclaimed, 'My, but I ask myself how people can focus thought, moral, custom, unity, without cattle. Why, look at these peoples we have been hearing about lately from your own children, who discovered African nations whose being is fixed on the banana. Yet this banana is an Indian thing after all, up in that Natal climate, is it not so?'

My father laughed tolerantly and didn't pursue this, as if knowing that the complexity of this unfamiliar territory of thought would take too long to elucidate to his less-travelled friend, even on such a leisurely Sunday morning. He only said, 'Yes, no! Yes, no, my dear friend. Even bananas are cattle, for some. And perhaps there is little harm in that. Don't forget, we cattle nations have painful adjustments to make because of this very way of life of ours. I don't have to remind you, of all people. What about this conservatism which impels every son-of-Xhosa to cling to mere numbers, as you said just now, regardless of quality? Hardening his brain against the fact demonstrated time and again in these enlightened days that we must cull our stock, reduce our herds and improve them instead?'

There was a sigh from the other, and for some time he sat in silence, thinking; for he had indeed been in the vanguard of modern-minded farmers in his limited way, devoted subscriber to my younger maternal uncle's monthly magazine on agriculture, stock-breeding, grain and such matters. At last he said, abandoning reflexions on bananas and what civilisations based on such things might be, to rejoin my father on familiar ground, 'Oh Jili, don't speak of that. Just don't speak of it!

'I am tired of talking nowadays. For forty years I have been preaching the gospel: "Limit your st-o-ck, O beloved people of ours, procure only the best, the milk yielders!" Forty years of preaching, yet how many converts, how many pelts to my name as hunter-preacher of progressive methods? I have the one or two of course, yet look at the *numbers* of unconverted.'

My father agreed, emphasising the sorry fact by using idiomatic phrases, finally saying:

'But one is only human. We are no longer young, you and I. One sits on one's verandah now and watches people carrying on their brainless ways of ancient Africa.' But here they had to laugh and then mutter affectionately. For they dearly loved Africa. To blend its ancient with its new had been their life's ambition. And I heard my father say:

'These daughters of mine here-at-home have come back to tell, as you have heard, how our people do up there, whence we Bantu came. And of course, looked on what they saw with impatient young eyes, although I am not saying the circumstances were not peculiar in some respects.'

It was my father's friend's turn now to encourage his tale, and he did so.

'O? *Utsho?* You say so? Continue, Jili.'

'Yes no. I say so. You know the proverb: *Ukuzala kukuzolula*, to bring forth children is to increase your own capacity (to do, learn, weigh up experience through what happens to or is done by your children). Well, I am a parent; you, coeval-of-mine, are a parent too: have increased your capacity also, in the way you were telling just now about your working son, for example.'

'Um-mh. Aha!'

'Therefore hear what I shall say to these children when they have stayed awhile and been revived in the bowels of their own customs, refreshed by familiar outlooks: when it will be proper time to speak with them.'

'—To speak with them. Say it.'

'I shall say: "Know this, children of mine. Those Africans are like us. They are our people. Never mind if we are as yet strangers to one another. We Ntlangwinis were strangers ourselves once, here among the Xhosas. Those people have been exposed to other vicissitudes from those *we* have known here down South. Their societies have evolved other ways of meeting other contingencies. Similarly, we have met *our* problems, are continuing to meet them, are devising differently. Thus there is no cause for alarm or distress or discouragement. This family-of-ours here at home may sojourn up East again and elsewhere another day, and will see what will then have come to pass. It will doubtless be the great-grandchildren who will go as our eyes next time, it won't be me or my daughters or their children. We shall no longer be here.'

'Continue!' His friend listened with concentration, for the idea was being put in language he could follow, so that although novel to him, and indeed not being progressive in all respects he could hardly visualise what he had heard of diverse customs and peoples, my father was successfully planting a thought in his mind too, not only in mine and my cousin's where we sat listening. To show that he followed and was willing to believe, he repeated the proverb my father had used as a premise:

'*Ukuzala kukuzolula!*'

And my father echoed it back and stopped, to mark that he was there resting his case, to be turned over in the mind at leisure, in the days to come.

There was a silence. Then the other exclaimed, in a new pitch of voice:

'By the way, what was I still saying when those pretty little calves came by?'

'Ah, you were telling about the medicine of that young slip of a doctor——', at which the other theme got under way again. In the end, our woman servant came out to them, respectfully holding her hands under her topmost apron which was utterly faded but clean and neat. She said:

'Peace, fathers. I have come to tell you that the second bell rang some time ago.' The old men were startled and exclaimed resoundingly; had clean forgotten the time. But they regained their calm when my father remembered that there had been a special service that morning, to which my new mother had gone. So the normal service would in any case have been postponed, wouldn't have reached its usual phase by the time of the second bell, they wouldn't be late.

I noticed how the maid stood about as though sorry to have

startled them. My father turned to her as though to forgive, wished her peace in his turn and said, interrupting his motion of rising from the wicker chair,

'By the way, MamZangwa, how is that child of yours? You took her to the doctor, am I right, yesterday?'

'Yes, father.' She respectfully waited to be drawn out. The other old man under the tree was also laboriously rising to his feet. At last, erect and straight as a soldier, he exclaimed:

'*Zangwa? Zangwa?* You are a Mpondomise, then? What on earth are you doing here in this Ciskei country so far from yours, what had you come to do here, what, what, what?' And all three smiled, my father delightedly laughing outright, since to touch the subject of clan names and clan migrations was of course to touch the love of his heart. He said:

'*Ah, lumka, wafa MamZangwa,* look out, being killed you are, Zangwa! Pay no attention! But what of the child now, since you took her to this African doctor of ours here?'

The woman's face brightened and I thought, she is a person too, her employers show that they regard her as one. And again I felt how good it was to be home. Having been suitably drawn out, she now told about the doctor's treatment of her child. Her voice rang as our elders rejoiced with her. Her statement re-iterated the feelings expressed earlier, before she had come on the scene, even to the 'explaining' and 'the trumpeting, *ukuxilonga*', so that my cousin and I exchanged glances.

Before setting off, my father looked in at us, inclining his head to one side, and on his face the special smile he reserved for the young, the 'tender in experience', and for calves and foals. He said:

'*Nonwabile bantwana bam,* you are happy, my children, are you not?' and turned to his friend who had now climbed on to the verandah and also stood at the door regarding us indulgently, supporting him in the pleasant contemplation of offspring. For to less sophisticated Africans everywhere, nothing was more precious than the coming generation. Not just one's own child-ren in the European biological family sense, but 'Children': symbols of continuity: satisfying, valuable in all manner of ways

207

that went deep into the past and future of existence. Like works of art. My father said, pointing at us with his pipe:

'The exchange of news is unending between these young, too, as between such as you and me. Man, I tell you, it keeps them talking all night long!' Then they walked away, sliding into reminiscence as they went.

My cousin and I sat on alone. It was quiet now that the big people had left; we did not speak. I breathed again, looking at the blue mountains and their granite crags through the clear dry Southern air. Surrounded as I was by the walls of my home, savouring the historical background and physical characteristics of the scene, I was aware of the personalities it had produced in my parents, their generation, others before and since. It was wonderful to be among my own again, the Southern Bantu. I was lost in thought.

Then hearing a friendly sound from my cousin, I looked round to find her brown eyes studying the expressions on my face. She had guessed something of what was in my mind for she said in Xhosa, laughing gently:

'Girl, this is home. The elders are still here, we will be elders for others in our turn. *Akukhonto, Jili. Alles sal reg kom.* All will come right!'